Your Money
The Missing Manual®

Your Money: The Missing Manual

BY J.D. ROTH

Published by O'Reilly Media, Inc., 1005 Gravenstein Highway North, Sebastopol, CA 95472.

O'Reilly books may be purchased for educational, business, or sales promotional use. Online editions are also available for most titles (http://my.*safaribooksonline.com*). For more information, contact our corporate/institutional sales department: 800.998.9938 or corporate@*oreilly.com*.

Editor: Dawn Frausto

Production Editor: Nellie McKesson

Copy Editor: Alison O'Byrne

Indexer: Jan Wright

Cover Designer: Karen Montgomery

Interior Designer: Ron Bilodeau

Print History:

March 2010:   First Edition.

ISBN: 9780596809409

[SB]

Contents

Part 1: Blueprint for Financial Prosperity

Part 2: Laying the Foundation

Part 3: Building a Rich Life

The Missing Credits

About the Author

J.D. Roth is an accidental personal-finance expert—a regular guy who found himself deep in debt. After deciding to turn his life around, he read everything he could about money and finance. To share what he'd learned, in 2006 J.D. started the award-winning website Get Rich Slowly (*www.get-richslowly.org*), which *Money* magazine named the Web's most inspiring personal-finance blog.

Over the past 4 years, Get Rich Slowly has grown into an active community where 500,000 monthly visitors share ideas on how to save money on food, find the best savings accounts, dig out of debt, and otherwise improve their financial lives.

J.D. lives with his wife and four cats in a 100-year-old house in Portland, Oregon. When he's not writing about money, he likes to read, eat, and laugh with his friends. You can read about his obsessions with books, cats, and comic books at *www.jdroth.com*. If you have questions, drop him a line at *jdroth@foldedspace.org*.

About the Creative Team

Dawn Frausto (editor) is assistant editor for the Missing Manual series. When not working, she likes rock climbing, playing soccer, and causing trouble. Email: *dawn@oreilly.com*.

Nellie McKesson (production editor) lives in Brighton, Mass., and spends her spare time studying graphic design and building a t-shirt business (*www.endplasticdesigns.com*). Email: *nellie@oreilly.com*.

Dylan Ross (technical reviewer) is a fee-only Certified Financial Planner practitioner and owner of Swan Financial Planning, LLC in New Jersey. He provides financial planning and investment advice on an hourly, as-needed basis. In his spare time, Dylan enjoys the outdoors, strumming his ukulele, and spending time with his wife and twin sons. Email: *dylan@swan-financialplanning.com*.

Charlie Park (technical reviewer), creator of the personal finance website PearBudget.com, is an indie web developer and family man. He lives in Williamsburg, VA.

Alison O'Byrne (copy editor) is a full-time freelance editor with over eight years' experience specializing in corporate and government projects for international clients. She "lives a rich and happy life" with her family in Dublin, Ireland. Email: *alison@alhaus.com*. Web: *www.alhaus.com*.

Jan Wright (indexer) lives in the mountains of New Mexico, and likes to ride an electric bike when she is not indexing, beading, or eating red chile. Email: *jancw@wrightinformation.com*. Web: *www.wrightinformation.com*.

Acknowledgements

You know, I've always skipped over the acknowledgement sections in books because they look so darn boring. What are they there for, anyhow? Now I know. After having devoted 4 months of more than full-time work to this project, I have a better appreciation for how much effort goes into producing a book.

First, I'd like to thank my editor, Dawn Frausto, without whom this book would be a dense, rambling mess. Dawn helped polish this rock into a shining gem. Along the way, Dawn and I were assisted by many folks, including tech reviewers Dylan Ross and Charlie Park, whose eagle eyes caught many stupid errors.

Many Get Rich Slowly readers contributed their stories and ideas to this book, including Courtney Cronk, Sabino Arredondo, Jason Corbett, Trent Hamm, Jessie Smith, Donna Freedman, Jim Wang, Mike Iannantuano, Matt Jabs, Jacob Laha, John Little, Sierra Black, Matt Haughey, Tim Ferriss, April Dykman, Adam Baker, and Ramit Sethi.

Thanks, too, to all the people who read chapters here and there and gave me feedback, including Jeremy Gingerich, Dave Carlson, Andrew Cronk, Paul Hosom, Josh Bennett, Tim Kutscha, Liz Weston, Bonnie Biafore, Adam Jusko, Curtis Arnold, and Chris Guillebeau.

Special thanks to Michael Hampton, without whom I never would have started my journey from debt to wealth. Without Michael's gentle prodding, I wouldn't have changed my profligate ways, destroyed my debt, started Get Rich Slowly, or written this book. Speaking of Get Rich Slowly, I'd be remiss if I didn't thank my blog's readers for the support and education they've given me over the years. You guys are awesome!

Finally, this book wouldn't have been possible without the support of my wife, Kris Gates, who has not only tolerated my long hours in front of the computer, but read every word in these pages many times, and provided much-needed moral support. This project has proved what I already knew: Kris Gates is always right.

This book is dedicated to Sparky: *http://tinyurl.com/GRS-sparky*.

Introduction

"What we get from this adventure is just sheer joy. And joy is, after all, the end of life. We do not live to eat and make money. We eat and make money to be able to live. That is what life means and what life is for." —George Mallory

For years, I lived paycheck to paycheck on an average American salary. Every month I struggled to pay my bills and make ends meet. I spent everything I had, and sometimes more. In the decade after I graduated from college, I racked up over $35,000 in debt. I knew how to spend money, but I didn't know how to save it.

2004 was a turning point for me. My wife and I bought a 100-year-old farmhouse that needed a lot of work. My budget was already stretched to the limit, and I didn't see how I'd be able to afford the plumber, electrician, and carpenter we needed. I felt like I was drowning.

With the help of some friends, I was able to keep my head above water: They loaned me some books about money. I read them, and then went to the public library and borrowed more books on the topic. I started picking up personal-finance magazines and browsing financial websites. All of the advice made sense, but there were so many numbers and terms involved that I couldn't keep them straight.

To make sense of it all for myself—and maybe to help some others along the way—I started writing about the things I learned and posting them at *GetRichSlowly.org*. I reviewed the books I read, shared the websites I found, and wrote down my thoughts about my relationship with money. I never expected anyone other than my family and friends to read the site, but to my surprise, others wanted to learn about this stuff, too.

Get Rich Slowly has grown into an amazing community of everyday folks who help each other tackle financial problems. (The site gets half a million visitors every month!) Want to learn how to cut your cable bill by 33%, where to find the best online savings account, or find out what a bond is? Get Rich Slowly readers have the answers.

Over the years, I've continued to use the site to share what I learn about managing money. I also share my own story, both the successes and the failures. I know a lot more about money than I did 5 years ago, but I still do dumb things from time to time. (We all make mistakes, right?) The key is to learn from them and move on.

This book is the culmination of everything I've learned while turning my financial life around. I've included the most important things I've discovered during 5 years of reading and writing about money every day. I've done my best to pack *Your Money: The Missing Manual* with tons of useful info while keeping it easy to understand and (I hope) fun to read. Above all, this book aims to give you the information you need to change your financial situation for the better.

About This Book

Based on my research—and my experiences with what does and doesn't work—I've developed a list of 14 guidelines that form the basis of my financial philosophy. These ideas lurk behind every page of this book:

1. **Financial success is more about mastering the *mental* game of money than about understanding the numbers.** The math is simple; it's controlling your habits and emotions that's hard.

2. **The road to wealth is paved with goals.** Without financial goals, you have no direction, so it's easy to spend money on things you'll regret later. But if you're saving for a house, your daughter's college education, or a new car, your goal will keep you focused.

3. **To build wealth, you've got to spend less than you earn.** Successful personal finance is all about building positive cash flow (which you'll learn about in Chapter 4). That's easy to say, but not always easy to do.

4. **Saving *must* be a priority.** Before you pay your bills, buy groceries, or do anything else, you should set aside some part of your income. Start small if you have to (even $25 a month is good), and then increase your saving rate with time.

5. **Small amounts matter.** Your everyday habits have a *huge* impact on your financial success, so don't be frustrated if you can only save $25 a month for now; I started small, too. Small changes help build good habits, and they can make a real difference over time.

6. **Large amounts matter, too.** It's good to clip coupons and to save money on groceries, but it's even *better* to save money on the big stuff like buying a car or house. By making smart choices on big-ticket items, you can save thousands of dollars in one blow.

7. **Financial balance lets you enjoy tomorrow *and* today.** Being smart with money isn't about giving up your plasma TV or your daily latte. It's about setting priorities and managing expectations: choosing to spend only on the things that matter to you, while cutting costs on the things that don't.

8. **Slow and steady wins the race.** The most successful folks are those who work longest and hardest at things they love to do. So try to find ways to make frugality fun, and recognize you're in this for the long haul. Remember that you're making a lifestyle change, not looking for a quick fix.

9. **The perfect is the enemy of the good.** Too many people are afraid to start getting their finances in order because they don't know what the "best" first step is. Don't worry about getting things exactly right—just choose a good option and do *something* to get started.

10. **Failure is okay.** Even billionaires like Warren Buffett make mistakes, so don't let one slip-up drag you down. Use failures to learn how to do better next time.

11. **Nobody cares more about your money than you do.** The advice that others give you is almost always in *their* best interest—which may or may not be the same as *your* best interest. Don't do what others tell you just because they're compelling. Get advice from various folks (and books like this one), but in the end, make your own decisions.

12. **Each person is different.** There's no one right way to save, invest, pay off debt, or buy a house, so don't believe anyone who says there is. Experiment until you find methods that work for you.

13. **Action beats inaction.** It's easy to put things off, but the sooner you start moving toward your goals, the easier they'll be to reach.

14. **It's more important to be happy than to be rich.** Don't be obsessed with money—it won't buy you happiness. It'll give you more options, sure, but *happiness* is what makes life worth living. If you can stay happy and in control of your life, money will be easier to manage.

Your Money: The Missing Manual will show you how to kick debt to the curb, save for the future, and pursue your financial dreams. I've done my best to write the book that I wish I'd read 20 years ago—*before* I got deep in debt. My hope is that I can help you avoid the same fate and build a brighter financial future.

About the Outline

This book is divided into three parts, each containing several chapters:

- In **Part One: Blueprint for Financial Prosperity,** you'll learn how to lay the groundwork for success; a little advance planning will pay off big in the long run. Chapter 1 explores the relationship between money and happiness, and suggests some ways of finding balance. Chapter 2 helps you set financial goals. In Chapter 3, you'll learn that budgeting isn't necessarily evil; in fact, it can be a great way to help you defeat debt, which is the subject of Chapter 4.

- **Part Two: Laying the Foundation** teaches you the importance of cash flow—the difference between what you earn and what you spend. In Chapter 5, you'll learn frugal tactics to help you save money on everyday spending. Chapter 6 looks at the other side of the equation: How to boost your income.

    Chapter 7 helps you find the best bank accounts for storing your money, and Chapter 8 will help you get your credit cards under control. Chapter 9 discusses how to be smart when buying big items, and Chapter 10 covers the biggest expense of all: housing. Finally, Chapter 11 provides the basic info you need to deal with taxes and insurance effectively.

- **Part Three: Building a Rich Life** shows you how to use your financial foundation to build a rich life—both today and in the future. Chapter 12 gives you a brief intro to investing, and Chapter 13 explains how and why to save for retirement. Chapter 14 wraps things up with a look at the relationship between love and money.

There's no way for one book to cover *everything* there is to know about personal finance. I've covered the essentials and included pointers to where you can learn more about any given topic by doing further reading in other books, on various websites, and in magazines. Along the way, I also share real-life stories from people like you.

About MissingManuals.com

At *www.missingmanuals.com*, you'll find articles, tips, and updates to *Your Money: The Missing Manual*. In fact, we invite and encourage you to submit such corrections and updates yourself. In an effort to keep this book as up-to-date and accurate as possible, each time we print more copies of it, we'll make any confirmed corrections you've suggested. We'll also note such changes on the website, so that you can mark important corrections into your own copy of the book, if you like. (Go to *www.missingmanuals. com/feedback*, choose the book's name from the pop-up menu, and then click Go to see the changes.)

Also, on our Feedback page, you can get expert answers to questions that come to you while reading this book, write a book review, and find groups for folks who share your interest in smart money management.

We'd love to hear your suggestions for new books in the Missing Manual line. There's a place for that on missingmanuals.com, too. And while you're online, you can also register this book at *www.oreilly.com* (you can jump directly to the registration page by going here: *http://tinyurl.com/yo82k3*). Registering means we can send you updates about this book, and you'll be eligible for special offers like discounts on future editions of *Your Money: The Missing Manual*.

Safari® Books Online

 Safari® Books Online is an on-demand digital library that lets you easily search over 7,500 technology and creative reference books and videos to find the answers you need quickly.

With a subscription, you can read any page and watch any video from our library online. Read books on your cellphone and mobile devices. Access new titles before they're available for print, and get exclusive access to manuscripts in development and post feedback for the authors. Copy and paste code samples, organize your favorites, download chapters, bookmark key sections, create notes, print out pages, and benefit from tons of other time-saving features.

O'Reilly Media has uploaded this book to the Safari Books Online service. To have full digital access to this book and others on similar topics from O'Reilly and other publishers, sign up for free at *http://my.safaribooksonline.com*.

1 It's More Important to Be Happy Than to Be Rich

"Happiness, not gold or prestige, is the ultimate currency." —Tal Ben-Shahar

You don't want to be rich—you want to be **happy**. Although the mass media has convinced many Americans that wealth leads to happiness, that's not always the case. Money can certainly help you achieve your goals, provide for your future, and make life more enjoyable, but merely having the stuff doesn't guarantee fulfillment.

This book will show you how to make the most of your money, but before we dive into the details, it's important to explore why you should care. It doesn't do much good to learn about compound interest or high-yield savings accounts if you don't know how money affects your well-being.

If personal finance were as simple as understanding math, this book wouldn't be necessary; people would never overspend, get into debt, or make foolish financial decisions. But research shows that our choices are based on more than just arithmetic—they're also influenced by a complex web of psychological and emotional factors.

This chapter gives you a quick overview of the relationship between money and happiness. You'll also learn techniques for escaping the mental traps that make it hard to be content with what you have. As you'll see, you don't need a million bucks to be happy.

How Money Affects Happiness

The big question is, "Can money buy happiness?" There's no simple answer.

"It seems natural to assume that rich people will be happier than others," write psychologists Ed Diener and Robert Biswas-Diener in *Happiness* (Blackwell Publishing, 2008). "But money is only one part of psychological wealth, so the picture is complicated."

There *is* a strong correlation between wealth and happiness, the authors say: "Rich people and nations are happier than their poor counterparts; don't let anyone tell you differently." But they note that money's impact on happiness isn't as large as you might think. If you have clothes to wear, food to eat, and a roof over your head, increased disposable income has just a small influence on your sense of well-being.

To put it another way, if you're living below the poverty line ($22,050 annual income for a family of four in 2009), an extra $5,000 a year can make a *huge* difference in your happiness. On the other hand, if your family earns $70,000 a year, $5,000 may be a welcome bonus, but it won't radically change your life.

So, yes, money *can* buy some happiness, but as you'll see, it's just one piece of the puzzle. And there's a real danger that increased income can actually make you miserable—if your desire to spend grows with it. But that's not to say you have to live like a monk. The key is finding a balance between having too little and having too much—and that's no easy task.

 Note A recent article in the *Journal of Consumer Research* showed that, in general, our feelings for material purchases fade more quickly than they do for experiential purchases. Material goods depreciate: The day after you buy something, it's usually worth less than you paid for it. Experiences, on the other hand, appreciate: Your memories of the things you do—vacations you take, concerts you go to—become fonder with time because you tend to recall the positives and forget the negatives.

The Fulfillment Curve

American culture is consumption-driven. The media teaches you to want the clothes and cars you see on TV and the watches and jewelry you see in magazine ads. Yet studies show that people who are materialistic tend to be less happy than those who aren't. In other words, if you want to be content, you should own—and want—less Stuff.

In their personal-finance classic *Your Money or Your Life* (Penguin, 2008), Joe Dominguez and Vicki Robin argue that the relationship between spending and happiness is non-linear, meaning every dollar you spend brings you a little less happiness than the one before it.

More spending *does* lead to more fulfillment—up to a point. But spending too much can actually have a negative impact on your quality of life. The authors suggest that personal fulfillment—that is, being content with your life—can be graphed on a curve that looks like this:

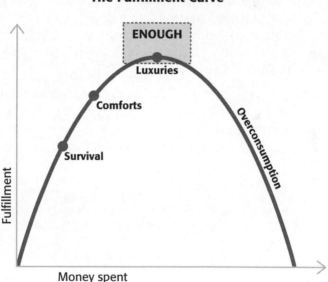

The Fulfillment Curve

This Fulfillment Curve has four sections:

- **Survival.** In this part of the curve, a little money brings a large gain in happiness. If you have nothing, buying things really does contribute to your well-being. You're much happier when your basic needs—food, clothing, and shelter—are provided for than when they're not.

- **Comforts.** After the basics are taken care of, you begin to spend on comforts: a chair to sit in, a pillow to sleep on, a second pair of pants. These purchases, too, bring increased fulfillment. They make you happy, but not as happy as the items that satisfied your survival needs. This part of the curve is still positive, but not as steep as the first section.

- **Luxuries.** Eventually your spending extends from comforts to outright luxuries. You move from a small apartment to a home in the suburbs, say, and you have an entire wardrobe of clothing. You drink hot chocolate on winter evenings, sit on a new sofa, and have a library of DVDs. These things are more than comforts—they're luxuries, and they make you happy. They push you to the peak of the Fulfillment Curve.

- **Overconsumption.** Beyond the peak, Stuff starts to take control of your life. Buying a sofa made you happy, so you buy recliners to match. Your DVD collection grows from 20 titles to 200, and you drink expensive hot chocolate made from Peruvian cocoa beans. Soon your house is so full of Stuff that you have to buy a bigger home—and rent a storage unit. But none of this makes you any happier. In fact, all of your things become a burden. Rather than adding to your fulfillment, buying new Stuff actually detracts from it.

The sweet spot on the Fulfillment Curve is in the Luxuries section, where money gives you the most happiness: You've provided for your survival needs, you have some creature comforts, and you even have a few luxuries. Life is grand. Your spending and your happiness are perfectly balanced. You have Enough.

 Yup, Enough gets a capital E, too. You'll learn more about deciding how much is Enough later in this chapter. (And don't worry: There aren't any more words with goofy capitals ahead.)

Unfortunately, in real life you don't have handy visual aids to show the relationship between your spending and your happiness; you have to figure out what Enough is on your own. But as you'll see in the next section, because we've been conditioned to believe that more money brings more happiness, most people reach the peak of the Fulfillment Curve and then keep on spending.

Caught Up in the Rat Race

Typically, as your income increases, your lifestyle grows with it. When your boss gives you a raise, you want to reward yourself (you deserve it!), so you spend more. All that new Stuff costs money to buy, store, and maintain. Gradually, your lifestyle becomes more expensive so you have to work harder to earn more. You think that if only you got another raise, then you'd have Enough. But in all likelihood, you'd just repeat the process by spending even more.

Psychologists call this vicious cycle the *hedonic treadmill,* though you probably know it as the "rat race." People on the hedonic treadmill think they'd be happy if they just had a little more money. But when they get more money, they discover something else they want. Because they're never content with what they have, they can never have Enough.

Most Americans are stuck on this treadmill. According to the U.S. Census Bureau (*http://tinyurl.com/census-inc*), in 1967 the median American household income was $38,771 (adjusted for inflation). Back then, less than one-fifth of U.S. families had color TVs and only one in 25 had cable. Compare that with 2007, when the median household income was $50,233 and nearly everyone had a widescreen color TV and cable. Americans now own twice as many cars as they did in 1967, and we have computers, iPods, and cellphones. Life is good, right? But despite our increased incomes and material wealth, we're no happier than were in the '60s.

 Note In case it's been a while since your last math class, here's a quick refresher: If you have a set of numbers, half of them will be greater than the *median*, and half will be less. The median is usually different from the average. For example, in the group of numbers 2, 3, 4, 5, and 101, the average is 23, but the median is only 4. (If economists talked about average incomes instead of median incomes, their numbers would be skewed by billionaires like Warren Buffett.)

Since 1972, the National Opinion Research Center has been polling Americans about their happiness (*http://tinyurl.com/norc-gss*). As you can see in the following graph, the numbers haven't changed much over the past 35 years. About one-third of Americans consistently say they're "very happy" with their lives (*http://tinyurl.com/gss-happy*), while a little less than one-third say they're "pretty well satisfied" with their financial situations (*http://tinyurl.com/gss-satfin*).

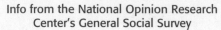
Info from the National Opinion Research
Center's General Social Survey

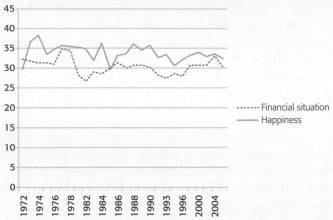

If Americans are earning more, why aren't they happier? We've been led to believe that prosperity brings peace of mind, but it turns out your grandfather was right: Money isn't everything.

The bottom line: **Money can't make you happy if your increased wealth brings increased expectations.** In other words, if you want more as you earn more, you'll never be content; there will always be something else you crave, so you'll need to work even harder to get the money to buy it. You'll be stuck on the hedonic treadmill, running like a hamster on a wheel.

The hedonic treadmill leads to lifestyle inflation, which is just as dangerous to your money as economic inflation; both destroy the value of your dollars. Fortunately, you can control lifestyle inflation. You can opt out, step off the treadmill, and escape from the rat race. To do that, you have to set priorities and decide how much is Enough. The next section shows you how.

How Much Is Enough?

Kurt Vonnegut used to recount a conversation he had with fellow author Joseph Heller (Vonnegut published this anecdote as a poem in the **New Yorker**). The two writers were at a party thrown by a billionaire when Vonnegut joked, "How does it feel to know that our host makes more in one day than **Catch-22** [Heller's best-known work] has made in its entire history?" Heller responded, "I've got something he can never have. I've got Enough."

Sudden Riches

Some folks believe their worries would vanish if only they had a six-figure salary. Others play the lottery because they think winning would solve their problems. But it's not how much you earn that determines how happy you are—it's how much you *spend* in relation to your income.

Take pro athletes: The average NFL player earns $1.1 million per year, and the average NBA player makes $4 million per year. Yet even these vast incomes sometimes aren't enough to cover what players spend. In a recent issue of *Sports Illustrated*, Pablo S. Torre described how and why athletes go broke (you can read his article at *http://tinyurl.com/brokeathletes*). He writes that after 2 years of retirement, "78% of former NFL players have gone bankrupt or are under financial stress."Within 5 years of retirement, roughly 60% of former NBA players are in similar positions.

Lottery winners have the same kinds of problems. A 2001 article in *The American Economic Review* found that after receiving half their jackpots, the typical lotto winner had only put about 16% of that money into savings. It's estimated that over a quarter of lottery winners go bankrupt. Take Bud Post: He won $16.2 million in 1988. Within weeks of receiving his first annual payment of nearly half a million dollars, he'd spent $300,000. During the next few years, Post bought boats, mansions, and airplanes, but trouble followed him everywhere. "I was much happier when I was broke," he's reported to have said. When he died in 2006, Post was living on a $450 monthly disability check. You can read more about him here: *http://tinyurl.com/budpost*.

Of course, not every wealthy person is so profligate. In fact, according to Thomas Stanley and William Danko, most millionaires are careful with their money. In their classic book *The Millionaire Next Door* (Pocket, 1998), Stanley and Danko catalog the characteristics of the quiet millionaires—those who live in average neighborhoods, drive average cars, and work average jobs. These folks are able to build and maintain wealth because they keep their spending in check—even as their incomes rise. The authors say the three words that best describe the affluent are "frugal frugal frugal."

So even if you come into a windfall like an inheritance or a bonus—or even a lottery jackpot—take your cue from the frugal millionaires: Don't spend it all in one place. (Page 304 has more about how to handle a windfall.)

Knowing that you have Enough can be better than having billions of dollars. If you're obscenely rich but aren't happy, what good is your money? Contentment comes from having Enough—not too little and not too much. But how much *is* Enough?

There's no simple answer. What's Enough for you may not be Enough for your best friend. And what you need to remain at the peak of the Fulfillment Curve (page 9) will change with time, so Enough is a bit of a moving target. It's tough to define Enough, but there are some steps you can take to figure out what it means to you.

Understand your goals and values

If you don't know why you're earning and spending money, then you can't say when you have Enough. So take time to really think about what having Enough means to you. Discuss it with your family, and explore the idea with your best friend. Is being debt-free Enough? Being able to pay cash for a new boat? Having a million dollars saved for retirement? Decide what Enough means to you, and then write it down. If you don't have an end in sight, you're at greater risk of getting stuck in the rat race.

 Note Personal goals are so critical to financial success that you'll spend all of Chapter 2 learning how to set them.

Practice conscious spending

Because the notion of Enough is so vague, the best way to approach it is to be mindful of your financial habits. The act of consciously choosing how you spend can help you make purchases that are in line with your goals and values.

Ramit Sethi popularized the concept of *conscious spending* in his book *I Will Teach You to Be Rich* (Workman Publishing, 2009). The idea is to spend with intent, deliberately deciding where to direct your money instead of spending impulsively. Sethi argues that it's okay to spend $5,000 a year on shoes—*if* that spending is aligned with your goals and values and you've made a conscious choice to spend this way (as opposed to spending compulsively—see page 65).

If you're new to conscious spending, try asking yourself the following questions:

- **Did I receive value from this equal to the amount I spent?** In other words, did you get your money's worth? You already know that $100 spent on one thing isn't always as good as $100 spent on another. Conscious spending is about striving to get the most bang for your buck.

- **Is this spending aligned with my goals and values?** Conscious spending means prioritizing: putting your money toward the things you love—and cutting costs mercilessly on the things you don't. If you're happy with the coffee at the office, then don't waste your money at Starbucks. But if your extra-hot nonfat caramel latte is the highlight of your day, then buy the latte! Spend only on the things that matter to you.

The box below tells the story of Chris Guillebeau, who has made a lot of unorthodox choices to be sure his spending matches his priorities.

Your Money and Your Life

The Art of Non-Conformity

Chris Guillebeau takes conscious spending to an extreme. At 32, he's defined what's important to him and is willing to make sacrifices to be sure his spending is aligned with his goals and values. One of his ambitions is to visit every country in the world by his 35th birthday. (As of this writing, he's visited 124 of 192 countries, and he's got 3 years to go.)

Travel is expensive, so in order to meet his goal, Guillebeau has made it his top priority. "Some people think I'm crazy," he says. "I don't own a car, so I walk everywhere. I don't even like spending a few bucks to use public transportation. But I spend thousands of dollars to fly all over the world."

By doing without the things that aren't meaningful to him—like a car—Guillebeau can afford the things he's passionate about. To read more about his unconventional life, check out his blog at *www.chrisguillebeau.com*, and look for his upcoming book, *The Art of Non-Conformity* (Perigee, 2010).

Reduce clutter

If you have so much Stuff that you need to rent a storage shed, you have more than Enough. If the Stuff leads to clutter that stresses you out, you've passed the peak of the Fulfillment Curve and your added luxuries are bringing you less happiness, not more.

Purging clutter can be a profound experience, but it can be difficult, too: You don't want to toss anything out because you might need it someday, or it has sentimental value, or it may be worth something.

Getting rid of Stuff only hurts for a little bit. Once you've pared your belongings, it's like a weight has been lifted; you feel free. Some people find the process so liberating that they go farther and practice **voluntary simplicity**, even to the point of moving into a smaller home. For example, Dave Bruno is chronicling his fight against materialism at his website (*http://tinyurl.com/100thingchallenge*); his goal is to own only 100 personal items.

 Tip *Living Green: The Missing Manual* suggests lots of great ways to de-clutter your life.

Seek balance

A balanced life is a fulfilling life. To find balance, you have to figure out how much is Enough for you—the point where you're content with what you have and can say "this much, but no more."

Once you define Enough, you gain a sense of freedom. You're no longer caught up in the rat race and have time to pursue your passions. You can surround yourself with family and friends, and rediscover the importance of *social capital*—the value you get from making personal connections with people in your community (see page 306). And because you no longer feel compelled to buy more Stuff, you can use your money to save for things that truly matter.

It's Not About the Money

If vast riches won't bring you peace of mind, what will?

In a 2005 issue of the **Review of General Psychology**, Sonja Lyubomirsky, Kennon Sheldon, and David Schkade looked at years of research to figure out what contributes to "chronic happiness" (as opposed to temporary happiness). Based on their survey, they came up with a three-part model:

- **About half of your happiness is biological.** Each person seems to have a happiness "set point," which accounts for roughly 50% of your sense of well-being. Because this set point is genetic, it's hard to change.

- **Another 10% of happiness is based on circumstances—external factors beyond your control.** These include biological traits like age, race, nationality, and gender, as well as things like marital status, occupational status, job security, and income. Your financial situation is part of this 10%—but only a part—which means it accounts for just a fraction of your total happiness.

- **The final 40% of happiness comes from *intentional activity*—the things you choose to do.** Whereas circumstances happen to you, intentional activity happens when *you* act by doing things like exercising, pursuing meaningful goals, or keeping a gratitude journal.

According to the authors, because circumstances—including your financial situation—play such a small role in your general contentment, it makes more sense to boost your bliss through intentional activity, by controlling the things you can and ignoring those you can't. (You can read the entire article at *http://tinyurl.com/hmodel*.)

Although your financial situation plays only a small role in your overall happiness, most people believe it's more important than that. Because of this, many Americans spend their lives striving for more money and possessions—but find that this materialism makes them *less* happy.

If you're caught up in the rat race, you may be dealing with things like credit card debt, living paycheck to paycheck, fighting with your spouse over money, and working a job you hate. These problems all stem from one issue: lack of control. When you feel like you have no control over money, you're worried and stressed. By taking charge of your finances, you can get rid of many of these stressors and be happier. Wealth gives you options and makes it easier to focus on things that can make you content.

This book will teach you specific ways to gain control of your finances. The first step to leading a rich life is learning how to set priorities.

Happiness by the Numbers

In their book *Happiness*, Ed Diener and Robert Biswas-Diener talk about the *happiness formula*, their attempt to quantify all this psychological stuff about money and well-being.

They found that a larger income generally makes people happier—but not always. It's not just how much you make that determines how satisfied you are with your life, but how that money relates to your desires. You might say that happiness is equal to what you have divided by what you want.

Say, for instance, that you're a famous author earning $200,000 a year. On paper, that sounds like a lot of money, but if you yearn for expensive luxuries and experiences, you may actually feel poor. On the other hand, if you're a struggling writer bringing in $40,000 a year, you can be happy as long as your expectations are low—that is, if you don't want more than you have. This is why frugality is so important. (Chapter 5 is chock-full of tips for spending less.)

For another attempt to quantify well-being, take a look at this happiness formula from *Dilbert* creator Scott Adams: *http://tinyurl.com/happy-dilbert*.

Living a Rich Life

Living richly means figuring out what to spend your time, money, and energy on—and what to ignore. Since you can't have everything, you have to prioritize. This means spending money on things that matter to you—and skimping on things that don't.

Psychologists generally agree that a life well-lived is rich in:

- **Security.** It's hard to be happy when you're constantly worrying about how to pay the bills. If you have money, you don't have to worry about those things. (But, as you now know, you don't have to be rich to be happy.) By living below your means and avoiding debt, you can gain some financial control over your life.

- **Relationships.** True wealth comes from relationships, not from dollars and cents. Wealthy or poor, people with five or more close friends are more apt to describe themselves as happy than those with fewer. A long-term, loving partnership goes hand in hand with this. And as you'll learn later (page 306), social capital can be worth as much as financial capital.

- **Experiences.** As explained in the Note on page 8, memories tend to grow more positive with time, but Stuff usually drops in value—both actual value and perceived value. As Gregory Karp writes in *The 1-2-3 Money Plan* (FT Press, 2009), "Experiences appreciate, assets depreciate." And in *Your Money and Your Brain* (Simon & Schuster, 2008), Jason Zweig notes, "Doing and being are better than having."

Remember these three pillars of happiness and you can build a rich life even on a limited income.

To further improve your relationship with money, keep these guidelines in mind:

- **Prioritize.** Spend on the things that make you happiest. There's nothing wrong with buying things you'll use and enjoy—that's the purpose of money. If you're spending less than you earn, meeting your needs, and saving for the future, you can afford things that make life easier and more enjoyable. (For another way to prioritize, see the box on page 20.)

- **Stay healthy.** There's a strong tie between health and happiness. Anyone who's experienced a prolonged injury or illness knows just how emotionally—and financially—devastating it can be. Eat right, exercise, and get enough sleep (*Your Body: The Missing Manual* has loads of tips on how to do all those things).

- **Don't compare yourself to others.** Financially, psychologically, and socially, keeping up with the Joneses is a trap. You'll always have friends who are wealthier and more successful in their careers than you. Focus on your *own* life and goals.

- **Limit media exposure.** Mass media—especially TV—tries to persuade you that happiness depends on things you don't really need and can't afford. Studies have found that watching lots of TV can influence your levels of materialism—how much you think you need to be happy.

- **Simplify.** The average Joe believes that materialism is the path to happiness—but the average Joe is wrong. Research shows that materialism actually leads to unhappiness and dissatisfaction. By simplifying your life and reducing the amount of Stuff you own (or *want* to own), you'll save money and be happier.

- **Help others.** Altruism is one of the best ways to boost your happiness. It may seem counter-intuitive (and maybe even a little self-serving), but donating to your church or favorite charity is a proven method for brightening your day.

- **Embrace routine.** Emerson wrote, "A foolish consistency is the hob-goblin of little minds," but there's evidence that *some* consistency is conducive to contentment. In *Happier* (McGraw-Hill, 2007), Tal Ben-Shahar recommends building routines around the things you love: reading, walking, gaming, knitting, whatever. Because it can be difficult to make the time for these activities, he argues that we should make rituals out of them. If you enjoy biking, make a ritual out of riding to the park every evening, for example. (See the box below for tips on finding time for what you love.)

- **Pursue meaningful goals.** As you'll learn in the next chapter, the road to wealth is paved with goals, and the same is true of the road to happiness. But for a goal to be worthwhile, it has to be related to your values and interests—it has to add something to your life. Chapter 2 will help you decide what goals to set.

On the Money

Fun Things First

You lead a busy life. There never seems to be enough time to do the things you really want, like doing yoga, running, or having a weekly night out with your sweetie. With so much already on your plate, how can you fit it all in?

In *Work Less, Live More* (Nolo Press, 2007), Bob Clyatt argues that you *can* make time for fun stuff. The secret, he says, is prioritizing:

> Imagine you have an empty jar, a collection of a few large rocks, and several handfuls of gravel. Your task is to put all the large and small rocks into the jar. One approach would be to pile all the gravel first, but doing so would leave room for only one or two of the large rocks; you wouldn't get everything to fit. Switch your approach and put the large rocks in first, and you'll find that the gravel will all fit nicely around the empty space. If a bit of gravel doesn't fit at the end, you've not lost much.

> Let too many little things take priority, and there never seems to be time for the big things. Consider the Big Rocks to be really important things you want to accomplish in life, the things that define you. Get the big things in first, work on the right projects and priorities, and let the little stuff fit in around the edges. Let your Big Rocks be non-negotiable priorities in your weekly calendar—and learn to say "no" when other things begin to intrude. Then fit those other things in where you can.

So if running makes you happy, schedule your runs—and then fit the rest of your life around them. Don't ignore your obligations, but make the stuff you have to do fit around the stuff you *want* to do, not the other way around.

The bottom line is that if you can't be content, you'll never lead a rich life, no matter how much money you have. The key to money management—and happiness—is being satisfied. It's not how much you *have* that makes you happy or unhappy, but how much you *want*. If you want less, you'll be happy with less. This isn't a psychological game or New Age mumbo-jumbo, it's fact: The lower your expectations, the easier they are to fulfill—and the happier you'll be.

That's not to say you should lead an aimless life of poverty; quite the opposite, in fact. But most people confuse the means with the ends. They chase after money and Stuff in an attempt to feel fulfilled, but their choices are impulsive and random. Their "retail therapy" doesn't address the root cause of their unhappiness: They lack goals and an underlying value system to help guide their decisions.

In the next chapter, you'll learn how to create meaningful financial goals that are aligned with your passions. Then you'll be able to use these goals to make better decisions about money. These choices will, in turn, help you live a happier life.

 Note For an excellent look at how to be happy, pick up a copy of Gretchen Rubin's *The Happiness Project* (Harper, 2009).

2 The Road to Wealth Is Paved with Goals

"If one moves confidently in the direction of his dreams, and endeavors to live the life which he has imagined, he will meet with a success unexpected in common hours."
—*Henry David Thoreau*

Whether you want to get rich or just get out of debt, you need to set goals. Goals give you purpose and help you know what your money is for. Think of goals as blueprints and money as the building material you can use to build the life you want.

When you have a fixed purpose, financial decisions are easy. You know that each night out with friends delays your ultimate objective, whether that's buying a house, saving for a wedding, or starting your own business.

In this chapter, you'll learn how to translate your dreams and passions into smart financial goals to help direct your saving and investing. But chasing your dreams isn't easy; you'll make mistakes and bad things will happen. That's why this chapter also includes tips for coping with setbacks, and equips you with tools to help you build the financial future you've dreamed of.

The Road to Success

Studies have shown again and again that people who pursue meaning-ful goals enjoy a greater sense of well-being and accomplish more than those without goals. In other words, having goals actually makes you hap-pier. And while some people succeed without setting goals, they're the exception, not the rule. For the rest of us, goals provide direction. Once you know where you're headed, you can create a budget, which (as you'll learn in Chapter 3) is like a roadmap that helps you find your way.

So how do you create goals that will guide you to financial success? The first step is discovering what brings meaning to your life.

The Importance of Passion

Goals are more than just wants: You *want* a chocolate chip cookie or the latest video game, but they're not your goals in life. Goals are about the Big Picture. You should be so passionate about your goals that you're willing to make sacrifices in order to achieve them.

You've probably set financial targets before, and it's likely you've met some of them and failed at others. Some of your goals were probably pretty cra-zy, like, "I want to be rich by the time I'm 30." That's an admirable aim, but odds are you didn't achieve it. Why not? For one thing, it's vague: What does "being rich" *mean?* And what would you do if you were?

For a goal to motivate you, it has to be specific. It should also be based on your values and desires. Do you really want to be rich in the sense of simply having lots of cash? Or were you just dreaming about what you could *do* with that wealth?

To you, being rich might mean owning a goat farm in South Carolina. For your best friend, it might mean being able to start her own business selling wine over the Internet. Whatever the case, you're probably not motivated by the money itself, but by what the money could let you be and do.

Some people have an easy time setting meaningful goals because they know *exactly* what they want. But it can be tough to know what you want, especially when you're young. With time and experience, you begin to learn what motivates you. You'll find that it's not enough to simply say, "Yeah, I might want to go to France someday. I'll make that a goal." Your goals should make you stand up and shout: "I've always wanted to spend a summer backpacking across France! How do I make that happen?"

If you're 20 years old, retirement probably seems pretty abstract—it's something that people talk about, but which has little relation to your own life. (Actually, retirement seems like a dream to many 30- and 40-year-olds, too!) Something this abstract makes for a poor goal. You know you should save for retirement, but that goal doesn't fill you with passion. But what if you re-framed the question? Think about what *does* matter to you and how saving for the future can help you to make that dream a reality.

With goals come tradeoffs, but having goals makes those tradeoffs easier to bear. If you're saving 25% of your take-home pay so you can quit your crummy job and start your own business, it's easier to pass up a ski weekend with friends because you know doing so will help you reach your goal that much sooner. When you have a why (in this case, to start your own business), the how (skipping the ski weekend) is a whole lot easier. Chris Guillebeau's story on page 15 gives a real-life example of someone who's made big tradeoffs to follow his dreams.

Once you've established your priorities, you can set meaningful goals that'll help you accomplish more and live a happier life. Your goals will form the foundation of your financial success and give you a framework that can help you decide how to spend money.

Chris Guillebeau's story on page 15

Your Money and Your Life

Life Planning

Life planning is a new approach to setting financial goals. Instead of focusing solely on maximum wealth, life planners work with people to find the point where the clients' money and happiness intersect. They help people align their spending with their values.

The father of the life-planning movement, George Kinder, is a Certified Financial Planner and the author of *The Seven Stages of Money Maturity* (Delacorte, 1999). To identify and clarify your goals, Kinder suggests thinking about three hypothetical situations:

- Imagine that you have enough money to take care of your needs, now and in the future. How would you live your life? Would you change anything? What would you do with the money?

- Now imagine that you visit your doctor and she tells you that you have 5–10 years left to live. She says that you won't feel sick, but you'll have no notice of the moment of your death. What would you do in the time you have left? Would you change your life? How?

- Finally, imagine your doctor shocks you with news that you have only 24 hours left to live. If you only had a day to live, what dreams would you have left unfulfilled? What would you wish you had finished? What would you wish you had done or been? What would you have missed?

These questions are powerful tools for figuring out what's important to you. If you take the time to really think about them and answer them honestly, they can help you clarify your personal values and set meaningful goals. For more about life planning, check out Kinder's website (*www.kinderinstitute.com*) or pick up a copy of his book.

Setting SMART Goals

Once you've decided what's important to you, it's time to set *SMART goals*.

Nobody's sure exactly who created the SMART goal framework (which you may have encountered at work), though some give credit to management consultant Peter Drucker. SMART goals are Specific, Measurable, Achievable, Relevant, and Timed. That might sound cheesy, but it's actually quite effective and can help guide you to success.

Here's a closer look at each aspect of a SMART goal:

- **Specific.** You're more likely to accomplish a specific goal than a vague one because you know exactly what you're supposed to do. In *The Power of Full Engagement* (Free Press, 2004), Jim Loehr and Tony Schwartz describe several studies that demonstrate the power of specific goals. In one, a group of women agreed to do a self-exam for breast cancer during the coming month. All of those who specified when and where they'd complete the exam did so, but only half of those weren't specific actually followed through. So don't just set a goal to fund your retirement; define when, where, and how you'll do this. For example, say "On Thursday, I'll contact HR to set things up so 10% of my paycheck automatically gets transferred to my 401(k)."

- **Measurable.** If you can't measure your progress, you can't know when you've met your goal. "I want to be rich" isn't measurable, but "I want to have $100,000 in savings" is. Such goals let you track your progress, stay focused, and know when you've finished.

- **Achievable.** There's magic in thinking big: Big goals force you to stretch, to look beyond yourself. But make sure your goals are realistic. There's a difference between, "I want to be the richest person in the world!" and "I want to have $500,000 saved by the time I'm 50." The latter might be tough, but it's doable; the former is just a pipe dream.

- **Relevant.** As discussed in the previous section, your financial goals should relate to your values and your situation. You're far more likely to achieve goals that reflect your priorities.

- **Timed.** The final step is to give your goal a timeline. It's okay to leave some goals open-ended, but most of your objectives should have a target completion date. For maximum impact, don't just pick a relative duration like "a few months"; specify an actual date when you want to complete your goal.

Why go to all this trouble? Because when you describe your goals in exact terms, you're more likely to succeed. If you create meaningful, smart financial goals—and follow through with them—you'll make better choices about money (and be happier, too).

The How of Happiness

During her nearly 20 years of research into goals and happiness, Sonja Lyubomirsky—author of *The How of Happiness* (Penguin, 2008)—has learned a lot about what makes an effective goal. In addition to the elements of the SMART framework, she says that goals should be:

- **Positive.** Positive goals (where you're attempting to reach a target, like saving for a vacation) yield better results than negative goals (where you're trying to avoid something, like cutting out your daily latte).

- **Flexible.** Your goals will evolve over time. As your priorities change, your goals should, too. This isn't an excuse to abandon a difficult goal or to quit just because you failed to meet it. But if you lose your job, say, you need to be willing to adapt your goals to take your new circumstances into account.

- **Activity-oriented.** Goals that involve doing rather than getting make people happier. Pursuing experiential goals will bring you more fulfillment than obtaining more Stuff.

SMART goals can help you achieve financial success. But setting goals with these three *extra* attributes can also help you find happiness.

To make sure you achieve your goals, keep these guidelines in mind:

- **Stay focused.** Pursue only a few goals at a time. It's tempting to multitask and work toward many things simultaneously, but you're more likely to succeed if you focus on as few goals as possible. If you try to take on several large goals at once, it's easy to get overwhelmed and lose your way. If you're focusing on debt reduction, just focus on debt reduction—worry about saving for a down payment after you've licked your debt. Do one thing at a time, and do it well.

- **Automate what you can.** One of the most effective ways to increase your odds of success is to take the choice out of your hands. You'll have better luck saving, for example, if you set up an automatic, repeating transfer from your checking account than if you have to remember to do it yourself every month. (To make this even *more* effective, deposit your income into your savings account and set up automatic transfers to checking.) Automation helps take the stress out of pursuing your goals.

- **Make it a habit.** In Chapter 1, you learned that rituals lead to happiness (page 20). Turns out they also help you reach financial goals. If you can't automate your monthly contributions to your savings account, make a ritual out of it: Get in the habit of sitting down and manually transferring the money each payday, for instance.

- **Break large goals into smaller pieces.** A goal like "save a $20,000 down payment for a house by 2014" can be daunting. You'll feel like you're making more progress if you break such long-term goals into sub-goals. So instead of trying to save $20,000 in 4 years, aim for $5,000 per year. It's easier to see progress when you're saving $400 a month toward a $5,000 target than when you're saving $400 a month toward a $20,000 target.

- **Do something for tomorrow *and* today.** As mentioned earlier, you're more likely to succeed if you focus on just a few goals at once. One way to multitask without becoming overwhelmed is to work on one short-term goal, one mid-term goal, and one long-term goal at the same time. If your long-term goal is to save for a down payment on a house, for example, you might also have a mid-term goal of saving for a holiday in Hawaii, and a short-term goal of asking your boss for a raise.

- **Review your progress.** In the next chapter, you'll learn how to create a budget and track your spending. Doing both of these things helps you see how far you've advanced toward your goals. If you don't keep tabs on where you've been, it's easy to lose track of where you're going.

- **Be patient.** You won't meet your objectives overnight. In fact, it can take years to meet some financial goals, so give it time. Trust the process and believe in yourself.

Ultimately, goals are a means, not an end. It's the process of working toward them that brings happiness—not the actual destination. That's not to say you should set goals you can never meet: You *do* want to pay off your debt or take that trip to Hawaii. But as you finish one big goal, set another. If you give yourself a series of challenges, you'll be happier and more successful.

The American Dream

Sabino's family moved to the United States when he was 10 years old. They were poor and didn't speak English. But from a young age, Sabino wanted to be part of the American Dream. Sabino learned English, worked hard, and put himself through college.

After Sabino got married, he and his wife Kim set financial goals. Their chief aim was for Kim to stay home and raise a family. So while their friends were buying homes and new cars, Sabino and Kim rented a mobile home in the country for $200 a month and paid $950 cash for a 1982 Honda Accord. They both worked full-time jobs, but they lived off Sabino's income alone and used Kim's salary to pay off $35,000 in student loans.

"We made sacrifices," Sabino says. "We made these choices because of the goals we had. We knew what we were working for, and we were happy to do it."

Today, Sabino is a successful business owner and Kim stays home to raise their three children, just as they'd planned. Because of their diligence, they now own a nice home in the country and a newer car that's fully paid for. By setting financial goals, staying focused, and making sacrifices, they were able to create the kind of life they'd dreamed about.

Tools and Resources to Help You Achieve Your Goals

Working toward goals isn't always easy. It can be a long slog, and sometimes you'll want to give up. To increase their odds of success, many people find it useful to set up systems to stay on track. This section explains several strategies and tools.

 Tip Positive reinforcement is more effective than negative reinforcement. Studies show that you'll do a better job of reaching your goals if you reward yourself for successes rather than beat yourself up over failures.

Accountability Partners

One of the best ways to stay on track is to find an **accountability partner,** somebody to share your progress with. You'll want to pair up with someone you can trust and who has a positive outlook. Preferably, she'll be in a financial situation similar to yours and will have similar goals, but that's certainly not a requirement. Sometimes the best accountability partners act as mentors, sharing their knowledge and wisdom.

Some people use their spouses as accountability partners, but that's not always the best choice because emotional baggage can get in the way. Others have success confiding in siblings or close friends. Whoever you pick, make sure it's someone you can trust, since you'll be sharing sensitive financial info.

When you've found an accountability partner:

- **Discuss your financial situations.** Be honest. Make a list of all your debts and account balances. Many people feel awkward about revealing financial data, but if you're not open about your situation, your partner can't do her job.

- **Share your goals.** Explain what you hope to accomplish and why. If you foresee challenges, let your partner know about them.

- **Schedule monthly reviews.** At the end of each month, update each other on your progress. What are your account balances now? Have you made progress toward your goals? What challenges have you faced?

- **Support each other.** The best part of having an accountability partner is that you're in the trenches together, so you can commiserate and encourage each other. But it's also important to speak up when you think your partner is being irresponsible. You're there to help each other achieve financial success, so you need to be honest.

For a real-life example of two sisters who act as accountability partners for each other, check out this article from Get Rich Slowly: *http://tinyurl.com/moneypartner*.

Web-Based Tools

An accountability partner will help you to stay on track, but she can't *always* be there for you. She's only human, after all. Sometimes it's useful to get help from a creature that never sleeps: the Internet. A variety of web-based tools can help you meet your goals. Here are a few good ones:

- **Joe's Goals** (*www.joesgoals.com*) is a simple website for tracking daily goals; it's meant to help you develop new habits. Inspired in part by Benjamin Franklin's 13 virtues (*http://tinyurl.com/virtuousben*), the site is perfect for reinforcing new financial routines. It lets you track positive and negative goals, and keeps a record of your progress. Cost: free.

- **43 Things** (*www.43things.com*) is ideal for tracking long-term goals. It lets you list your goals and keep a journal of your progress. You can also cheer on other people as they pursue their goals. Cost: free.

- **StickK** (*www.stickk.com*) takes a unique approach: You set goals, and then commit to a consequence if you don't meet them. For example, you might decide to pay off your credit cards by the end of next year—and if you don't, you'll mow your best friend's lawn for a whole summer. StickK tracks these commitments and consequences, and lets others view your progress. Cost: free.

- **The Prioritizer** (*http://tinyurl.com/prioritizer*) is a simple tool from CNN Money: You create a list of up to 15 goals, and the site then asks you to choose between each possible pair of goals. When you're finished, you have a prioritized list of objectives. Cost: free.

- **Lifetick** (*www.lifetick.com*) may be the most comprehensive goal-tracking site on the Internet. It lets you enter your core values, and then encourages you to set SMART goals (page 26). Each goal is broken into sub-tasks that are easy to track. There's also a Lifetick iPhone app. Cost: A free account lets you track four goals. For $20 per year, you can track unlimited goals and use advanced tracking features.

There are other options, of course. If you're a do-it-yourself type, you may find that Google Docs (*http://docs.google.com*), which is free, provides all the goal-tracking power you need. You could keep a word-processing document of your big goals, and track your daily goals in a spreadsheet, say. Some people use Wordpress blogs (*http://wordpress.org*) to record their progress. Experiment to find which method works best for you.

Old-School Tools

Not everyone is comfortable with web-based tools, especially when it comes to tracking their financial lives. If you're one of these people, there are plenty of other ways to stay focused.

For example, I, your humble author, use a spiral notebook. Every day, I make a list of my short- and long-term goals; paying the bills and paying off the mortgage both go on the list. As I accomplish a goal, I cross it off the list. At the end of the day, I copy all of my unfinished goals to a new page. In this way, the stuff I haven't finished floats to the top of the list and I add new goals at the bottom. You can use this same technique to track goals in your favorite text editor or spreadsheet program (including Google Docs; see the previous section).

Other people like visual reminders of their progress. You can draw a debt thermometer and stick it to the fridge, or write your annual savings goal on an index card and tape it to the bathroom mirror. Or create a chart with 360 checkboxes—one for every mortgage payment—and check off the boxes one by one as you make payments.

There are many ways to track the progress toward your financial goals, and no one method is right for everyone. Go with whatever works for you.

Coping with Mistakes and Setbacks

It's unlikely you'll achieve all your goals without encountering setbacks or making mistakes. When you get sidetracked from your goals, it's easy to get discouraged. You can waste a lot of time reacting to problems—bounced checks, emergency car repairs, and so on. The best way to deal with financial setbacks is to prepare for them.

There are two main ways to lessen the impact of setbacks. You can do both of these *before* disaster strikes:

- **Educate yourself.** The more you know, the better you can anticipate problems. Read personal-finance books, magazines, and blogs. Most importantly, talk to the people you know who have control of their finances; they'll probably be happy to offer advice.

 Tip For more recommended sources of financial info, head to this book's Missing CD page at *www.missingmanuals.com*.

- **Be prepared.** Start an emergency fund (page 59). Setting aside $500–$1,000 in savings is cheap insurance. If you have a cash cushion, your financial plans can't be derailed by a single mistake or crisis (unless it's *big*). Your emergency fund can grow as you become more financially stable.

Even if you're prepared and educated, you're still going to make mistakes now and then, so you need to know how to pick up the pieces after things fall apart. Here are some strategies for minimizing the damage:

- **Don't panic.** When you suffer a setback or realize you've made a mistake, try to relax and do not freak out. Take an hour or two to distract yourself. Better yet, sleep on the problem—it's amazing how a little time can provide some perspective.

- **Believe in yourself.** Though you may not know exactly how to solve the problem at hand, trust that you'll find a solution. Stay positive, solve the problem, and learn from the experience.

- **If possible, undo it.** You can reverse some mistakes. Say you just blew a bunch of money on new clothes or are feeling buyer's remorse over your new Nintendo Wii. Return the items, if you can. If that's not an option, sell them to recoup some of your loss.

- **Evaluate your options.** Some mistakes and setbacks aren't reversible: If a little old lady runs a red light and totals your car, there's no undoing the damage. So make the best of the situation: Create a list of your options, keeping your long-term goals in mind. This will help you avoid making rash decisions.

- **Don't let it get you down.** When things go wrong, it can be tempting to ease the pain by spending more money. But compulsive spending (page 65) just makes it harder to reach your goals, which will make you feel worse, not better. So fight the urge to practice "retail therapy." Don't let one problem snowball into two or three.

- **Learn from your mistakes.** Figure out where you went wrong. How did that traveling salesman sell you those overpriced steak knives? What can you do in the future to avoid doing the same thing again? This is a fine line to walk: You don't want to beat yourself up, but you don't want to keep making the same mistakes, either.

- **Don't dig a deeper hole.** Money spent is money spent. Just because you've already sunk $200 into a gym membership you never use doesn't mean you need to *keep* spending money on it. Cut your losses by getting out as soon as possible.

- **Keep your goals in mind.** A setback is just that: a temporary roadblock on your journey to something more important. Make peace with the past and keep your mind on the future.

Setbacks are disheartening, but remember: Failure is okay. Mistakes are lessons in disguise. There's a Japanese proverb about perseverance that translates as "Fall down seven times, get up eight." Successful people fail just as often as the unsuccessful; the only difference is that successful people learn from their mistakes, get back on their feet, and resolutely march toward their goals.

If you've made some poor choices or had some bad stuff happen to you—or both—don't give up. Use the mistakes to launch yourself on a new path. It's never too late to change direction and start making smart choices. Build your future on the ashes of the past.

 Tip For more on transforming failure to success, read John C. Maxwell's *Failing Forward* (Thomas Nelson, 2007).

Fighting Financial Trolls

As you travel the path to wealth, you'll inevitably run into *financial trolls*, which Steve Pavlina describes on his website (*http://tinyurl.com/wealthlessons*) this way:

> Financial trolls strive to sabotage your financial pursuits. These trolls can be internal or external. They're the people who make comments like, "Wealthy people are so greedy. They only care about themselves and will take advantage of anyone to make money." Financial trolls are also the internal voices that say, "If you make too much money, people will judge you harshly for it. They'll assume that's all you care about."

External trolls are people with chips on their shoulders who cling to preconceived notions or just want to argue. They're not worth your time, so dealing with them is easy: Ignore them. Redirect the conversation, leave the room, or hang up the phone. Above all, don't argue—any time you argue with a troll, the troll wins.

Internal trolls are more insidious than their external cousins because they're part of you, so eradicating them requires self-discipline. Internal trolls include:

- **Self-defeating thoughts and behaviors:** "I can't do this—it's too difficult", "I'm not smart enough", "It's too much work", "I don't deserve to have money."
- **Procrastination:** "I'll start next week", "I'll worry about this later", "I can start saving next month." For more on how to beat the procrastination habit, see *http://tinyurl.com/GRS-putoff*.
- **Rationalization:** "Buying just one pair of shoes won't blow my budget", "I'm out with my friends—I should have fun", "I deserve to reward myself for how well I've been doing lately."
- **Barriers:** "I don't know how to open a Roth IRA", "It's too much bother to set up automatic deposits", "Sure I could shop around for lower rates, but I don't like talking on the phone." (There's more on how to knock down the barriers that hold you back at *http://tinyurl.com/GRS-barriers*.)

Most internal trolls are a product of self-doubt and can be best combated through exercise, discipline, positive social interaction, and a healthy diet. (Yes, exercise and a healthy diet can help you with your finances!)

Some trolls are difficult to defeat: What do you do about a partner who insists on sabotaging your family's financial security? How do you cope with your own compulsive spending? Problems like these may require the assistance of a trained professional like an accountant, lawyer, psychologist, or financial planner. The important thing is to deal with them; otherwise, they'll hold you back and keep you from achieving your goals. For more on defeating both kinds of trolls, read T. Harv Eker's *Secrets of the Millionaire Mind* (Collins, 2005).

Final Thoughts on Pursuing Goals

Setting meaningful goals that are closely aligned with your passions can help you make better decisions about money. When you're tempted to spend on something that doesn't match your priorities, you can resist because you know that your money is better used somewhere else. (The next chapter has detailed info about using goals to direct your spending.)

One thing more than any other can help you achieve your financial goals: action. If you want to pay off your debt, own your home, or retire early, the best thing you can possibly do is *start today*. Commit to your goal and take the first step. The sooner you start, the sooner you'll be living the life of your dreams.

3 "Budget" Is Not a Four-Letter Word

"A budget is telling your money where to go instead of wondering where it went."
—John C. Maxwell

As you learned in the last chapter, your financial goals are your destinations. But to get from here to there, you need a map to show the way. In other words, you need a budget.

To most people, budgeting sounds about as much fun as a trip to the dentist. But creating and sticking to a budget doesn't *have* to be a giant chore, and it can have huge benefits. You probably think of a budget as a restrictive, tedious accounting of every penny you earn or spend. Turns out budgets don't need to be super detailed to be helpful.

For a lot of people, a broad, general budget gives them the guidance they need to reach their financial goals without making them feel like they're in a straightjacket. But some people prefer a detailed budget with lots of categories. If you pick a budget that fits the way you live, it can help you meet your goals more quickly than you ever imagined.

This chapter will give you some basic budget frameworks that lots of people have road-tested and found helpful. You can use them as is, or build on them to create a more detailed budget. You'll also learn why many budgets fail, and find out how to avoid common pitfalls. Finally, you'll get a rundown of some of the best computer programs for tracking your budget.

Mapping Your Financial Future

You may have the wrong idea about budgets—lots of folks do. Budgets aren't meant to control you, and they shouldn't prevent you from enjoying life. In fact, when done properly, budgeting doesn't make you spend less on the stuff you want; it helps you spend more on the stuff that *matters*.

In their classic **The Millionaire Next Door**, Thomas Stanley and William Danko write, "Operating a household without a budget is akin to operating a business without a plan, without goals, without direction." In Chapter 2, you learned how to set meaningful goals. A budget is simply a plan that helps you reach those goals; it's a way to specify how and where you want to spend your money.

Your budget can show you where you've already spent your money (expense tracking), what you have available to spend now, and where you want to spend your money in the future (expense planning).

If you don't look at what you've spent in the past, you have no way of knowing how your current spending relates to your habits; in other words, you can't know what your "typical" spending looks like. And if you don't look at the future, you're not taking an active role in directing your money, which makes it hard to reach your goals. A good budget helps you look at the past, present, *and* future so you can evaluate your spending decisions in relation to your past choices and future plans.

Many budget skeptics turn into budget evangelists once they discover that budgeting can take them from deficit spending (spending more than they earn) to actually having a cash surplus (earning more than they spend); see the box on page 39 for a real-life example. In this way, rather than making you feel confined, a budget can actually be liberating. Keep reading to learn more about the joys of budgeting.

Building a Budget That Works

As mentioned earlier, your budget is your roadmap to success. It should help you take charge of your financial situation and steer you toward your goals. The key is choosing the right map. Maps are designed to make your journey easier, and the same is true of budgets. Yet when most people budget, they create elaborate, detailed lists of categories and impose so many rules on themselves that their budgets hinder their progress instead of helping, and they eventually give up. But it doesn't have to be that way.

This section will show you some simple yet effective budget frameworks you can adapt to suit your life. Some of them have as few as three categories. You can't get much simpler than that, now can you?

Budgeting Your Way to Success

In 2005, Jason was living paycheck to paycheck when his wife gave birth to their second child. Jason realized that unless he started saving, he wouldn't be able to afford clothes for his kids, let alone send them to college. So he decided to do something about it.

Jason had tried budgeting before, but without success. The systems he used were too complex and they felt restrictive. "I tried to account for every nickel, every dime," he says. "That didn't work for me. I always gave up after a day or two."

Then he had his *aha!* moment. "One day I sat down and made a spreadsheet," he says. "My wife and I earned a certain amount of money, and we decided that was all we were going to spend. I took my bank statement and put the numbers into the computer. I just made the simplest budget I could: income, fixed expenses, and whatever was left over. Nothing fancy. The first few months of budgeting were hit-and-miss, but that was okay. I made adjustments and learned to set priorities. I learned from my mistakes. After a few months, the budget was liberating."

Jason started with a basic budget and added complexity with time. Eventually he was able to pay off over $11,000 in debt *and* break the cycle of paycheck-to-paycheck living. Today he still uses a budget—but now he only has to fuss with it once a year.

Jason now runs a blog called No Credit Needed (*www.ncnblog.com*), where he helps others tackle their debt and spending issues. He tells his readers that keeping a budget was central to overcoming his financial problems.

"If you had told me 5 years ago that today I'd be debt free, my retirement accounts would be fully funded, *and* I'd have plenty of money to live on, I would have thought you were crazy," he says. "But all of these things are true. And it's because my budget helped me paint a picture of my spending."

Simple Budget Frameworks

Many budgets fail because they're too complex. When something is difficult, it can become a chore, and if it's a chore, you're not going to stick with it. Your first budget should guide your spending in broad ways rather than determining how you spend every single penny.

The key is to start simple. Don't begin by tracking 50 spending categories—you'll get overwhelmed. Instead, try starting with 10 categories, or five, or even just two. Simple budgets provide a general framework for spending. This may sound a little sloppy, but loose budgeting is actually surprisingly powerful.

In *The Only Investment Guide You'll Ever Need* (Harvest Books, 2005), Andrew Tobias offers the following simple yet effective budget: Destroy all your credit cards; invest 20% of all that you earn and never touch it; live on the remaining 80%, no matter what. Although Tobias is being glib, budgeting really can be that easy if you're disciplined. If you follow his three steps—and you start early enough—you can become rich.

In *All Your Worth* (Free Press, 2005), Elizabeth Warren and Amelia Tyagi propose a budgeting method similar to Tobias's, though they're less tongue-in-cheek than he is. The authors argue that, in order to succeed financially, you need to balance three broad areas of your finances. They say to divide your monthly net income (that's *after*-tax income—what you actually take home each paycheck) as follows:

- Allocate no more than 50% to needs, including housing, transportation, groceries, insurance, and a basic wardrobe.

- Spend up to 30% on wants like cable TV, clothing beyond the basics, dining out, concert tickets, comic books, knitting supplies, and so on.

- Set aside at least 20% for savings, including paying off debt.

The Balanced Money Formula

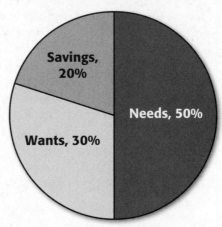

Savings, 20%

Wants, 30%

Needs, 50%

> **Tip** When creating a budget, think of savings and debt reduction as interchangeable. While you have debt, your main focus is to get rid of it—saving money is secondary. Conquering debt takes time, but it can be done. See Chapter 4 for debt-defeating pointers.

This budget framework lets you save for the future *and* have fun today. The authors insist that to maintain financial balance and be happy, you can't spend more than 50% on needs (spending less than that is even better). For example, if you take out an enormous mortgage and overload yourself with a bunch of monthly bills, you'll feel swamped and unhappy.

> **Tip** You can think of financial happiness as inversely related to how much you spend on needs: The lower your needs, the higher your happiness. (See page 21 for more about how expectations affect happiness.)

Warren and Tyagi say most budgets fail because they don't leave room for fun. Their formula lets you spend 30% of your money on the things you want, with no restrictions. So spend it all on baseball cards or a trip to Europe if that makes you happy. The final 20% of your income should go to savings—or debt reduction.

Finally, let's look at a budget framework shared by Richard Jenkins in an article for MSN Money (*http://tinyurl.com/60pct-solution*). After 20 years of budgeting, Jenkins decided that a detailed budget was too much work for too little information, so he developed a simpler framework.

Jenkins's goal is to keep committed expenses manageable. (Committed expenses are the wants and needs you can't or won't compromise on; you're committed to them.) He suggests allocating your monthly gross (that's *pre*-tax) income like this:

- 60% to committed expenses like taxes, clothing, basic living expenses, insurance, charity (including tithing), and regular bills (like cable).

- 10% to short-term savings for things like vacations, home repairs, new appliances, and so on.

- 10% to long-term savings including car purchases, home renovations, emergency savings, *and* paying down debt.

- 10% to retirement savings through Roth IRAs, 401(k)s, and the like.

- 10% for fun money you can spend on anything you want: hobbies, dining out, whatever.

The 60% Solution

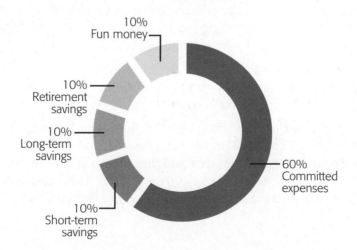

When your committed expenses rise, so does your stress level. So Jenkins says that the best way to relieve money pressure is to reduce committed expenses: cut the cable TV, spend less on clothing, reduce your rent, and so on. If you can keep these costs under 60% of your income, you'll have more money to spend on other things—like having fun.

The budget frameworks listed in this section are starting points, and if you follow them, you'll be in good shape. But there's no reason you can't do more by going beyond the percentages they suggest. If you choose the Balanced Money Formula, say, and you can reduce your needs to *below* 50% of your income, great. If you can get them down to 40% or 30% of your income, that's even better.

Next, let's take a look at how you can use these frameworks to build an actual budget.

Budgeting in Practice

Budget frameworks can help you wrap your head around the big picture, but most people need at least a *little* more detail to create a budget that'll actually help them change their spending habits. Whereas budget frameworks have broad, general categories like savings, wants, and needs, actual budgets usually have *specific* categories like groceries, car payment, mortgage, and so on.

How can you decide what categories to use? One way is to get ideas from budget templates, which you can find online at places like *http://tinyurl. com/ramseybudget* and *http://tinyurl.com/googlebudgets*, or in books like Mary Hunt's *Debt-Proof Living* (DPL Press, 2005) or Dave Ramsey's *The Total Money Makeover* (Thomas Nelson, 2003). But it's important to not just blindly use a budget that belongs to somebody else; your budget should fit *your* life. You may want to use your budget to:

- **Track problem areas.** Do you buy a lot of music or spend too much on dining out? If these habits make it hard for you to achieve your goals, incorporate them into your budget. By adding a budget category to track your music expenses, for example, you can continue to indulge your hobby—within reason.

- **Save for specific goals.** Maybe you plan to visit your aunt in Cleveland next year, and want to save $1,200 for the trip. Add a category to your budget so you'll save $100 per month toward this goal.

It's up to you how detailed to make your budget. To get started, take one of the budget frameworks from earlier in this chapter, like the Balanced Money Formula, and break each of the broad categories into three to five more specific categories.

Let's say, for example, that your family's take-home pay totals $4,000 per month. You'd use this number to construct your budget. (Always budget with only your actual income; don't include bonuses or raises you've been promised.) Based on this hypothetical income, you might split the Balanced Money Formula into the following categories:

Sample Balanced Money Formula Budget		
Needs: 50%, or $2,000	**Wants: 30%, or $1,200**	**Savings: 20%, or $800**
Rent: $800	Entertainment: $400	Credit card payments: $300
Utilities: $150	Dining out: $300	Your retirement savings: $200
Transportation: $300	Clothes and grooming: $200	Your spouse's retirement savings: $200
Insurance: $150	Miscellaneous: $150	Your kid's college fund: $100
Groceries: $500	Charitable giving: $150	
Health care: $100		

These numbers are *targets*. Every month, do your best to stay within the goals you set, but be willing to make course corrections based on your actual habits. For instance, if your family struggles to keep your dining out expenses under $300, you might bump your target spending in that category to $400 and drop your entertainment target to $300.

If you really wanted to get more detailed about your spending in a certain category, you could break things down further. Say you wanted to know where all of your entertainment spending is going. To find out, you might create sub-categories for movies, concerts, and sporting events.

This is just one way to create a more detailed budget; you need to choose a level of detail that's right for you. I recommend starting broad—maybe just using a basic framework for a month or two—and then adding detail as needed. One reason budgets fail is that people try to get *too* detailed; so start basic, and then add enough structure to meet your needs. The benefit of starting simple and adding complexity—rather than doing the reverse—is that you add only the details you need instead of being overwhelmed with too much noise at the start.

You're more likely to stick to a budget if the categories you track reflect *your* situation and spending habits, not somebody else's. Make sure your budget reflects your goals and values: If you want to travel, then budget for travel; if you want to donate 10% to your church, then budget for tithing. The next section has more tips for sticking to your budget.

Sticking to a Budget

There's more to budgeting than just putting numbers down on paper. Drafting your framework and setting up categories is all well and good, but it doesn't mean a hill of beans unless you adjust your behavior accordingly. Whether you stick to your budget depends on how you spend money on a daily basis. The following sections offer strategies that can increase your odds of success.

Note It can take time to get your spending to match your budget, so be patient. It may take several months to get the kinks out. If you're struggling, change tactics: Switch from a detailed budget to a loose budget—or vice versa. And if you suffer setbacks, the list on page 33 has strategies to help you cope.

Tracking Your Spending

If you struggle to stick to your budget (or struggle with money in general), it may help to track your spending. It can be a tedious process, but what you learn about your spending habits makes tracking worth the effort. Without doing this, it can be hard to know how much you've really been spending—and what you've been spending it on.

Tracking your spending demystifies money and puts you in control. You'll have a heightened awareness of your financial habits, which will let you make changes to improve your situation. By looking at the details, you'll have a better sense of your overall spending and begin to understand how your one-DVD-a-week buying habit affects other parts of you your life.

The classic book *Your Money or Your Life* recommends that you keep a daily money log to record your spending. This log can take any form: a pocket-sized memo book, a computer text file, a spreadsheet, personal-finance software—whatever.

Every time you get money—from a paycheck or a garage sale or by picking up change off the ground—write it down. Every time you spend money—paying bills or buying coffee or paying bus fare—write it down. Keep track of *every penny* that enters or leaves your life.

 Note When you track your spending, it's important not to make judgments. This activity is meant to *describe* your money habits, not to change them. (You probably do want to change them, but that's a different task.) So write everything down, whether you're proud of it or not.

Some transactions are easy to forget, like when you pay with cash or buy stuff online. To help you remember:

• **Get a receipt for everything.** Make a habit of asking for receipts, and keep them in one place so you know where to find them.

- **Record your transactions weekly.** Some people track their spending daily, but it can be hard to detect patterns when you look that closely. Besides, daily bookkeeping can be a chore. You'll probably have more success if you record your transactions weekly. A good strategy is to make it a habit—do it at the same time every Saturday morning, for example.

This process will show you your actual spending habits—which may not match what you think they are. You can then use this knowledge to fine-tune your budget and set financial goals. At the very least, you'll get a snapshot of where your money has been going.

Frequently Asked Question

How Detailed Should My Records Be?

When you first begin budgeting and tracking your spending, it's tough to know how detailed you should get. Should your budget simply include a Food category, or should you break Food into Groceries and Dining Out? Should you track produce separately? If you go to the store and buy a $3.19 bottle of shampoo and an $0.89 pack of bubblegum, should you record both as groceries?

The answer is: Track what's important to you. Remember that what gets measured gets managed. In other words, the things you track are things you'll be better able to control.

If you think you spend too much on candy, then track it. If you want to know how much you spend on beauty products, track that. But don't go overboard; if you have too many categories, tracking gets tedious. Also, be consistent: If you decide that shampoo counts as groceries because you buy it at the grocery store, then include it in that category every time.

Envelope Budgeting

The envelope budgeting system is a simple method that you can use with any sort of budget to help you manage your spending. The basic process is this: When you get paid, you put cash in various envelopes designated for specific budget categories. Here's how it works:

1. **Choose your categories.** You should have one envelope for each category you plan to track. Write the category's name on each envelope.

2. **Set money aside.** After you deposit your paycheck, withdraw cash for each budgeted category. So if you've budgeted $200 for groceries, put $200 in your Grocery envelope and note the amount on the back.

3. **Spend as usual.** Throughout the month, take cash from the envelopes to make your purchases. Write your withdrawals on the back: If you spend $77 at the grocery store, note that you have $123 left for the pay period. After you buy something, put the receipt and the change back in the envelope.

4. **When an envelope is empty, you're done.** If you run out of money in an envelope, you have two options. Hardcore budgeters argue that you should suck it up until your next paycheck rolls around; once you've spent your entertainment budget, that's it. ("How else will you learn discipline?" they ask.) Others say that it's okay to take from one envelope to fund another. Whichever route you choose, the important thing is *not* to resort to credit—that would defeat the whole purpose of this cash-based system.

5. **Decide what to do with the leftovers.** At the end of the pay period, if you have money left in an envelope, you can leave it there to bulk up that category for the next round. Better yet, use the surplus to pay down your debt or make a deposit into long-term savings.

6. **Do it all over again with your next paycheck.** If you discover that you always have a deficit or surplus in certain categories, adjust your budget accordingly.

 Tip This YouTube video does a fantastic job of explaining envelope budgets: *http://tinyurl.com/envelope-budget*. The Frugal Dad blog has a more in-depth explanation of the system: *http://tinyurl.com/frugal-envelope*.

You can use this method whether your budget is simple or complex. If you don't want to hassle with actual envelopes—or carry around large amounts of cash—check out Mvelopes (*www.mvelopes.com*) or YNAB (*www.youneedabudget.com*), software that lets you manage your budget using virtual envelopes; learn more on page 49.

Think Yearly

If you're having a tough time staying within your budget, the problem could be that you're trying to predict your spending over too small a time frame. A study published in the *Journal of Consumer Research* in August 2008 found that folks who made annual budgets did a better job of predicting what they'd spend than those who made monthly budgets.

Yearly budgets are more accurate because people consider more expense categories when thinking long-term. If you build a monthly budget in April, for example, will you remember to include a category for Christmas gifts? If you instead take the whole year into account, you'll remember to include stuff like that.

The downside of yearly budgets is that they aren't very useful for planning day-to-day spending. The solution is to get the best of both worlds:

- **Create an annual budget first.** It's easier for most people to estimate yearly expenses than monthly ones.

- **Make a monthly budget based on your annual one.** Once you have your annual budget, divide the estimated expenses in each category by 12 to get monthly numbers.

Voilà—you've got yourself a monthly budget that takes seasonal expenses into account.

Automating Your Budget

Whether you use a simple budget or a more detailed one, do yourself a favor and automate the budgeting process.

The past two decades have seen a revolution in personal finance. It used to be that you had to balance your checkbook by hand every month. You'd take your bank statement, your receipts, and your checkbook register, record all of your transactions, and then try to make sure everything matched; it was a laborious and often maddening process. And if you tried to keep a budget at the same time, it could be even more frustrating.

Some people like using pencil and paper to track their money; for the rest of us, personal-finance programs make it easy to track spending and build a budget. Your biggest decision is whether to use software you install on your computer or an online program. The next two sections explain your options.

Desktop Software

A few years ago, you could choose from several well-known personal finance programs for your computer, but now there's only one: Quicken. With the extinction of Microsoft Money, Inuit's Quicken is the last major money-management program out there.

Despite being the sole survivor, Quicken is far from perfect: It has some bugs, it has so many features that it can be overwhelming, and many people report being frustrated with Intuit's customer service.

These caveats aside, if you want to automate your finances offline, Quicken is a great option. You can enter transactions just like in a checkbook register, or download account data from your bank or credit-card company. The program also lets you track your investments and create budgets. And Quicken offers a wide range of reports, charts, and graphs to help you see where you've been and where you're going.

Date	Number	Payee/Category/Memo		Payment	Clr	Deposit	Balance
		J.D.'s Checking: Register					
8/20/05		Powell's		60.85	R		647.43
		split	book group				
8/20/05		Caprial's Bistro		110.02	R		537.41
		Food:Dining Out					
8/21/05		Carmen Drive Chevron		27.76	R		509.65
		Auto:Fuel	10.681g @ 2.599				
8/24/05		Rejuvenation		70.00	R		439.65
		Home Repair:Remodeling	bathtub rack, etc.				
8/24/05		Mike's Drive In	⬍	15.90	R	Deposit	423.75
	▼	Food:Dining Out	▼	▶ Open Split			

Record   Restore   Balance Today: $1,350.18

Quicken is available in lots of versions for Windows computers and Macs; figuring out which is which and how much they cost can be confusing. Don't sweat it: For most people, the cheapest version works just fine. Pick up a copy at Amazon.com or your local office-supply store.

But Quicken isn't your *only* option. You may want to check out these lesser-known programs:

- **Moneydance** enjoys a fine reputation among the folks who use it. It has lots of features and can read various Quicken file formats in case you're looking to make a switch. You can set up Moneydance to talk to your bank, manage your budget, and track your investments. It costs $40 and is available for Mac, Windows, and Linux computers. You can download it from *http://moneydance.com*.

- **You Need a Budget** lets you download info from your bank, schedule recurring transactions, and budget for the future. The program has a variety of budget-related features, including a virtual envelope system. It's available for Macs and Windows computers; you can download it from *www.youneedabudget.com* for $60.

There are other desktop programs out there, but they seem to be a dying breed. Web-based tools (covered next) now rule the roost.

Tip For a list of 16 great personal finance programs (both the online and desktop variety), head to *http://tinyurl.com/PFprograms*.

Web-Based Tools

If you're comfortable using web applications, you can choose from at least a dozen online personal-finance programs. Most of the sites on the following list are free, and many of them feature blogs with financial advice and important money-related news. Though they all have similar features, each one has its own special twist. Many also offer iPhone applications so you can track your money while you're on the go.

- **BudgetPulse** (*www.budgetpulse.com*) bills itself as "the free and upbeat way to manage your money." This site *doesn't* sync with your bank (which helps if you're worried about identity theft), but you can upload files from Quicken or your favorite spreadsheet program. BudgetPulse can be used by anyone in the world (not just Americans). One of the site's stated goals is simplicity; it doesn't do a whole lot other than track your major accounts.

- **Mint** (*www.mint.com*) has become the Big Daddy of online personal-finance programs, with more than a million registered users. (It was recently acquired by Intuit, the folks behind Quicken.) Mint can help you track investment accounts, which is a cool feature not all sites have. It also includes basic budgeting features, automatic synchronization with your bank accounts, and can display your financial info in spiffy graphs. (Downsides? You have to enter your bank account passwords, and Mint doesn't work for accounts at many small banks.) There's a Mint iPhone app, too.

- **moneyStrands** (*https://money.strands.com/*) lets you set up budgeting goals and create custom alerts (like "let me know when I've spent $30 on coffee this month"). And if you'd like to manage your finances in Spanish, you're in luck—there's a setting in moneyStrands that'll let you track your cash *en Español*. There's also an iPhone app available.

- **Mvelopes** (*www.mvelopes.com*) is a web-based version of the envelope budgeting system (page 46) that lets you allocate your money to virtual envelopes. Mvelopes automatically connects to most banks and lets you pay your bills online. The site isn't free: Monthly fees range from $8 to $13 depending on the length of your subscription. Despite this fee, many find that Mvelopes helps them take control of their money when all else has failed, so it's definitely worth a shot if you're at your wits' end.

- **PearBudget** (*www.pearbudget.com*) doesn't pretend to be a total financial-management package. It's streamlined so it just lets you do simple budgeting and expense tracking, but it does a great job of that. It costs

$3 per month, but there's a 30-day free trial. (There's also a PearBudget spreadsheet you can download for free from *www.pearbudget.com/spreadsheet*.)

- **Wesabe** (*www.wesabe.com*) was the first online personal-finance program. It has a dedicated fan base; in fact, one of Wesabe's strengths is its active community: people on the site support each other, sharing tips and ideas. This program lets you track cash accounts (how much money you have in your pocket), something most other online programs don't do. Also, Wesabe is *very* security-conscious: If you don't want the site to automatically sync with your bank, you don't have to let it; you can upload data manually instead. And yes, there's a Wesabe iPhone app.

- **Thrive** (*www.justthrive.com*) is designed to help you plan for the future. It offers budgeting tools as well as reminders about when to pay bills and how much to pay. The site also sports features to let you set and track savings goals.

- **Yodlee MoneyCenter** (*www.yodlee.com*) lets you track your spending and set budget limits; view balances and transactions for banking, credit, and investment accounts; and pay bills with your checking account or credit card.

Why Budgets Fail

As you've seen, building a budget doesn't have to be a chore; you can use a variety of tricks to make the task more fun and more personal. All the same, simply creating a budget doesn't guarantee that it'll work; a lot of people try to budget, and a lot of people fail. You may encounter trouble with your budget if:

- **It's too complicated.** Folks tend to make budgets more complicated than they need to be. Keep it simple; include only the details you need.

- **It doesn't reflect your values.** Chapter 2 helped you figure out our financial goals. A budget is meant to help you achieve your goals, so make it personal. For example, if you want to budget for fancy coffee, add a category for that. But don't just drink the stuff out of habit.

- **It doesn't reflect reality.** Too often budgets are based on wishful thinking—*possible* salary increases and *ideal* spending habits. These are doomed to failure. When you draft a budget, build it around your actual income and behavior. If you spend a lot of money on CDs and MP3s, then budget for music. And don't count on a raise you haven't received yet.

- **It seems like a chore.** It's important to review your budget regularly, but don't let the system bog you down. If checking your progress feels like a chore, you won't do it. So use a pencil and paper if that works for you, or download a budget app if you're an iPhone addict. Your goal is to have a budget that works—so pick whatever method suits you.

The truth is your spending will *rarely* be in line with your expectations, especially if you have a detailed budget. Sometimes you'll overspend on a category; other times, you'll underspend. Life doesn't stand still, so just make your best guesses and when you're wrong, make adjustments. It's nothing to be discouraged about. The point is to keep learning and keep improving.

Remember: Your goal isn't to keep a budget, it's to live a rich and happy life. Your budget is merely a tool to help you build a successful financial life. Just as you have to tinker with your lawnmower—adjust the belts, change the oil, sharpen the blade—so too you'll need to adjust your budget from time to time.

On the Money

Make It a Habit

In Chapter 1, you learned that habits and routines make people happier (page 20). In Chapter 2, you learned that habits help you achieve your goals. Let's go for the habit trifecta. When you first start using a budget, it's easy to be overwhelmed. The best way to avoid this? That's right: Make budgeting a habit.

Designate a time and a place every week to review your budget (you can call it "doing your finances" if you think that makes you sound nice and grown up). This routine will help you cope when something unexpected comes up—and you know it will. Remember: When your goals are specific, you know exactly what you're supposed to do—and you're more likely to do it. So make budgeting once a week one of your goals and you'll be more likely to follow through. Without such a plan, it's all too easy to slip back into the habit of not budgeting at all.

How you *think* you spend money is likely very different from how you *want* to spend it—and how you *actually* spend it. A budget can help you bring these three into alignment.

The next chapter will teach you how to defeat your debt so that you can begin to save for the things you really want.

4 Defeating Debt

"It gives much more pain to the mind to be in debt, than to do without any article which we may seem to want." —Thomas Jefferson

Let's be honest: There's no quick and easy way to get out of debt; it takes time and effort. That said, it can be done—and *has* been done by millions of people just like you.

Before you can begin to destroy debt, you have to understand the basics of *cash flow*, since cash flow problems were what got you into debt in the first place. After you've got that concept under your belt, you can begin to focus on reducing debt. Although there's just one basic debt-elimination process, you can apply it in a couple of ways. The key is to find the method that works best for you. This chapter explains your options.

The Power of Positive Cash Flow

"The first step to happiness is spending less than you earn," write Arun Abey and Andrew Ford in *How Much is Enough?* (Greenleaf, 2009). You've probably heard that before, and if you're in debt, you might think it's lame advice. But the truth is, *spending less than you earn is the key to all personal finance*.

When you spend more than you earn, there's never enough money to go around. You're always $50 or $100 short of what you need, and you fall further behind every month. You end up spending money you don't have—using credit cards, taking out loans—which leads to more debt, which puts you deeper in the hole.

You can't possibly get ahead when you spend like that. The math simply doesn't work. In order to save money and pay off debt, you need to spend less than you earn. Although it's easy to understand this intellectually, it's only when you actually see the concept applied to your own life that you'll be able to appreciate the power of positive cash flow.

Cash Flow Basics

If "cash flow" sounds like an accounting term, that's because it is. But don't let that scare you—it's easy to understand. For any given time period:

```
Cash Flow = What you earn - What You Spend
```

Simple, right? That's second-grade math. But don't let the simplicity fool you—this is a powerful concept. This formula tells us two things:

- **If you spend more than you earn, you have a negative cash flow.** You're losing wealth and in danger of going into debt—or, if you're already in debt, you're digging the hole deeper.

- **If you spend less than you earn, you have a positive cash flow,** which will let you climb out of debt and build wealth.

The greater the gap between earning and spending, the faster you build (or lose) wealth. This may seem obvious, but smart personal finance really is this simple. Everything else—clipping coupons, saving for retirement, asking for a raise—is done in support of this basic idea.

Tip Only two things will increase your cash flow: spending less (Chapter 5) and earning more (Chapter 6).

Here's an example: Joe Spendsalot has been living paycheck to paycheck, making minimum payments on his $5,000 credit card debt. Joe brings in $2,500 per month after taxes, but he spends $2,600 a month, including $100 per month on his credit card bill, which barely covers the 15% interest. Because he spends more than he earns, his cash flow is negative, and he's sinking into debt.

Salary	$2,500.00		Rent	$1,000.00
			Car Payment	$250.00
			Credit Cards	$100.00
			Food	$500.00
			Utilities	$250.00
			Other	$500.00
Income	$2,500.00		**Expenses**	$2,600.00
	Cash Flow: $2500.00 − $2600.00 = −$100.00			

Eventually Joe realizes he can't continue to spend more than he earns; he's just digging himself a deeper hole. He decides to make some small changes to cut his costs, including biking to work and using the public library for free entertainment. Together, these save him $100 per month. Now his monthly income and expenses are both $2,500, so his cash flow is zero: He's not saving anything, but he's not taking on any more debt, either.

Joe continues to pay $100 per month to his credit card bill, but the balance never seems to drop. Running the numbers, he realizes that at this rate it'll take him decades to pay off his credit card. In fact, according to the Federal Reserve's credit card repayment calculator (*http://tinyurl.com/CCcalculator*), he'll be paying on that debt for *24 years*.

Joe decides to increase his cash flow by taking a part-time job at the local mini mart, where he earns an extra $250 per month. He also cancels his cellphone plan, begins cooking more meals at home, and switches to store-brand groceries, all of which saves him $250 per month.

Salary	$2,500.00		Rent	$1,000.00
KwikMart	$250.00		Car Payment	$250.00
			Credit Cards	$100.00
			Food	$350.00
			Utilities	$150.00
			Other	$400.00
Income	$2,750.00		**Expenses**	$2,250.00
Cash Flow: $2750.00 − $2250.00 = +$500.00				

Now Joe's bringing in $2,750 per month after taxes and spending $2,250 per month, giving him a positive cash flow of $500. If he's disciplined and uses all this surplus to pay down his credit card, he can be debt-free in just 9 months. And once he eliminates his credit card debt, he'll no longer have that $100 monthly payment, so his monthly cash flow will increase to $600. He can quit his job at the mini mart and still set aside $350 a month for saving and investing—and fun.

You might be saying "There's no way I can find an extra 600 bucks every month!" That's okay. Say you can manage to cut your spending so that you have a positive cash flow of $100 per month. Psychologically, the difference between losing $100 each month and gaining $100 is huge: It's the difference between feeling like you're being buried alive and feeling like you're climbing out of the pit. Even if your $100 positive cash flow is all going toward debt, you're still making progress.

People make these sorts of changes every day. In fact, this is exactly how I, your humble author, got out of debt (see the box on page 57), and how many of the readers at Get Rich Slowly (*www.getrichslowly.org*) have done the same.

The bottom line is that in order to conquer debt you need to have a positive cash flow. We'll explore ways to cut your spending in Chapter 5, and we'll boost your income in Chapter 6. For now, let's look at how to use a positive cash flow to pay off debt.

Saying Goodbye to 20 Years of Debt

How can I be so sure that the techniques discussed in this book will help you get out of debt? Well, I can't be 100% certain, but I do know one thing: these are the methods I used to pay off $35,000 in consumer debt—credit cards, car loans, and so on—and they've worked for thousands of other people, too.

I first got into debt in the fall of 1987, when I was a freshman in college. I used a department-store charge card to buy a fancy electric razor and a bottle of cologne. (I had to impress the sorority girls, after all.) It was all downhill from there: By the time I graduated, I had several thousand dollars of debt. Within just a few years, that had grown to over $20,000. I had a problem.

I did my best to turn things around using the standard advice (like "pay your high-interest debt first"—page 61), but nothing seemed to work. It didn't help that I was a compulsive spender (page 65). By the fall of 2004, I'd accumulated over $35,000 in consumer debt, and I felt like I was drowning.

When I decided to turn things around, I used the exact methods described in this book: I set a big goal (be debt-free within 5 years), and broke it into sub-goals (start by paying my smallest debt first). I used a "spending plan" (I refused to call it a budget). I tracked every penny that came into or went out of my life. I cut spending and boosted income. And I used the debt snowball (which you'll learn about on page 60) to destroy my debt.

It worked! In December 2007, 39 months after I'd started, I paid off the last of my $35,000 debt. It took a lot of hard work to get there, but it felt awesome when I'd finished. (Along the way, I shared my progress on *getrichslowly.org*.)

So, I don't know *for sure* that these techniques will work for you. But I know from experience that they worked for me. And I'm confident that if you try to apply them to your life and you're patient, you too can kick debt to the curb.

The Basics of Debt Reduction

Many people look for magic bullets to get them out of debt: They play the lottery hoping for a big payout, or they listen to the snake-oil salesmen on TV who promise instant solutions. The truth is, there aren't any instant solutions. There are, however, some time-tested, proven techniques.

Real debt elimination involves three main steps: Stop accumulating new debt, establish an emergency fund, and destroy existing debt. In the next three sections, you'll learn about each step in turn.

Tip Being in debt because of student loans or a medical emergency is different from being in debt because you spend too much. If spending isn't your problem, you can skip to the section on establishing an emergency fund (page 59). For advice on paying off student loans, check out *http://tinyurl.com/st-loans*; and you can find an article about medical debt from *Smart Money* at *http://tinyurl.com/doc-debt*.

Stop Accumulating Debt

If your debt is out of control, it's because you have a negative cash flow—you're spending more than you earn. The first step on the path to debt-free living is to reverse this cash flow. For most people, that means it's time to stop using credit; credit makes it way too easy to spend more than you have.

Nobody needs credit cards. Don't try to make excuses for why you have to keep them: You don't need them as a safety net, for convenience, or for cash-back bonuses—you can get by without them. (Turn to page 158 to read about someone who lives without credit cards.) If you've had problems with credit cards, the worst thing you can do is hold on to them. It's like an alcoholic keeping a couple beers in the fridge in case he gets thirsty. When your debts are gone and your finances are under control, *then* you can get a credit card; in the meantime, make do with a debit card.

It can be tough to quit credit cold turkey; I know from first-hand experience that it's easy to find reasons to whip out the plastic. If you're really struggling with credit-card debt, your best move is to remove the temptation completely: Destroy your credit cards. Don't put them in a desk drawer, and don't freeze them in a block of ice; you're better off shredding them, burning them, or cutting them into tiny pieces with scissors.

After you destroy your cards, halt any recurring charges. If you have a gym membership, cancel it. If you automatically renew your *World of Warcraft* account every month, cancel it. Cancel anything that automatically charges your credit card. The point is to *completely* stop using credit.

Once you've done this, you'll need to decide whether you're going to close your credit card accounts or leave them open. If you try to cancel a card that has a balance on it, the issuer may want to jack up your rates or do other evil things. Plus, it'll ding your credit score (see page 156). But so what? If you have trouble with credit card debt, you've got to remove the temptation; if you don't close your account, you can still use it to shop online even if you've destroyed the card. Besides, when you call to close your account, some card issuers will let you lock in a lower rate by putting you on a payment plan.

If you simply **have to** leave your account open, then ask for a better deal. Find an offer online to use as a bargaining chip. When you call, say something like this:

> "Hi. I was just browsing online at CardRatings.com and I see they have a card from [Other Bank] that has an APR of just 10%. I'm paying 18% APR on the card I have with you. I'd rather not switch, but 8% is a lot. Is there anything you can do to help me out?"

Your bank may not agree to match the terms, but then again it might. You'll have better luck if you've been a long-time customer, paid on time, and used the card regularly. Be friendly but insistent, and don't make any threats you're not prepared to follow through on.

Establish an Emergency Fund

The next step is to sock away some savings. Use that positive cash flow you're building to set aside a little *self insurance*, money you keep on hand in case of emergencies. This helps you cut costs because it's cheaper than paying an insurance company to handle unexpected catastrophes. (See page 223 for more about self insurance.)

It may seem counter-intuitive to try to save up a little bit of money while you're still in debt, but if you don't save **before** you begin paying down debt, you'll struggle to cope with unexpected expenses.

 Tip Whatever you do, **don't** use a credit card to pay for emergencies; a credit card is not an emergency fund. Instead, destroy your credit cards and save for emergencies.

How much should you save? Ideally, $1,000 is a good amount to start with. (If your expenses are low, you might be able to get by with $500.) Keep this money liquid, but not immediately accessible. In other words, make it easy to get to—but not **too** easy. Don't keep your emergency fund in your main checking account, for example; consider opening a separate account at a new bank. (Chapter 7 has tons of info about bank accounts.)

Don't tie your emergency fund to a debit card; that just makes it easier to sabotage your efforts by using the debit card to pay for non-essentials. This money is for emergencies only, not for beer, clothes, or a new iPhone. It's for when your furnace croaks or you break your arm or you lose your job.

A good option is to open a high-interest savings account at an online bank like ING Direct or HSBC Direct. (For a list of online banks, check out *http://tinyurl.com/savingACT* or flip to page 132.) That way, when an emergency arises, you can transfer the money to your regular checking account. It'll be there when you need it, but you won't be tempted to spend it rashly.

Is There Such a Thing As Good Debt?

Some experts, like Dave Ramsey, argue that there's no such thing as a good debt. But most financial gurus agree that certain debts make sense.

As a general rule, you shouldn't borrow money to buy things that are likely to decrease in value. That means you shouldn't buy your new plasma TV on credit—next week, it'll be worth less than you paid for it. Nor should you go into debt to buy food, clothes, or computers.

But many experts say that it's okay to take on *reasonable* debt to pay for a handful of things that are likely to increase in value. This good debt includes an affordable mortgage on your home, student loans to pay for education, and loans to start a new business.

Car loans are borderline: They generally carry low interest rates, but as you well know, cars lose value the moment you drive them off the lot.

Even when you take on these kinds of "good" debts, be smart. Don't borrow more than you can afford. Shop around for the best interest rate (see Chapter 7 for more on this). And remember: The best debt is debt that's paid off.

Destroy Existing Debt

After you've stopped using credit and created an emergency fund, *then* go after your existing debt. Attack it with vigor—throw whatever you can at it. The best way to do this is to use a technique called the *debt snowball*, which lets you build and maintain debt-destroying momentum. Here's the basic method:

- Make a list of your debts in the order you want to destroy them. (You'll learn a couple of good ways to prioritize debts in a moment.)

- Set aside a certain amount of money to pay toward debts each month ($500, say).

- Make the minimum payment on all debts except the first one on your list.

- Throw every other penny at the first debt on the list.

But here's the key to making the debt snowball work: After you've destroyed your first debt, you'll find you've freed up a bit of cash; because one of your debts is gone, you have one less monthly payment. You could take this money and use it for something else, but you're going to do something smarter: keep paying the same total amount—$500, in our example—toward debt every month.

Clear as mud? Let's look at a couple of examples that prioritize debt reduction in different ways.

Destroying high-interest debt first

Conventional wisdom says that you should pay off debt from the highest interest rate to the lowest interest rate. Let's say our friend Joe Spendsalot (page 55) is dating a woman named Karen Kashout. Karen is a typical twenty-something who wakes one morning to realize that she's in debt, and she decides to do something about it. She's burdened with the following liabilities:

- $20,000 student loan at 5% interest
- $8,000 credit card balance at 12%
- $2,000 computer loan at 10%
- $3,000 car loan at 4%

Technically, the quickest way for Karen to conquer her debt is to pay off the balances with the higher interest rates first, so she'd tackle them in this order:

- $8,000 credit card balance at 12%
- $2,000 computer loan at 10%
- $20,000 college loan at 5%
- $3,000 car loan at 4%

Using the debt snowball method described above, Karen would pay the minimums on the bottom three debts and throw all the money she could at her credit card balance. Once she destroys that debt, she'd pay the minimums on the bottom two debts and throw all of her money at the computer loan, and so on.

Mathematically, the high-interest payoff plan does indeed make the most sense. That's because paying interest works *against* you in the same way that earning interest works *for* you (see page 277), so paying off your highest interest debt first is technically the best use of your money—if you follow this plan, you'll pay less in the long run. But this plan works only if you have the discipline to stick to it, and even if you know it's the right thing to do, that's no guarantee it'll work for you.

I struggled with debt for a decade (see the box on page 57). I made several attempts to pay off my debt using this highest-to-lowest interest method, and each time I failed. My highest interest rate debt was also my debt with the highest balance, so I felt like I was paying and paying but the balance never dropped. I'd get discouraged and give up on ever paying off my debt.

That's not to say you shouldn't try this method: If it works for you, use it! But if you struggle, consider the next method, which is the one that helped me succeed.

 Tip It might help you to have a visual representation of your debt-paying progress. Try this: Take a piece of graph paper and block off squares to represent your debt. (You might use one square for every $100, say.) When you make a payment, mark off a square—and give yourself a pat on the back. (If you're a geek, build yourself an Excel spreadsheet that does something similar.) These little progress reports are cheesy, but they can keep you on track.

Destroying low-balance debt first

If you've tried following the highest-interest-rate-first advice and still struggle with debt, there's another way. In his book, *The Total Money Makeover*, Dave Ramsey advocates an approach to the debt snowball that tackles accounts with *low balances* first. (Ramsey didn't invent this method, but he's popularized it over the past decade.)

With this version of the debt snowball, you ignore interest rates when determining the order in which you'll pay off your debts. All you look at is how much you owe, organizing the debts from smallest balance to largest balance.

Our friend Karen Kashout, for example, would arrange her debts like this:

- $2,000 computer loan at 10%
- $3,000 car loan at 4%
- $8,000 credit card balance at 12%
- $20,000 college loan at 5%

After she lists her debts from smallest to largest, she'd make the minimum payment on all of them except the smallest: the computer loan. She'd throw every dollar she can at the computer loan until it's gone, and then move on to her next smallest debt, the car loan.

This method may not be as quick as paying your high-interest debt first, but it provides tremendous psychological reinforcement. You get some quick wins—checking creditors off your list— that encourage you to keep at it. Dave Ramsey calls this "behavior modification over math," and he's right: The most important thing when paying off your debts is to, well, pay off your debts; the order in which you do so is irrelevant.

Critics of this approach argue that the math doesn't make sense, and they're right: If you use this method, you *will* pay more interest than if you had the discipline to pay off your debts based on interest rate. But humans are complex psychological creatures, not adding machines. We usually know what we *ought* to do, but that doesn't mean we always do it. If we were adding machines and always made the best choices, we wouldn't get into debt in the first place!

Other approaches

You can use the debt snowball to get out of debt in other ways. For instance, you might decide to first target the debts that give you the biggest headaches. Do you have a loan from your sister and her husband? Do you hate the fact that you borrowed money to buy a new computer? Whichever debt bugs you most, pay it off first.

 Tip To learn more about the debt snowball and the various ways to use it, download this free spreadsheet from Vertex 42: *http://tinyurl.com/v42-debt*. (You can see a video demo of the spreadsheet at *http://tinyurl.com/v42-video*.)

Regardless of which order you use to destroy your debt, put as much money as possible toward this goal. Apply raises and windfalls (like tax refunds) directly to your bills. Sure, you'd rather spend that birthday check from grandma on a night out with your friends, but it'll do you more good if you use it to pay off that *last* night on the town. You'll have plenty of time to spend future windfalls; for now, use the money to get debt off your back.

And if someone tells you that you you're being stupid if you don't follow a debt-repayment plan that minimizes interest payments, just ignore him. The ultimate goal is to get your debts paid off. Know yourself and choose whichever method makes the most sense for you and your financial situation.

Tip For the lowdown on the pros and cons of using home-equity loans to pay off credit card debt, head to this book's Missing CD page at *www.missingmanuals.com*.

Other Tips and Tricks

You can do lots of other things to improve your situation while you're working on the three main steps of debt elimination. But all the debt-reduction tips you'll find are based on one simple fact: To pay off debt, save money, or accumulate wealth, you have to spend less than you earn—in other words, financial success comes from having a positive cash flow.

It's not always easy to find ways to earn more money, but almost everyone can find ways to curb their spending. Developing frugal habits is a great first step toward being debt-free. Some people think that frugal living is equivalent to being "cheap," but that's not the case. Frugality and thrift used to be core values in our society, but we lost touch with these ideals during the age of easy credit. Thrift can be a fun way to stretch your hard-earned dollars. (The next chapter discusses ways to be frugal.)

While you learn to spend less, do what you can to increase your income. Try selling some of the Stuff you bought when you got into debt. This can be painful, but ask yourself: Do you really use that weight bench? Is your DVD collection really doing you any good? Use eBay.com and Craigslist.org or the Amazon Marketplace to get some cash for the things you own. Consider taking an extra job or working longer hours. (For more on boosting your income, see Chapter 6.)

Finally, go to your public library and borrow a book on debt reduction. After you finish it, borrow another book about money. The more you learn about smart money management, the easier it'll be to make the right choices.

The most important thing is to ***start now***. Not tomorrow, not next week—start tackling your debt now. Have patience and don't get discouraged if your efforts seem small and insignificant at first. Trust me: Most of us started paying off our debts the same way. In time, your efforts will bear fruit. If you're willing to persevere, you'll have your debt paid off sooner than you think.

 Tip Conquering debt is like playing baseball: Go out there and do your best every single day. If you make an error, don't give up—make the play next time. If you strike out, shake it off and step up to the plate for your next at-bat.

The Paradox of Choice

In *The Paradox of Choice* (Harper, 2005), Barry Schwartz describes his research on two groups of people that he calls Maximizers and Satisficers:

- **Maximizers only accept the best.** Every time they make a purchase (or do anything else), they need to be sure they've made the best possible decision.
- **Satisficers are willing to settle for "good enough."** These people still have expectations and standards, but they're willing to settle for something other than the absolute best in order to save time, money, or effort.

Maximizers believe that Satisficers are comfortable with mediocrity, but that's not necessarily true. Satisficers are just as interested in quality as Maximizers—but they recognize that sometimes the extra effort required to move from "good" to "best" isn't worth it.

What does this have to do with your money? Tons. Don't get hung up on looking for the "best" way to manage your finances. Find methods that work for you and your lifestyle, methods that you'll actually use.

Who cares if the debt snowball isn't the best way to pay down debt? Who cares if you don't find the best interest rate for your savings account? Who cares if you don't own the best mutual fund? You've found some good ones, right? Just pick one and get in the game.

The perfect is the enemy of the good. When you spend so much time looking for the "best" choice that you never actually do anything, you're sabotaging yourself. No matter what you're trying to accomplish, simply starting the process plays a larger role in your success than any other factor.

Curbing Compulsive Spending

Many people get into debt because of compulsive spending. They can't keep from buying more—even when that means spending money they don't have. "Overspenders...have confused and confusing relationships with money," write psychologists Brad and Ted Klontz in *Mind Over Money* (Broadway, 2009). "On one hand, they're convinced that money and the things it can buy will make them happy; yet they're often broke because they can't control their spending."

A spending addiction is a scary, dangerous thing. Like other addictions, it makes victims feel out of control. (The Illinois Institute for Addiction Recovery has a list of money habits that indicate a problem with compulsive shopping or spending: *http://tinyurl.com/shoppingsigns*.)

In *Mind Over Money*, the authors note, "Overspending can become a vicious cycle. Overspenders experience an irresistible impulse to spend; they lose control over their spending, and then, to ease the anxiety over having lost control, they continue to buy."

People who've never suffered from compulsive spending can't understand the problem, and you may have a hard time explaining it to them. They don't know what it's like to see something and feel the urge to buy it *now*. They don't know the lure of the shopping "rush"—and the subsequent nausea from the guilt of having spent money they don't have.

Here are some steps—based on my own experience and that of many Get Rich Slowly readers—that you can use to curb compulsive spending:

- **Cut up your credit cards.** Don't make excuses to keep them—if you have a problem with compulsive spending, destroy your credit cards *now*. Don't jot the numbers down someplace "just in case"; that makes it too easy to go to your desk drawer, pull out the numbers, and place an order online. Get rid of your credit cards completely.

- **Carry only cash.** Don't use your checkbook or a debit card. Inconvenient? Absolutely, but that's the point. If you're a compulsive spender, your goal is to break the habit. To do this, you've got to make sacrifices. Spending cash will help remind you that when you buy something you're actually spending money. Plastic (and to some degree checks) make this connection fuzzy.

 Tip When you're tempted to buy something on credit, stop and ask yourself, "Would I pay cash for this?" If the answer is "no," then why in the world would you pay more for it by using a credit card, which is also going to charge you interest and fees?

- **Track every penny you spend.** You may not even be aware of how much you're spending. Lunch every day at McDonald's—how much could that possibly cost? Picking up a few magazines on the way home from work—what harm is there in that? Once you begin to track your spending, patterns become clear. When you see these patterns, you can act on them. (For more on how to track your spending, see page 45.)

- **Play mind games.** For some people, money isn't an emotional issue. They're able to make logical choices and not be tempted to do otherwise. For most of us, though, it doesn't work that way. If you're in this majority, it can be useful to play tricks on yourself. You might train yourself to use the 30-day rule (see page 68), for instance. I've found that I can often keep myself from spending by simply adding the Stuff I want to my wish list at Amazon.com; I come back weeks later and can't remember why I wanted it in the first place. Here are some questions to ask yourself when you're tempted to buy: *http://tinyurl.com/ GRS-tempted*.

- **Avoid temptation.** The best way to keep from spending money is to avoid situations that tempt you to spend. If your weakness is music, stay out of record stores and de-activate your iTunes account. If you tend to overspend at big department stores, stay away from the mall. Avoid the places where you normally spend.

- **Ask for help.** It's tough to beat an addiction alone. Seek support from your friends, family, and spouse—and don't get angry when they call you on your missteps.

- **Consider professional help.** There's no shame in seeking therapy for help with problems that seem bigger than you. You have to look inward to overcome any form of addiction; a therapist is like a trained guide who can help you to find the way.

The good news is that you *can* break free from emotional spending. The bad news is that it's going to take work and it won't happen overnight. You'll make mistakes and backslide, but when you do, don't give up and don't beat yourself up over it. You're human, after all. Stay focused on your long-term goals, and resolve to do better next time.

Where to Find Help

The sad truth is that not everyone can dig out of debt alone. For some, life just deals too many blows, or they can't seem to control their spending, or they don't earn enough money to make headway on their payments.

The 30-Day Rule

There's no shame in using mind games to keep from buying things you don't need. In fact, these little tricks (or "money hacks", as some call them) can be a fun way to use psychology in your favor. For example, the 30-day rule is a simple way to control impulse spending. Here's how it works:

1. Whenever you feel the urge to splurge—whether it's for new shoes, a new video game, or a new car—force yourself to stop. If you're already holding the item, put it down. Now *leave the store*.

2. When you get home, take a piece of paper and write down the name of the item, the store where you found it, the price you were going to pay, and the date.

3. Post this note someplace obvious: on a calendar, the fridge, or a bulletin board.

4. For the next 30 days, think about the item and whether you really want it, but *don't* buy it—not yet.

5. If, at the end of a month, you still have the urge, then consider purchasing it (but *don't* pay with credit).

That's all there is to it. It's simple, but surprisingly effective.

The 30-day rule works because you aren't actually denying yourself—you're simply delaying gratification. This process also teaches you to think through your purchases and breaks the cycle of instant gratification that can lead to compulsive spending.

This rule has another advantage: It gives you a chance to research the item you want to purchase. You may find that there's a better product out there, or that you can get it for a better price at another store!

If you feel like you've tried everything but you still need help, don't turn to the debt-settlement companies that advertise on TV and radio. They don't have your best interests at heart—they're in it to make money. (For more on the problems with debt-settlement companies, check out this article at MSN Money: *http://tinyurl.com/msn-debtsettlement*.)

If you need help with debt, turn to reputable sources. First, go to your public library and borrow two books: *How to Get Out of Debt, Stay Out of Debt & Live Prosperously* by Jerrold Mundis (Bantam, 2003) and *The Total Money Makeover* by Dave Ramsey.

 Tip In his book, Mundis recommends one simple action to start you on the path to debt-free living: "Just for today, one day, do not incur any new debt. Not one." Make—and keep—this promise to yourself, just for today. (And then make and keep the same promise tomorrow.)

This chapter has already covered many of the key lessons from these books, but they go into a lot greater detail than we can here. If you're struggling, take the time to read these books and apply their lessons. If you still need help, the next few sections discuss a few different places you can turn.

Debtors Anonymous

Debtors Anonymous (DA) is a twelve-step program for people struggling with debt and compulsive spending. DA started in 1968 when a group of Alcoholics Anonymous members noticed that, for them, debting (spending money they didn't have) was an addiction just like alcoholism.

Debtors Anonymous believes that many people get into trouble with debt because they don't really pay attention to their spending. They spend without thinking about the consequences. To fight this habit, DA encourages members to track their spending (as described on page 45) and develop some sort of budget. (Many DA members use the envelope method explained on page 46.) The Jerrold Mundis book recommended above is based on DA's principles.

To learn more about DA, go to *www.debtorsanonymous.org* or call 1-800-421-2383.

 Tip Being hounded by debt collectors? Know your rights! The Federal Trade Commission has a handy guide to the Fair Debt Collection Practices Act at *http:// tinyurl.com/FTCcollections*. Don't let creditors push you around.

Consumer credit counseling

The National Foundation for Credit Counseling (NFCC) is a network of non-profit credit counseling agencies that help people take control of their finances and get out of debt. When you contact an NFCC agency, they'll work with you to create a *debt management plan* (DMP).

With a DMP, you pay off your debts by making monthly payments to the credit agency you're working with; they then send these funds to your creditors. Some creditors may be willing to reduce interest rates or waive fees if you're using a DMP. In a lot of cases, if you show a good faith effort to work with them, they'll work with you.

 Note A debt management plan can ding your credit score (see page 161), but it's not a permanent penalty. Since you shouldn't be taking out new lines of credit if you're in this situation anyway, that's a small price to pay to break free from the chains of debt, don't you think?

One added benefit of working with a credit-counseling agency is that they'll act as the go-between for you and your creditors. If you're being hounded by debt collectors, the agency will take the calls for you—how cool is that?

Credit counseling isn't always free, but some agencies do offer their services for low (or no) fees. For more information, contact the National Foundation for Credit Counseling at 1-800-388-22727 or *www.nfcc.org*, and check out the box below for tips on selecting a counselor.

Financial Peace University

There's been a lot of Dave Ramsey in this chapter, and there's a reason for that: Ramsey is the guru of debt reduction. His advice has helped hundreds of thousands of people—including me—to stop spending and start living debt free.

Ramsey's company, The Lampo Group, offers a 13-week course called Financial Peace University (FPU) that provides hands-on training in debt reduction and money management. FPU takes 2 hours per week and costs about a hundred bucks for the entire course. The classes teach you how to save, budget, invest, and—of course—pay off debt.

One thing to know about Financial Peace University: Ramsey is a devoted Christian, so his program incorporates Biblical principles and the classes are usually held at churches. For many people, this isn't an issue, but it might bug you. If you're a non-Christian considering FPU, you may have to just deal with the religious language. Or you can use the class finder at *http://tinyurl.com/FPUfinder* to see if any credit unions or nonprofits in your area are offering the course. There's also an online version of the class available: *http://tinyurl.com/FPUonline*.

You can learn more about Financial Peace University at *www.daveramsey. com/fpu/*. For a first-hand account from somebody who completed FPU, check out *http://tinyurl.com/FPUsteps*.

Start Now

It's not getting out of debt that's important—it's the freedom that being debt-free can bring you. When you're chained to the shackles of credit card payments and student loans, your choices are limited. You feel trapped in your crummy job because you can't afford to quit.

Debt can feel so overwhelming that you think you'll never escape, but the good news is you can. It'll take hard work, but you can do it. Although debt repayment can seem daunting at first, it *won't* take forever.

The most important thing is to start now. Waiting to get out of debt is a fool's game—it doesn't help anything. Begin with baby steps if you need to, but do *something*. For starters, turn the page to Chapter 5, where you'll learn ways to cut your spending.

 Note The toughest part of taking control of your finances is getting started. I recommend setting aside a single day (a "Money Day") to tackle all of your financial chores at once. To learn more, head to this book's Missing CD page at *www.missingmanuals.com*.

5 The Magic of Thinking Small

"Be industrious and frugal, and you will be rich." —Benjamin Franklin

Frugality. Thrift. Economy. Whatever you call it, the idea is the same: using your money and resources carefully. If you don't spend mindfully, your hard-earned dollars slip through your fingers and it's hard to get ahead. By being frugal, you make conscious choices that'll help you live well tomorrow *and* today.

As you'll see in the following pages, you can be frugal and still wear nice clothes, dine out on occasion, and buy new things. Frugality means making the most of your money by focusing on everyday expenses (as opposed to big-ticket items, which you'll learn more about in Chapter 9) and recognizing that small amounts matter. It's a skill that anyone can hone, and it lays the groundwork for sound financial habits throughout your life. This chapter explains why it's important to cut costs on the small things—and suggests strategies for doing just that.

 Tip To commit fully to changing your lifestyle and embracing frugality, you have to keep your goals in mind. (Hop back to Chapter 2 for a refresher on goals.) If you lose track of *why* you're making sacrifices, frugality will become a burden and you won't stick to your plan.

Why Frugality Matters

Thrift is nothing new. In fact, it used to be fashionable—you were admired if you watched your nickels and dimes—but that's no longer the case. Over the past 50 years, frugality has gained something of a bad reputation.

Many people equate being frugal with being cheap. But there's a difference: When you eat stale crackers with your soup for lunch, you're being frugal. When you serve stale crackers to your guests to eat with *their* soup, you're being cheap. You cross the line when your habits affect others, not just you.

Part of the reason thrift fell from grace is that there's no profit in it. Nobody's going to run a Super Bowl commercial to promote being careful with your money, or shell out for a magazine ad campaign that tells you not to go into debt. If you want to be thrifty, you have to advertise to yourself (see the box on page 32).

Even though there aren't any big corporations to sing its praises, frugality is an important part of personal finance. Packing a sack lunch may only save you a buck or two each day, but when you make many small changes over months and years, they really add up.

Here are a few reasons it's important to develop thrifty habits:

- **Quick wins.** As you learned in Chapter 4, the two ways to improve your cash flow are to reduce expenses and boost income. Both are important, but reducing expenses offers the quickest results. It takes time to find a new job or to ask for a raise, but you can start being frugal *right now*.

- **Lots of opportunities.** Our society idolizes big winners: million-dollar athletes, lottery winners, and Wall Street billionaires. Nobody celebrates the guy next door who bikes to work, grows his own food, shops at the thrift store, and gets his books from the library. That sort of life isn't glitzy, yet it can—and does—lead to true wealth (see the box on the next page). Of course, it's also important to save money on the big stuff, like a home or a car (see Chapters 9 and 10), but large transactions are rare. (How often do you spend more than $1,000 on *anything?*) You have many more chances to save on the small stuff you buy regularly, like groceries.

- **Small steps lead to big savings.** As you'll see, small savings here and there really do add up over time. And there's an interesting side effect to making small, thrifty changes: They spread to affect *all* your buying decisions. If you learn to comparison shop for shoes, you can use that same skill when you buy something big, like a car. Or if you learn to slash recurring monthly payments on things like magazines and newspapers, you can apply this same principle when shopping for a mortgage.

Thrift is about more than just saving money. It also:

- Highlights the value of things.
- Provides for the future.
- Lets you focus your time and money on what's really important to you.
- Reduces your consumption and waste.
- Gives you a sense of accomplishment.

When you practice frugality, you're developing habits that'll help you save money and build wealth throughout your life.

On the Money

Thrifty Millionaires

Some financial gurus argue that building wealth is all about earning more. A huge income is great, but research shows it's not how much you earn that matters, but how much you *spend.*

You'll never become a millionaire if you spend every penny you earn—or spend even *more* and wind up in debt. In their book *The Millionaire Next Door* (Pocket, 1998), Thomas Stanley and William Danko write, "Being frugal is the cornerstone of wealth-building." As mentioned in the box on page 13, the three words they feel best describe most millionaires are "frugal frugal frugal." They also found that millionaires usually:

- **Budget.** "They became millionaires by budgeting and controlling expenses, and they maintain their affluent status the same way." Of the millionaires who don't budget, more than half save and invest their income first, and then spend what remains. (You'll learn about this "pay yourself first" strategy on page 145.)
- **Track their spending.** They know how much they spend each year on food, clothing, and shelter.
- **Set goals.** This is especially true of those who've built their wealth through frugality.
- **Actively plan and manage their finances.** Wealthy Americans spend nearly twice as much time planning their financial futures as the rest of us.

If you want to build wealth, copy the subjects of *The Millionaire Next Door*. The best place to start is by being thrifty.

The Power of Small Change

Saving 50 cents a week on milk doesn't mean much if you do it just once, but over the course of the year, it adds up to $26. Taken together, many such small economies make a noticeable difference. Small amounts really *do* matter.

 Tip Because you earn pre-tax dollars but spend after-tax dollars, a penny saved is actually *more* than a penny earned. Depending on your tax bracket, you might have to earn $111, $133, or even $150 to put $100 in your pocket. So if you're in the 25% tax bracket, saving $750 a year is like giving yourself a $1,000 raise! (You'll learn more about tax brackets in Chapter 11.)

Rather than give you pie-in-the-sky examples of how much you could save, here are some real examples from my own life. While trying to improve my cash flow and pay off over $35,000 in debt (see page 57), I made many small changes, including:

- Switching my cable TV package from $65.82 per month to $12.01 per month, saving $645.72 every year.

- Getting rid of my home phone line (roughly $46.50 per month) and my subscription to Audible.com ($21.95 per month), saving $821.40 per year.

- Cancelling my magazine and newspaper subscriptions, saving $137 per year.

- Going to the public library instead of shopping at bookstores, saving $391.95 in the first year.

- Planting a vegetable garden to grow my own produce, saving about $300 in 2008 (see box on page 84).

With just these few changes, I boosted my cash flow by $2,281.61 per year—that's almost $200 every month.

Changes like these don't affect just your short-term finances—they also help you build long-term savings. Here's a look at the cumulative gains I can expect by investing the money I've saved thanks to the changes listed above. (This chart assumes a 6% return on investment; page 277 has more on the power of compound interest.)

	Monthly	1 year	2 years	5 years	10 years	20 years
Cable	$53.81	$663.78	$1,368.49	$3,754.33	$8,818.35	$24,862.42
Phone/Audible	$68.45	$844.37	$1,740.82	$4,775.76	$11,217.54	$31,626.70
Subscriptions	$11.42	$140.87	$290.43	$796.77	$1,871.50	$5,276.51
Books	$32.66	$402.88	$830.61	$2,278.69	$5,352.30	$15,090.26
Garden	$23.80	$293.59	$605.28	$1,660.53	$3,900.33	$10,996.57
Total	**$190.14**	**$2,345.48**	**$4,835.63**	**$13,266.07**	**$31,160.02**	**$87,852.46**

You won't get rich—slowly or otherwise—by simply cutting your cable bill or growing your own tomatoes. But as this chart shows, when you make small changes part of an ongoing campaign of saving and investing, they can lead to a very large change indeed.

Frugal Tactics Anyone Can Use

Every year, the U.S. Bureau of Labor Statistics looks at data about millions of households to create a profile of the average American consumer. In 2008, the typical U.S. family spent the following amounts each month:

- $1,747.83 on housing, including $372.08 on utilities.
- $954.17 on transportation.
- $687.92 on food.
- $332.00 on healthcare.
- $316.50 on entertainment.

Your Money and Your Life

It Never Hurts to Ask

A willingness to ask questions is one of the best weapons you can add to your financial arsenal. If you're able to overcome a little shyness, you can ask your bank to waive overdraft charges, your landlord to give you a break on the rent (see page 198), the cable company to lower your monthly fee, and your employer for a pay raise.

If you ask, you might be able to save money on almost anything. Be careful, though: It's not your *right* to get a better price—only to ask for it. For best results, arm yourself with information (like a competitor's ad showing a sale price) and be polite.

One reader at Get Rich Slowly sits down once a year to call all of his service providers to ask if he can save money. He simply calls the customer service line and asks about specials and promotions. This only takes a few minutes, but yields repeated savings. For more on this tactic, check out Ramit Sethi's post about asking to have bank fees removed: *http://tinyurl.com/RAMITnofees*.

Chapters 9 and 10 discuss ways to spend less on housing and big purchases, but there are plenty of opportunities to cut spending on smaller stuff, too. The next few sections cover the best techniques for saving on four large chunks of your family's budget: food, utilities, healthcare, and entertainment.

 Note It's impossible to list all the great ways to save on small stuff here, so think of what follows as a sort of "greatest hits" collection. You can find tons more money-saving tips at *www.getrichslowly.org*.

Eat Well for Less

If you work at it, you can probably save $80 or $100 or more on food every month. The four keys to fighting food costs are saving at the supermarket, making your own meals, dining out sensibly, and growing what you can. Since this isn't a cookbook, you won't find any make-at-home recipes here. But the following sections elaborate on each of the other three strategies with specific tips to inspire you.

Supermarket savings

The easiest place to trim your food budget is at the grocery store. Because you spend so many of your food dollars on groceries, you have lots of opportunities to save. You can find whole books devoted to supermarket savings, but here are some top tips:

 Note For the most part, smart grocery shopping hasn't changed in decades—your grandmother could have written most of these tips. For a fun look at the shopping advice of yesteryear, watch this 1950 film about buying food: *http://tinyurl.com/1950shopping*.

- **Make a list—and stick to it.** This is the cardinal rule of shopping. Your list should include only the stuff you really need: staples you're out of and ingredients for upcoming meals. This will help you avoid buying on impulse—which is how shopping trips get out of control.

- **Compare unit pricing.** An item's *unit price* tells you the cost for each unit of measurement. For example, the unit price of a box of cereal tells you how much you're paying for each ounce. If you're lucky, your grocery store already posts unit pricing for most items, which makes comparing them easy. If not, carry a calculator.

 Note The biggest package isn't *always* the most cost-effective. Stores know that people want to buy in bulk, so sometimes they actually make the larger package's unit price higher than the smaller package's.

- **Choose a store and learn its prices.** Because supermarkets monkey with prices, you can't be sure a deal is *really* a deal unless you know what the store usually charges. Use a price book (see the box on the next page) to uncover regular and sale prices. Once you know one store's prices, you can save even more by learning another store's prices and comparing them to the first store's.

- **Buy only what you can carry.** If you're dashing into a store to pick up milk and bread, don't use a basket—it'll just tempt you to buy more. Similarly, try walking, biking, or taking the bus to the store. When you're limited to what you can actually carry, you're more likely to avoid impulse buys.

- **Discard brand loyalties.** You may have a favorite brand of diced tomatoes, but does it really matter? Buy whatever has the lowest unit price, even if that means getting the store brand or a generic. You may find you like the less-expensive product just as well. (The box on page 81 has more on generics.)

Your Money and Your Life

The Power of the Price Book

In *The Complete Tightwad Gazette* (Villard, 1998), Amy Dacyczyn advocates using a *price book* to save big bucks at the supermarket. A price book is an ongoing list of the items you buy most often, where and when you buy them, and how much you pay. That info can help you figure out sales cycles, spot bargains, and plan your shopping trips for maximum savings. You also learn which stores offer the best prices on which items.

"At first you may think this is too much work and the idea of shopping at so many stores will be inconceivable. It will pay off," Dacyczyn writes. "The keeping of a price book revolutionized our shopping strategy more than anything else we did. For the first time we had a feeling of control over our food budget."

By keeping a price book, you'll learn the *strike point* for your favorite items—the price that's low enough to let you snap up a supply until the next time the strike-point price rolls around.

- **Shop less.** Studies show that when people shop more often, they buy more stuff. (Shocking, huh?) Every time you enter the grocery store is another chance to spend. Fewer trips mean you'll avoid temptation *and* save time and gas.

Tip Steve and Annette Economides, authors of ***America's Cheapest Family*** (Three Rivers Press, 2007), are extreme non-shoppers: They've been making just one grocery shopping trip per month since 1984—and they have five kids!

- **Use coupons wisely.** Coupons get a bad rap, but they really can save you money. Clip coupons only for products you'll use or for stuff you'd like to try. And if your store lets you, combine coupons with sales.

- **Take advantage of special offers.** You may not need two pot roasts, but it's the same as getting one for half price if you can find somebody to share the deal with. And if your store offers a "get $10 if you spend $50" deal, use it.

- **Buy in bulk—when it makes sense.** For example, check your calendar to see if you've got any upcoming events that you'll need lots of food for. But don't go for bulk items if the larger package has a higher unit price, you don't have room to store it, or you won't use the product before it spoils. (Nobody likes stale Lucky Charms.)

 Tip If you eat a lot of meat and have the storage space, buying beef in bulk can be an excellent value. The price is generally about the same as in the supermarket, but the quality is much better. Pool your resources with other families and buy from a local rancher or butcher. For more info, read this article about buying and freezing beef: *http://tinyurl.com/buyingbeef*.

- **Check your receipt.** At the register, make sure your items and coupons scan correctly. Sale items, especially, have a tendency to ring up wrong, yet few people notice. You don't need to hold up the line: If you suspect an error, step to the side and check the receipt as the clerk begins the next order. If there's a problem, politely point it out. It's your money—ask for it.

- **Buy from produce stands and farmers markets.** During the summer months, produce stands and farmers markets offer fresh, local food at excellent prices. Even better, these kinds of places usually don't have a lot of impulse items to tempt you. Also look at community-supported agriculture (CSA) programs, which let you "subscribe" to fresh produce from a local farm (see *www.localharvest.org* for more info).

- **Waste not.** One of the best ways to save money on food is to not let it go to waste. According to various estimates, Americans throw away 12–25% of their food. So if you spend $400 on groceries every month, you may be able to save $50 to $100 simply by never throwing food away. (Here's a **New York Times** article on the subject: *http://tinyurl. com/fwaste*.)

How Good Are Store Brands Really?

You used to have to sacrifice quality when choosing store brands, but not anymore. The October 2009 issue of *Consumer Reports* compared 29 name-brand foods to their store-brand counterparts in blind taste tests. The store brands offered roughly the same quality as national brands, but at much lower prices.

The magazine found that the store brands they tested cost an average of 27% less than the name brands. In my own research of 25 store-brand products (*http://tinyurl. com/store-brands*), I found I could save 22% at one nearby store and **36%** at another.

Many store brands are actually made by the same companies that make their name-brand competition, which means you may be getting a nearly identical product for much less. So why do name brands cost more? Marketing: You recognize name brands because of the money companies spend promoting them.

A few other notes about store brands:

- Many stores offer a money-back guarantee on their house-brand products, so if you don't like something, ask for a refund.
- Store brands aren't *always* a bargain; be sure to compare prices. Sometimes the name brand is actually a better deal, especially if it's on sale.
- Some stores have a wider selection of generics than others. Most will carry staple items—beans, rice, toilet paper, tomato sauce, and so on—but some markets have a better selection.

If you decide to give store brands a try, take it slow: Buy a small amount of the product to see if you like it before buying more. If you're satisfied, make the switch. If you hate it, lesson learned. And if you're undecided, then keep using it until you make up your mind. (Remember: Most tastes are acquired—you may need time to get used to a new product.)

 Tip If your family throws away a lot of spoiled food, create a leftover list and post it on the fridge. Every time you store leftovers, note the date, the name of the dish, and how many servings are left. When you're hungry, check the list!

Dining out

More than a third of U.S. food spending happens outside the home, and dining out can be costly. But you can enjoy a nice restaurant meal without blowing your monthly food budget—you just have to practice a little conscious spending (page 14). Here are a few tips:

- **Eat a healthy snack before you go.** Grab a banana or some carrot sticks to take the edge off your hunger so you won't be tempted to order too much when you look at the menu.

- **Order appetizers as your meal.** At many eateries, appetizers are a cheap and tasty alternative to ordering a main dish, and they're often plenty big to fill you up.

- **Share food.** Portion sizes in American restaurants have grown enormous over the past few decades, so try splitting an entrée. Many restaurants charge a few bucks extra for this, but it's much less than paying for a second main dish.

- **Watch what you drink.** Restaurants make a big profit on soft drinks and alcohol (meaning they're a bad deal for customers), so if you're looking to save money, skip the drink order. Water may be boring, but it's cheap and good for you.

- **Order in sequence.** When you order everything at once, it's easy to end up with too much food. If the restaurant lets you, order and eat your appetizer *before* you order your main dish. That way you can plan the rest of our meal based on how hungry you are. (If you order this way, be sure to leave a bigger tip.)

- **Take food home.** One excellent way to stretch your food dollars is to *plan* to take leftovers home. (Some people ask for a box when their meal arrives so they can divide the portions immediately.) A $12 enchilada plate only costs $6 per meal if you also have it for lunch the next day.

- **Eat lunch, not dinner.** If it fits your schedule, enjoy your meals out in the afternoon instead of evening—you'll often pay much less for the exact same food.

- **Skip (or share) dessert.** If you crave just a bite or two of something sweet after a meal, try splitting a dessert. Or some people keep a bar of chocolate (or other sweet treat) in their purses or cars for such occasions.

Greens from the garden

Once you begin to master your grocery shopping, you'll find that you sometimes want more than the supermarket can provide, like fresh herbs at a moment's notice or strawberries that don't cost $3 per pound.

Food fresh from your yard is convenient and generally tastes better than what you find in the supermarket. If you have a suitable spot for a garden, growing your own food is a fun and rewarding way to save money. Here are some pointers for starting your own vegetable patch:

- **Plan ahead.** Decide what you'd like to grow and figure out how much time and space you're willing to devote to the project. A container garden (*http://tinyurl.com/container-garden*) might be a good place to start. Or try square-foot gardening (*http://tinyurl.com/SF-gardening*), which lets you maximize food production in a small space.

 Tip Your public library probably has lots of great gardening books, including some tailored to where you live. Two excellent ones are *Square-Foot Gardening* (Cool Springs Press, 2006) by Mel Bartholomew and *The Bountiful Container* (Workman Publishing, 2002) by McGee and Stuckey. You might also want to check out You Grow Girl (*www.yougrowgirl.com*), a blog about gardening.

- **Start small.** When planning your garden, don't be overly ambitious. If you want to test the waters, try herbs, which are easy to manage and *much* cheaper to grow than buy.

- **Choose productive plants.** It's frustrating to plant a bunch of seeds that don't yield anything. If you want a rewarding and productive garden, do some research to find out what grows well in your area. One excellent resource is your state's extension office (*www.nifa.usda.gov/Extension/*), or ask your friends and neighbors for advice.

- **Share with others**. When you buy a packet of seeds, you'll generally get more than you need. It's fun and frugal to split the costs with others. Same goes for equipment: You may own a rototiller while your neighbor has a trailer for hauling manure; share them to save money.

- **Buy quality tools.** When you buy garden tools, it pays to get top-quality items. Thrift and frugality are about getting value for your dollar—not just paying the lowest price. Find garden tools that'll last and be a pleasure to use for years.

- **Have fun.** Don't make gardening more work than it has to be. Your garden doesn't need to be perfect: Pick a favorite fruit or vegetable, plant a few seeds, and have fun watching them grow. If you have kids, get them involved, too.

With a little effort, your yard can produce food that tastes great and saves you money!

How Much Can a Garden Save Me?

Many prominent penny pinchers claim that gardening is a great way to save money: Michelle Obama is growing vegetables at the White House, and the Burpee seed company boasts that $50 in seeds and fertilizer will yield $1,250 in produce (*http://tinyurl.com/burpee-claim*). Burpee CEO George Ball told the *Wall Street Journal* that $1 in seeds will produce $75 worth of beans.

But how much does a garden really save? My wife and I set out to answer that question in 2008. For 12 months, we tracked the costs of seeds, fertilizer, water, and electricity. We carefully weighed every fruit and vegetable we harvested, comparing costs with local supermarkets and produce stands. We also logged the time we spent working in the garden.

At the end of the year, we tallied the results. We'd spent 60 hours working on our crops and $318.43 on seeds and supplies. We harvested $606.97 worth of food, including $225.74 in berries, $294.59 in vegetables, $66.63 in fruit, and $20.10 in herbs.

We repeated the experiment in 2009. This time, we spent $351.37 (and 63.5 hours) and harvested $809.74 worth of food. So we didn't get the kinds of results Mr. Ball claims, but we doubled our investment in just a year. That's a better return than mutual funds—and tastier, too. For more about the Get Rich Slowly garden project, check out: *http://tinyurl.com/GRSgarden*.

 Tip Saving on food is always a popular topic at Get Rich Slowly. If you crave more tips, here's 3 years' worth of articles on the subject: *http://tinyurl.com/GRSfoodlist*.

Pay Less for Power

The Bureau of Labor Statistics reports that the average family spent $372.08 per month on utilities in 2008. You can't do without light and heat, but as the following sections explain, you can cut utility costs, adding more money to your cash flow.

The electric company

Michael Bluejay has a great website about saving electricity (*http://tinyurl.com/saving-electricity*), where he describes how electricity works and, more importantly, gives real-world examples of how you can use less energy (and thereby save money). The best tactic, he says, is "dealing with the biggest electricity-guzzlers rather than worrying about items that don't use much electricity." This chart from the Department of Energy shows how the average American household used electricity in 2005:

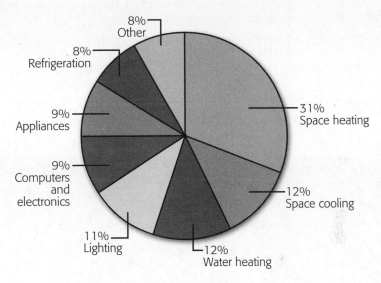

8% Other

8% Refrigeration

9% Appliances

9% Computers and electronics

11% Lighting

12% Water heating

12% Space cooling

31% Space heating

Source: *www1.eere.energy.gov/consumer/tips/home_energy.html*

Because heating and cooling use the most energy, they also offer the best opportunities for saving. Bluejay estimates that the typical family can save about:

- $1,200 a year by using space heaters instead of central heating. (And you can save even more with a heat pump—after you recoup the installation costs.)

- $600 a year by using fans instead of AC.

- $150 a year by drying clothes on a line instead of in a dryer.

- $150 a year by washing laundry in cold water instead of hot.

- $100 a year by replacing regular light bulbs with compact fluorescents.

- $75 a year by getting rid of your TV.

- $60 a year by putting your computer in sleep mode when you're not using it.

 Tip A programmable thermostat is an easy way to reduce utility bills. It lets you turn off the furnace automatically when you're asleep or not home. The government estimates the average homeowner could save $180 per year by installing an Energy Star programmable thermostat (see *http://tinyurl.com/ES-thermostat*).

If you're gung-ho about cutting your power bill, Bluejay recommends the Kill-a-Watt electricity meter (*http://tinyurl.com/killwatt*), which measures how much energy an item is using so you can identify your home's power hogs.

 Tip *Living Green: The Missing Manual* has a whole chapter about saving energy.

On the Money

Level Payment Plans

Utility bills can make it hard to budget: You might pay $250 for natural gas in December but only $50 in July. Fortunately, many utility companies now offer *level payment plans*.

When you sign up for such a plan, the company looks at how much energy you used over the past year and divides the total amount by 11 to get a fixed monthly payment. You pay this fixed amount for 11 months, and in the twelfth month you settle up, either paying more (if you used more energy) or getting a refund or credit (if you used less). At the end of each year, your monthly payment rises or falls based on recent usage patterns. (Some utility companies make adjustments more than once per year, but the same principle applies.)

To make budgeting really easy, sign up for a level payment plan *and* automated billing. Then you only have to deal with your utility bill once a year; the rest of the time, it's paid automatically.

If you're in the market for a new dishwasher, clothes dryer, or other major appliance, be sure to visit the Energy Star website (*www.energystar.gov*). (Energy Star is a joint program of the Environmental Protection Agency and the Department of Energy; its goal is to "help us all save money and protect the environment through energy efficient products and practices.") The website has lots of useful resources, including a list of Energy Star–qualified products, home improvement tips, and info about home energy audits.

Tip Many areas have nonprofit organizations that provide in-home energy audits, which can help you improve your home's energy efficiency and turn you on to available tax credits. (They might even give you free compact fluorescent bulbs along with the audit!) Contact your power company and ask for a referral.

The phone company

If your family has a home phone line in addition to a cellphone or two, you're paying too much. Choose one or the other. More and more people are ditching landlines and discovering they don't miss 'em.

Most major cellphone companies give discounts to employees of specific companies and students of specific schools. To see if your school or company qualifies, visit:

- **Alltel**: *http://tinyurl.com/alltel-discounts*
- **AT&T**: *http://tinyurl.com/att-discounts*
- **Sprint**: *http://tinyurl.com/sprint-discounts*
- **T-Mobile**: *http://tinyurl.com/tmobile-discounts*
- **Verizon**: *http://tinyurl.com/verizon-discounts*

A quick check of these discount programs could save you 20% or more on your phone plan; plus, you might be able to score a great deal on a new phone.

But that's not the only way to save on phone service. When was the last time you checked to be sure your monthly plan matches your usage? If your plan doesn't have enough minutes, you can get hit with exorbitant fees; if your plan has too many minutes, you're paying for something you never use. Either way, it's time to change plans.

And be sure to check out prepaid phones from providers like Tracfone (*www.tracfone.com*), NET10 (*www.net10.com*), T-Mobile (*http://tinyurl.com/ TM-prepaid*), and Virgin Mobile (*http://tinyurl.com/VM-prepaid*).

With prepaid wireless, you can buy an older, name-brand phone for 10 or 20 bucks. You then pay in advance for as many minutes as you want. When you use them all, you simply "top off" as needed. Light phone users (fewer than 200 minutes per month) will almost certainly save by giving up a monthly contract. Even if you use 400 minutes or more each month, there's a chance that prepaid could cut your costs. (If you need a phone with the latest features, prepaid wireless probably isn't your best bet, but don't rule it out.)

 Tip For more on prepaid phones, check out this article from *The Red Tape Chronicles* (*http://tinyurl.com/MSNBC-prepaid*) and this one from Greg Karp's "Spending Smart" column (*http://tinyurl.com/karp-prepaid*).

Slashing Recurring Expenses

Saving money on one-time purchases is great, but if you really want to boost your cash flow, try cutting costs on things you pay for every month.

For many services—cellphones, fitness clubs—you pay a flat fee that grants you a certain amount of use (or in some cases, as with cable TV, unlimited use). This means you often pay for things you never use, like extra cellphone minutes, cable channels you never watch, and days you don't go to the gym.

You may be able to save money by paying only for what you use instead of shelling out a recurring fee. Each situation is different, but it's not hard to run the numbers.

For example, pull out your most recent cellphone bill. Divide the total amount by the number of minutes you used to find out your per-minute cost. Then visit a prepaid wireless company's website and see what it would cost you to pay as you go. You may be able to save a lot of money.

If you don't actually use the service you're paying for, it's easy to make the call. Don't go to the gym? Cancel your membership. Only read the newspaper once a week? Stop getting it delivered every day. Cutting a recurring expense is a one-time task, but it pays you back with improved cash flow every single month. Plus it's one less thing to worry about.

The cable company

The Internet may just kill cable television. Not only can you get amateur (and some professional) content on YouTube, you can also watch network programming for free or cheap—often from the networks' own sites. Three great alternatives to cable are:

- The **iTunes Store**, where you can buy episodes of your favorite programs or subscribe to whole seasons. If you miss *Mad Men* and just have to see it, this is a great choice.

- **Hulu.com** offers a variety of current TV shows, like *30 Rock* and *Family Guy*, as well as a growing library of classic programs from years gone by. This is the place to go if you want to watch *Adam-12* or *The Mary Tyler Moore Show*. Hulu also has a limited library of movies.

- **Netflix** isn't just a DVD-by-mail company anymore. They also let members watch old movies and TV shows directly in a web browser.

In early 2007, I dropped my cable from a $65.82 deluxe monthly package to a plain-vanilla basic rate of $12.01 per month. To make up for some of what got cut, I started buying some shows through the iTunes Store and watching others on various websites. Since making the switch, I've paid an average of $27.90 per month for TV shows (including basic cable), a savings of $37.92 per month—that's more than $450 a year!

Cutting cable isn't for everyone. If you're a big sports fan, for example, it may be hard to find the games you want online. But slashing—or cancelling—your cable plan is a great way to save money.

 Tip If you want to explore the world of web-based TV, check out this amazing list of online options: *http://tinyurl.com/byebye-cable*. (It even includes sources for sports.)

Doctors and Drugs

Few things can blow a budget like unexpected medical bills. Even if you save and invest, unforeseen health problems can smash your financial plans to bits. And a medical crisis can be devastating for those who don't have their finances in order.

If you have health insurance, here are three steps you can take to make sure you're not paying more than you have to:

- **Understand your policy.** Insurance rules can be confusing. Take the time to read your policy to be sure you grasp the basics. At the very least, know how your plan works in the case of emergencies. Any time you have a concern about coverage, call your insurer and ask questions.

- **Read your bill.** Don't assume your medical bills are accurate. Take time to read them, and ask about anything that seems wrong. Nobody cares more about your money than you do, so take charge of the situation.

- **Strike a deal.** Always ask for a discount. Some places will offer them and some won't, but it never hurts to ask (see the box on page 77). You may be able to save big bucks by picking up the phone and negotiating with your provider. (For more on negotiating, see page 75.) If they do agree to reduce your bill, be sure to get the details in writing.

 Note If you don't have health insurance, your situation is more complicated, and sadly there's no such thing as *Buying Health Insurance: The Missing Manual*. These three articles are a good place to start: *http://tinyurl.com/GRSsolo-insurance*, *http://tinyurl. com/KIPsolo-insurance*, and *http://tinyurl.com/WSJsolo-insurance*.

Another great place to save is at the pharmacy. Here are some ways to cut costs on medications:

- **Use older remedies.** Don't let ads for new drugs fool you: In many cases, the most effective choice is a tried-and-trued medication that's been on the market for years. The drug companies want to sell you the new stuff because they make more money off it.

- **Buy generic.** When a drug's patent expires, other companies can make similar products to compete with the original manufacturer. This increases competition and drives prices down.

 Generic drugs are just as good as their name-brand counterparts. The FDA requires that all generics have the same dosage, safety, strength, quality, and performance as the "real thing". You can read more about generics at *http://tinyurl.com/FDAgeneric*.

- **Shop around.** Don't assume that a given drug will cost the same at different stores. At the Freakonomics blog (*http://tinyurl.com/NYTdrugs*), Stephen Dubner reports that price differences can be extreme. He cites one case where Walgreens was charging $117 for 90 tablets of generic Prozac while Costco was charging *$12*.

- **Look for discounts.** Believe it or not, you *can* find coupons for prescription drugs. Before your next trip to the pharmacy, do a quick Google search for coupons and rebates, or try going to the website for the medication you're interested in.

- **Consider pill splitting.** Because of the way drugs are priced, it's sometimes possible to get a tablet that's twice as strong for the same (or slightly higher) cost as your normal dose. You then simply cut the pill in two before taking it. To learn more about this option, ask your doctor or pharmacist. (You can read more about pill splitting at WebMD: *http://tinyurl.com/pill-splitting*.)

- **Think long term.** If you use maintenance drugs (like blood-pressure medication) or have long-term prescriptions, you might save by ordering a 90-day supply. Mail-order programs, like Walmart's (*http://tinyurl. com/WM-homepharm*), can often get you a 3-month supply for the price of 2 months' worth.

For more info on the costs and benefits of various prescription drugs, visit these sites:

- **Consumer Reports Best Buy Drugs** is a free site that lets you search for drugs by category and offers tips for managing your prescriptions. (You can download a PDF that explains their advice for getting the best price from *http://tinyurl.com/CRdrugs*.)

- **WorstPills.org** is a subscription-based site from Public Citizen, a watchdog group that aims to warn consumers about possible side effects of various prescription drugs and drug combinations.

And don't forget the best way to save money on medical costs: Stay healthy. It sounds trite, but your health really is your most important asset. Regular exercise and a proper diet reduce the risk of many diseases and improve self-esteem, both of which will help your pocketbook.

Maximum Fun at Minimum Cost

Some people are afraid to embrace thrift because they think they'll have to give up everything fun, but nothing could be further from the truth. In many ways, free fun is even better than the stuff you pay for. There's nothing like the satisfaction you get from enjoying a great evening that costs next to nothing.

Your Money and Your Life

Cheap Thrills

Does being frugal mean you can't have fun? "No way," says Trent Hamm from The Simple Dollar (*www.thesimpledollar.com*). This Iowa father—and author of *365 Ways to Live Cheap!* (Adams Media, 2009) and *The Simple Dollar* (Financial Times Press, 2010)—believes a thrifty lifestyle can be *more* fulfilling than one where you shell out cash to find happiness.

"I used to run with a crowd that spent a lot of money," Hamm says. "We went golfing all the time. We'd go out for drinks after work several times a week. We had gadget wars, competing to see who could buy the latest and greatest toys." Hamm says it was fun—but costly. "I didn't even use all the stuff I bought!" He had piles of debt and lots of Stuff (page 8).

Things changed when he and his wife had their first child. Instead of going out frequently, he was staying home with his family. This forced him to find other ways to spend his leisure time, and he learned that he didn't need money to have fun.

"I spent a lot of time walking around town, holding my son," Hamm says. "I began to notice things. Like, I was vaguely aware that my town had parks, but I had no idea the parks had free Ultimate Frisbee leagues. And I didn't know about all the hiking trails nearby."

Hamm recommends you look for the fun, not the price: "The mistake most people make is looking for the free stuff first. Look at the things you *really* enjoy doing. Once you know what you like to do, there's almost always ways to do these cheaply." For example, Hamm still goes golfing with his friends—but he's found cheaper ways to do it. He doesn't play as often, and when he does he uses public courses and cheap golf balls. "Why would I spend $30 on a ball?" he says. "I'm not Tiger Woods."

Here are some ways to have a good time without spending your last dime:

- **Play games.** A deck of cards costs a couple of bucks. A fancy board game costs about $40—or less if you find it on Craigslist.org. Either one will provide hours of fun with friends and family. (You can still have poker nights with your buddies, just do away with the high-stakes jackpots.)

- **Take up a hobby.** Some of the best times you'll ever have come from pursuing your favorite interests. Gardening and playing music are two great examples of hobbies that cost something up front, but which yield great rewards down the road. Things like knitting and wood-working can be expensive, but if you're knitting a scarf or building a table, those useful items mitigate some of the cost. And if you sell the things you make, you can even *earn* money.

- **Read.** Don't overlook your public library, which has a wealth of en-tertainment options, including books, magazines, CDs, DVDs, audio books, lectures, Internet access, board games, story time, and more. Some libraries even give passes to zoos, museums, and other cultural institutions. The library is like a giant entertainment warehouse, and since you pay for it with your tax dollars, you might as well get some use out of it!

- **Take a class.** Strictly speaking, this option isn't low cost. Community-ed classes usually run about $50, and classes at your local community college might be up to $200. Even though you have to shell out some money for these classes, you're not only having a good time while you learn about woodworking or French or computer programming, you're also picking up a skill you can use to improve your life.

- **Exercise.** Physical fitness is some of the cheapest fun there is, and study after study shows that exercise improves both physical and mental well-being. If you're bored by walking, running, or biking, check into city league sports.

- **Use what you own.** If you're like most Americans, you have stacks of CDs, DVDs, books, and magazines sitting around your house. When was the last time you watched your complete set of *Star Trek* tapes? That's weeks (or months) of fun right there. If you start using the Stuff you own, you might never run out of things to do.

- **Explore your community.** Search out the cheapest deals in your town, like movie theaters or museums or Mexican restaurants. Spend a Saturday touring yard sales or browsing the local shops you've never bothered to visit before. Attend a high school musical or an open-mic night at the coffee shop. Stroll through nearby parks. Your city or town likely has tons of cheap entertainment, but most people are too busy to notice.

The key, as always, is to do what works for you. Choose activities that you enjoy and find ways to do them for less. No matter what you're into—photography, knitting, restoring old cars—there are people who have found ways to do it without spending lots of money. If you're clever and resourceful, you can connect with these frugal folks and learn their techniques. (The Internet is always a good place to start.)

You can find dozens of other ideas for frugal fun in this discussion at Get Rich Slowly: *http://tinyurl.com/GRSfrugalfun*. And don't forget what you learned in Chapter 1: A life well-lived is rich in relationships and experiences, so get out there and *do* things with other people.

Save While Shopping

If you're trying to save money, shopping can be dangerous. Sure, you have to buy some things like food, pet supplies, and new underwear, but, especially if you're a recovering shopaholic (page 65), shopping can tempt you to buy things just for the thrill of it.

Thrifty people still shop, but they shop for things they need, not just for fun. They understand that shopping is a means to an end—and they realize the dangers of being burdened by too much Stuff (page 96).

Some people recommend window-shopping as a substitute for the real thing. If you think you can do that without spending, go ahead. But be careful: It's often better to avoid the temptation altogether.

 Tip Some savvy shoppers save money by playing the "drugstore game" (*http://tinyurl. com/drugstore-game*). By combining coupons and sales, they score amazing bargains from free toothbrushes to cartloads of household goods for just 5 or 10 bucks. For more on this sort of saving, visit *www.moneysavingmom.com*.

When you do shop, keep these guidelines in mind:

- **Shop with a purpose.** The key to keeping your shopping under control is to buy only what you need. It may help you to shop with a list, just like at the grocery store. Knowing exactly why you're shopping can help keep you from getting distracted.

- **Don't be afraid of used.** Buying used items has something of a stigma in the U.S. But a recent poll by Harris Interactive showed that 70% of American adults say that it's now more acceptable to buy used than it was a decade ago. If you're on a tight budget, used stuff can be awesome. You can find all sorts of great bargains on Craigslist.org and eBay. com and at yard sales around town. And don't forget to check your local thrift stores, which carry more than just clothes: Many are great places to find furniture, kitchenware, and even inexpensive entertainment. (For more thrifting tips, check out *www.thethriftshopper.com*.)

 Note Some things are actually *better* used. Here's Liz Weston's list of 10 things you shouldn't buy new: *http://tinyurl.com/Liznonew*.

- **Beware of shopping momentum.** Researchers at Stanford University warn that shopping can lead to more shopping: At first you deliberate over whether to buy something, weighing the pros and cons. But once you've made the decision to buy, you spend less time deciding on additional purchases. This phenomenon, dubbed *shopping momentum*, increases the likelihood you'll buy more.

- **Something you'll never use isn't a bargain.** It's tempting to pick up stuff you know is dirt cheap. But even if you save 90% on a salad spinner, it's money wasted if you never use it. A deal is only a deal if it's something you had a need for before you saw it. So only buy what you know you'll use—everything else is just Stuff (page 96).

Finally, here's a flowchart April Dykman created to help her stay on track while shopping (*http://aprildawnwrites.wordpress.com/*). It helps her keep emotions out of the buying process so she can focus on just the things she needs.

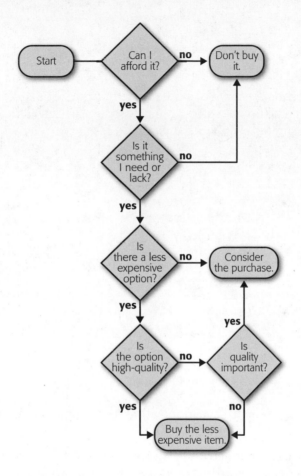

Using such a flowchart may be a little too much for you, but a tool like this can help people who struggle with compulsive spending (page 65) make conscious choices instead of buying impulsively. If you don't need the flowchart but want a little help, here are 10 questions to ask when you're tempted to buy: *http://tinyurl.com/GRS10questions*.

Online Tools

Sometimes you can find the best deals at the mall by turning to your computer. A growing number of websites can help you save money—even if you're not shopping online. Here are some good ones:

- **FatWallet** (*www.fatwallet.com*) is one of the oldest, largest, and most-respected money-saving sites. It lists coupons and cash-back offers, and has a section highlighting top deals. But the best part is the discussion forum, where you can find out about the best bank accounts, travel deals, and more.

- **RetailMeNot** (*www.retailmenot.com*) started as a database of online coupon codes for discounts at popular shopping websites. It now also includes printable coupons for supermarkets and other stores.

- **PriceProtectr** (*www.priceprotectr.com*) lets you save money *after* you buy things. A lot of stores have price-protection policies—if they lower the price on an item you've bought, they'll refund the difference. The catch: You have to notice the price drop, and who has time for that? PriceProtectr does! Simply tell it you bought a new plasma TV from Target, for example, and the site will email you if the price falls.

- **Wishpot** (*www.wishpot.com*) lets you save all the things you're shopping for online in a wish list or registry. This keeps you from buying impulsively and creates a place for your friends and family to go to see what sorts of gifts you might want.

The Tyranny of Stuff

There's one huge way to save money that few people talk about: Own less Stuff.

In his brilliant essay entitled "Stuff" (*www.paulgraham.com/stuff.html*), Paul Graham writes that before you buy **anything**, you should ask yourself, "Will this be something I use constantly?"

Graham used to pick up free Stuff from the side of the road. He'd buy something at a garage sale simply because he could get it for a tenth of what it cost new. Eventually he realized that nothing is a bargain if it just sits in the garage or a storage unit. Things only have value if you use them. (For info on the outrageous cost of storing Stuff, check out *http://tinyurl.com/cost-of-stuff*.)

The Science of Shopping

If you want to spend less at the supermarket or shoe store, get a copy of *Why We Buy: The Science of Shopping* (Simon & Schuster, 2008) from your local library. In the book, Paco Underhill suggests ways to win the retail battle, including:

- **Spend less time in stores.** Underhill writes, "The amount of time a shopper spends in a store (assuming he or she is shopping, not waiting in line) is perhaps the single most important factor in determining how much he or she will buy." The takeaway: Don't browse; shop with a purpose (page 94).

- **Only seek employee contact when you need help.** There's a reason the employees are so eager to please at your favorite store: Interacting with staff makes people buy more. Underhill notes "the more shopper-employee contacts that take place, the greater the average sale." So steer clear of clerks unless you have a specific question.

- **Just say no to samples.** Research shows that people are more likely to buy something if they sample it first. So don't try the samples at the giant warehouse store—they'll just tempt you to spend more.

- **Hands off.** The more you interact with something, the more likely you are to buy it. According to Underhill, "Virtually all unplanned purchases—and many planned ones, too—come as a result of the shopper seeing, touching, smelling, or tasting something that promises pleasure, if not fulfillment." So when you're out shopping, keep your hands (and nose, and mouth) to yourself.

- **Have Mom do the shopping.** 60–70% of supermarket purchases are unplanned, and men are bigger culprits than women. One study found that almost all women take shopping lists to the supermarket, but less than a quarter of men do.

For many compulsive spenders, Stuff is comforting. When these people buy things (even on credit), they feel wealthy. But in time, Stuff becomes clutter. One of the great things about setting goals and recognizing what gives meaning to your life is that it helps you differentiate the Stuff from what's important. For example, to you, that weight bench in the basement may be an integral piece of your life plan, but to someone else, it's just another piece of Stuff.

Stuff plays a huge role in your happiness—or unhappiness. Stuff costs money to buy, store, move, and maintain. But the costs aren't just financial. There's a real mental toll to having too much Stuff: You think about it and worry about it; it becomes a burden.

There's nothing wrong with owning things you use and value. The problem is accumulating Stuff you never use. The best way to cope with Stuff? Don't let it into your home in the first place.

 Tip Every time you buy something, it has an impact on the world around you. Buying fewer things means a little more money in your pocket and a little less pollution in the world. So do your part for the environment: Buy less Stuff.

Here are some ways to guard against Stuff:

- **Ignore the Joneses.** Peer pressure is powerful, and one of the most dangerous paths to clutter (and overspending) is the urge to own as much as your friends do. But life isn't a competition. Learn to be content with what you have; owning more Stuff won't make you happier.

- **If you don't need it, don't buy it.** In his book *Clutter's Last Stand*, Don Aslett argues that the value is in the using, not the owning. "No matter how you look at it," he writes, "clutter is a poor investment." So buy only what you need.

- **Focus on experiences, not things.** As you learned in Chapter 1, experiences are more likely to make you happy than material goods. Of course, experiences cost money, but a trip to Thailand, a nice dinner with friends, and the entrance fee for a marathon all have one thing in common: They don't take up space. You get value for your money without any residual Stuff.

- **Practice the one-in, one-out rule.** Try to keep a steady state of Stuff. If, for example, you have 12 pairs of pants and buy another, get rid of an old pair to prevent Stuff from building up.

 Tip Here's another strategy: Every week, fill a bag with Stuff you no longer want or need. At the end of the month, give the four bags you've filled to the charity of your choice—and start filling another bag. This is an easy way to slowly purge clutter from your life. (If you itemize your tax deductions, make a note of what goes into the bags so you can save on taxes at the end of the year.)

- **Focus on quality.** Base your buying decisions on the value an item will give you. Often it makes more sense to have one excellent, expensive item than several lousy, cheap ones that just clutter up your home.

- **Borrow and lend.** When you borrow and lend among friends, each person needs to own less, so you share the joy of having less Stuff. And why own thousands of books when there's a public library down the street?

- **Ditch packaging.** Why buy DVDs when you can use Hulu.com or Netflix? Why purchase CDs when you can get songs through iTunes? If you don't need the packaging, don't buy it.

- **Reduce advertising exposure.** Many people report that they buy much less Stuff when they stop watching TV. But radio programs, newspapers, magazines, and the Internet are all filled with ads, too. The more you avoid—or ignore—advertising, the less you'll be tempted to buy.

 Tip Many web browsers let you install plug-ins (little additions to the program) that help block ads, like this one for Firefox: *http://tinyurl.com/FFadblock*. Search around online to see what's available for your browser or ask your geeky friends for recommendations.

For more about the tyranny of Stuff, check out ***Unclutter Your Life in One Week*** by Erin Doland (Simon Spotlight Entertainment, 2009), ***Clutter's Last Stand*** by Don Aslett (Marsh Creek Press, 2005), and ***It's All Too Much*** by Peter Walsh (Free Press, 2007). These three websites are also great resources: *http://unclutterer.com*, *www.flylady.com*, and *http://mnmlist.com*.

As you purge Stuff from your life, you come to realize that all you *really* need are the bare essentials—everything else is just Stuff.

Leading a Rich Life on a Budget

Frugality keeps you focused on your goals. When you buy generic food at the grocery store or get your clothes at a thrift shop you're not being cheap—you're prioritizing and working toward a greater goal. You're not depriving yourself—you've decided to live debt-free or follow a spiritual ideal or save for a trip around the world. Small, frugal, everyday choices can help you attain these big aims.

 Tip Over the years, the readers at Get Rich Slowly have suggested tons of ways to feel rich while being frugal. The most common suggestion? Give to or volunteer at a church or charity. (For more on this, see page 304.)

It's all about balance. When you cut spending on things you don't need, you can indulge in things that really matter to you. Frugality isn't about depriving yourself of everything you enjoy; it's about making smart choices to reach your goals.

We all like nice things, and there are plenty of ways you can have nice things without spending a lot. More importantly, being frugal can help you feel a sense of achievement from money saved, not money spent. Remember that buying things won't make you a better person—you *aren't* what you own. As Tyler Durden says in *Fight Club*, "You're not your job. You're not how much money you have in the bank. You're not the car you drive. You're not the contents of your wallet."

When you stop wanting to always have the newest, best things and you realize that money is in no way connected to your self-worth, you'll not only be better at managing your finances, you'll be happier, too.

6 How to Make More Money

"Your greatest asset is your earning ability." —Brian Tracy

As you learned in the last chapter, frugality is an important part of personal finance: By managing your expectations and living within your means, you're more likely to be wealthier *and* happier. But cutting costs isn't the only way to boost your cash flow. If your goal is to build wealth, you'll get the best results by looking beyond frugality to increasing your income.

For most people, this means managing a career effectively: finding the right job, learning how to ask for a raise, and knowing when to move on. Others can up their incomes by selling stuff they already own, pursuing money-making hobbies, or starting their own businesses. This chapter explores all these ways to get more cash coming in.

Working for Others

Your health is your most valuable financial asset, but your career is a close second. Few things affect your financial situation—and your happiness—as much as what you do for a living.

Positive cash flow (page 54) is important. It lets you avoid debt, buy things you need, and save for the future. But you can't have positive cash flow without income. And unless you've won the lottery or inherited a ton of money from Aunt Mabel, your main source of income is your job, so you should make the most of it. This section offers pointers on how to do just that.

For Love or Money: Which Career Should You Choose?

Before you can start down a career path, you have to decide what to do for a living. Should you pursue your passion, doing work you love regardless of how much you earn? Or should you focus simply on the money? In his essay on how to do what you love (*www.paulgraham.com/love.html*), Paul Graham writes:

> Finding work you love is very difficult. Most people fail. Even if you succeed, it's rare to be free to work on what you want till your thirties or forties. But if you have the destination in sight you'll be more likely to arrive at it. If you know you can love work, you're in the home stretch, and if you know what work you love, you're practically there.

Some folks claim that if you do what you love, the money will follow. Others say that a job is just a job—you're not meant to like it. The truth is somewhere in between. There are few things worse than a job you hate. Lots of people do enjoy fun, fulfilling careers—and earn a good living at it—but these dream jobs don't just magically appear.

To find a promising career, you have to take certain steps:

1. **Decide what you want to be when you grow up.** Don't just pick a job because it pays well; have a goal in mind (see page 26). Choose a field based on your interests and experience, and know where you want to go in that field. If you don't know what you want to do, explore: read, take classes, and talk to people about their jobs (see the box on page 110). For more inspiration, read Richard Bolles's classic book *What Color Is Your Parachute?* (Ten Speed Press, 2009).

Finding Your Sweet Spot

In his book *Good to Great* (HarperBusiness, 2001), Jim Collins describes how successful businesses are built by finding the sweet spot where passion, excellence, and economics meet. You can apply this idea to your own career. To help decide what you want to do, think about what you're passionate about, what you do best, and what people will pay you to do.

There's a sweet spot where these three things overlap. In real life, that spot is where you find work you love, are good at, and can earn a living at. But if one of these pieces is missing, you haven't found your sweet spot. For example, if you're good at something and people will pay you to do it, but you're not passionate about it, you'll still hate your job.

Once you find your sweet spot, try to organize life so you can spend your time doing that thing. Whether you work for yourself (page 111) or somebody else, this is the key to a meaningful, rewarding career.

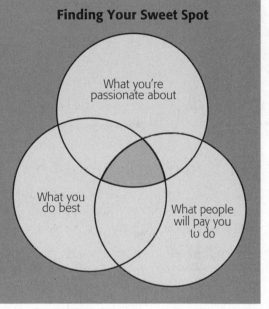

Finding Your Sweet Spot

What you're passionate about

What you do best

What people will pay you to do

 Tip The Department of Labor's *Occupational Outlook Handbook* (*www.bls.gov/oco/*) lists hundreds of different jobs and describes their educational requirements, earning potentials, future prospects, and typical working conditions.

2. **Start at the beginning.** Once you've picked a field—and received the required education or training—find a job, but be patient: Don't expect to graduate with a degree in library science and immediately be the head librarian at a prestigious university. It would be great if we could all have our dream jobs by age 21, but that's not how it works. You have to start low on the totem pole and work your way up. The sooner you start, the sooner you'll reach your goals.

3. **Get the most from the grunt work.** Since entry-level jobs are unavoidable, use them to your advantage. If you're a receptionist or a file clerk, make the most of it: Use your time to learn the jargon, make connections, and understand the industry. To excel in any field, you have to be in it every day. So do the drudgework, but make it count.

No matter what career you choose, follow the age-old advice: Keep a good attitude. Learn how to deal with your boss and coworkers. Rise above the gossip. Help others succeed by sharing credit and taking your share of the blame. Know when to ask for help and when to take charge. Be curious. Solve problems. Learn from those around you. Work hard and be professional. Do these things and you'll gain knowledge and skills you can apply to every job you ever have.

 Tip For 20 tips on how to nail a job interview, visit *www.howtonailaninterview.com*.

Starting on the Right Foot: Salary Negotiations

Your pay doesn't necessarily reflect your performance or seniority. In fact, your buddy who does the same work you do (and just as well) may get paid twice as much. Why? Because he's a better negotiator.

One of the best ways to increase your income is through salary negotiations, either when you're first offered the job or when you have a performance review. Salary negotiations make a lot of people uncomfortable, but they're extremely important.

"We spend years thinking about what we'll be when we grow up," Jack Chapman writes in **Negotiating Your Salary** (Ten Speed Press, 2001). "But when it's time for a raise, most of us just accept whatever we're offered. How many minutes do we spend negotiating the money? *Zero*."

Chapman argues that with just a little effort, you can make the case for a higher salary during a review or a job interview. Asking for what you're worth during those few minutes can make a difference of hundreds of thousands of dollars over your lifetime.

 Note The best way to get the salary you want is to make yourself a desirable employee. This means you have to work hard and well, which puts you in a position to ask for—and get—a better salary.

Here are Chapman's five rules for negotiating your salary when interviewing for a job:

1. **Postpone salary negotiations until you're offered the job.** Let your potential employer decide whether you're the right candidate, and *then* talk about money. The same is true of raises—discuss them *after* you have your performance review. (The next section has more about asking for a raise.)

2. **Let them go first.** It's hard to come out ahead by naming a number, so let your employer suggest a salary. Lots of people find it awkward to evade direct questions about salary history. For these folks, Chapman has posted a short video that explains how to answer questions about salary expectations: *http://salarynegotiations.com/Video.htm*. (Also see Penelope Trunk's advice on the subject: *http://tinyurl.com/BCsalary*.)

3. **When you hear their offer, repeat the top value—and then stop talking.** "The most likely outcome of this silence is a raise," Chapman writes. This technique buys you some time to think while putting pressure on the employer. For more on this step, check out Chapman's video about it: *http://tinyurl.com/theflinch*.

4. **Counter their offer with a researched response.** Next, make a counteroffer based on what you know about yourself, the market, and the company. This means you have to do some research beforehand so you know the reasonable salary range for the position.

5. **Clinch the deal—then deal some more.** Finally, lock in the offer, and then negotiate additional benefits like extra vacation days or a company car. This is like agreeing on the price of a car before you negotiate the value of your trade-in (see page 177).

Chapman's book has detailed info on each of these five steps. It also offers tips for determining your fair-market value (though you can do a lot of that online at sites like PayScale.com, SalaryScout.com, and GlassDoor.com) and applying these techniques to raises and performance reviews. It also explores situations where you should break these rules.

The average person doesn't spend enough time looking for ways to boost his income. Learning how to negotiate your salary when applying for a job is one of the best ways to improve your financial position. And as the next section explains, once you have a job, it's important to know how to ask for a raise.

The Value of a College Education

Does earning a college degree make a difference in your financial future? Absolutely! The facts are striking: On average, people with college degrees earn almost *twice* as much folks who never attend college.

Here are the U.S. Census Bureau's median 2007 income levels based on education (see page 11 for a refresher on medians):

Highest Level of Education Completed	Median Income	Increase over Level Below
Some high school	$19,405	—
High school degree	$26,894	38.6%
Some college	$32,875	22.2%
College	$46,805	42.4%
Advanced degree	$61.287	30.9%

Of course, these are just statistics: Getting a college education doesn't *guarantee* you'll end up earning more money than you would otherwise. Some English majors wind up working in convenience stores and some high-school dropouts end up running multi-million dollar corporations. But in general, completing college has a huge impact on how much you earn in your lifetime—it can be worth a million dollars!

For more on the financial benefits of a college education, check out *http://tinyurl. com/college-census*.

How to Ask for a Raise

If you do a good job, keep a positive attitude, and help your boss meet her goals, you should expect regular raises. But not every company is as free with the salary bumps as they ought to be. (In fact, some employers—such as government agencies—can't give discretionary raises at all!) And, of course, if the economy is in the toilet, even companies that used to regularly give raises may have to tighten their belts.

The best way to get a raise is, well, to ask for one. If you think you deserve a raise but haven't heard that anything is in the works, schedule a meeting with your manager. Keep these tips in mind:

- **Make your case.** Draw up a list of ways you've helped the company, and try to state these achievements in dollar terms, if you can. For example: "By creating the new maintenance schedule for our delivery trucks, I've saved the business $10,000 over the past 3 months." Be honest and don't exaggerate. Try to think of things from the company's point of view—nobody's going to give you a raise just because you need extra cash.

- **Do your homework.** Before you meet with your boss, have a target salary in mind. Use sites like PayScale.com, SalaryScout.com, and Glass-Door.com to research the going rate for similar jobs in your area. (Better yet, ask around to see what colleagues at other firms are earning.)

- **Seize the moment.** The best time to ask for a raise is after a strong performance review or after your boss gives you new responsibilities. You're not *entitled* to a raise simply for coming to work every day, but you've got a right to request one if you're doing good work.

- **Don't complain.** Be positive and professional: Emphasize your strengths and accomplishments, and give examples of how you've helped the company. Don't gripe about your workload or other employees.

- **Follow up.** After your meeting, be sure to follow up on any promises your boss made. Get the details of the raise in writing, and keep an eye on your paycheck to make sure it goes up when it's supposed to.

 If your boss turns down your request for a raise, ask what you need to do to earn one and when you can meet to discuss the subject again.

If you're really an asset to the company, they can almost always find enough money for a raise. Businesses know that it's better to pay a bit more to keep a proven performer than to go through the hassle and risk of hiring somebody new.

 Don't ask for a raise if your work isn't up to snuff. Raises are rewards, not entitlements. Your boss will be more willing to give you a raise if you make her life easier. That doesn't mean you have to suck up—just make her look good.

Earning More *Without* a Raise

Raises and promotions aren't always options—especially in a rocky economy. Here are a few ways to get more for your labors—even if your paycheck stays the same:

- **Use your company's retirement plan.** If your employer offers a retirement plan, take advantage of it—*especially* if the company matches your contributions. Never turn down free money! (See Chapter 13 for more on retirement savings.)

- **Refer a new employee.** Some companies will pay you a bonus if you refer someone who ends up getting hired. (Check with your HR department for specifics.) At the very least, helping the company out this way will earn you some goodwill.

- **Improve your skills.** Even if you didn't get a raise this year, you can increase your odds of future salary bumps by learning new things. Attend training sessions, go to seminars and conferences, and get certified in job-related skills. (Many companies will even pay for your classes.) You can then use your new skills at your current job—or to help you find a new one.

- **Ask for non-monetary rewards.** If there's no room in your company's budget for a raise, ask for other compensation, like an extra week of vacation, a more flexible schedule, or a better parking space.

- **Network.** Consciously build new connections inside and outside your company by doing things like joining committees and volunteering for the tasks nobody wants (taking on the tough jobs can bring you to the attention of your boss—or even your boss's boss).

- **Know the rules.** Make sure you're familiar with all your company's policies. Reading the employee handbook is tedious, but you might find out about some little-known perks you can ask for.

Moving On

Few things last forever. Even if you love your job, you'll eventually want to try something new. And if you hate your job, it's important to know how to quit without burning bridges. You don't want to let your guard down during your final days and do something foolish that could damage your career.

On eWeek.com (*http://tinyurl.com/jobquit*), Deb Perelman offers some excellent advice for leaving a job:

- **Be sure you're making the right choice.** Sometimes that dream job *isn't*. If possible, "test-drive" the new job first—by working at it part-time during weekends or evenings—so you don't give up what you already have for something that isn't a good fit for you.

- **Give written notice.** Be sure to submit a written letter of resignation to your boss (or HR department); it makes you look professional and makes everything official. In your letter, stick to the facts, don't let your emotions get the better of you, and don't lie about why you're leaving. Whether your letter is simple or complex, keep it positive. You can read sample letters at Emurse: *http://tinyurl.com/rletters*.

 Note If you're thinking about switching jobs, pick up a copy of Alexandra Levit's *New Job, New You* (Ballantine, 2009). Levit profiles 35 people who've managed to reinvent themselves with new careers.

- **Tell your boss first.** Respect the chain of command: Talk to your manager before telling your buddies you're leaving.

- **Be ready for a counter-offer.** If you're a valuable part of the company's plans, they may try to get you to stay. Be prepared for this, and know what you're going to say. (This is one reason it's important not to lie when resigning: If the company offers to fix the things you claimed were wrong but they aren't your *real* reasons for leaving, you could end up in an awkward position.)

- **Leave in good standing.** As tempting as it is to mentally check out before you're done working for your old company, resist that urge. If you said you'd stay 2 more weeks, *work* during those 2 weeks. If you don't, you put the company in a tough spot and make yourself look bad. You never know when you'll need a reference from a former boss or find yourself working with former coworkers again.

Informational Interviews

Finding a job can be tough. Competition is fierce, and even if you've got the right skills, it's challenging to make yourself known to the right people. *Informational interviews* are a way to get an edge on your competition. These aren't the same as job interviews—they're an opportunity to learn more about a career or company.

The first step in setting up one of these interviews is to find people with jobs that interest you. Prepare a simple list of questions to make sure you get the info you need when you contact these folks. It may help calm your nerves to approach the interview as if you were a reporter: Pretend you're gathering facts for a news story.

The cardinal rule of informational interviews is *don't ask for a job*. If you tell somebody you're just gathering info but then turn the meeting into a job interview, you're just going to make her angry. (If she thinks you're a promising candidate and she has a position available, she'll contact you.)

Here are some more guidelines:

- **Ask politely.** If the subject agrees to an interview, set a time and a date. If she's not up for such an interview, respect her boundaries.
- **Be prepared.** Dress appropriately, be punctual, do your homework about the company or field, and be ready to ask intelligent, relevant questions.
- **Listen.** Ask open-ended questions, and then let the subject talk about herself and the company. Good questions include "What's your typical workday like?" and "How is your company different from its competitors?"
- **Take notes.** You're conducting this interview to learn more about a possible career, so write things down and ask follow-up questions.
- **Be brief.** Keep track of time. Don't rush, but don't overstay your welcome.

Afterward, remember to send an email or hand-written note to thank the person for taking time to meet with you.

For more about informational interviews, check out *http://tinyurl.com/NYTinfoview*.

Taking a Second Job

One of the best ways to earn extra income is to get a second job. Earning a few bucks in your spare time is a great way to boost your cash flow, and it's something that almost anyone can do.

Some people don't like the idea of a second job; they feel like it's beneath them. But if you can get over that, it's a simple and straightforward way to bring in predictable income. You should be able to find *something* you're willing to do at a place that needs part-time (or even full-time) help on evenings and weekends: a bookstore, coffee shop, amusement park, whatever.

When I needed extra income to pay off my debt, for example, I taught my-self computer programming, and then landed a part-time job using my new skills. And I know a biologist who picked up a few hours a week at an upscale clothing store (which let her earn extra cash *and* use the employee discount to save money on her wardrobe).

Working a second job involves less risk and planning than some of the other ideas in this chapter, and it's likely to cause you far less stress than your main job. But before you go out and pick up a shift at the local Starbucks, make sure your regular job doesn't have a policy against moonlighting. It's not worth jeopardizing your career over a job at the Kwik-Mart.

For tips on landing the perfect second job, head over to the *Good Morning America* website: *http://tinyurl.com/2ndjob*.

Working for Yourself

Working for a big company isn't for everyone. In 2008, there were 29.6 million businesses in the United States. According to the Small Business Administration, about 75% of these had no employees. That means that three quarters of all American businesses are owned by people working for themselves.

People choose self-employment for lots of reasons. Some can't stand working for somebody else. Others see it as an opportunity to make more money. And a few recognize it as a way to do work they're passionate about. Working for yourself can be freeing, increase your income, and let you focus on doing what you love. But as wonderful as self-employment is, there are plenty of pitfalls.

The Pros and Cons of Entrepreneurship

There's a big difference between doing what you love as a hobby and hav-ing it for a job. When you make a little money from your hobby (see page 115), that's extra income, which is part of the fun. But when you flip the switch and it becomes your sole means of making a living, some of that fun vanishes—sometimes all of it disappears.

Working for somebody else is like renting an apartment, whereas working for yourself is like owning your own home; both have their rewards and drawbacks. Having to generate your own income can add a lot of stress to your life: You have to draft the business plan, find the customers, send the invoices, and pay the bills. Sure, there's pressure when you work for somebody else, too, but there's also a sense of freedom: You're not responsible for the daily decisions, and if you don't like the job, you can quit. Plus, unless you're in sales, the actual source of income probably isn't your responsibility; it's something management worries about.

Despite the downsides, owning your own businesses can be tremendously rewarding, both emotionally and monetarily. The authors of *The Millionaire Next Door* write that, "self-employed people are four times more likely to be millionaires than those who work for others."

If you decide to make the leap, be careful. Take your time, do research, and make smart choices. Here are some other things to keep in mind:

- **Have a plan.** Just as a budget is important for your personal finances, a business plan is key to entrepreneurial success. If your business is small, the plan can be as simple as a list of goals. But if you're looking for outside funding or hope to take over the world, your plan needs to be as detailed as possible. You can find free sample business plans at *www.Bplans.com*.

- **Don't quit your day job—at least not at first.** If possible, start by going solo on evenings and weekends to get a feel for your business and find out if you really want to pursue it full time. You may discover your new gig isn't what you'd hoped for.

- **Find advisors you trust.** A new business is uncharted territory, so it's really helpful to have guides. Heed the advice of your mentors, and find a good lawyer and accountant and follow their instructions.

- **Play by the rules.** Some small-business owners strike out on their own because they're mavericks. This independence may make them think they can cut corners by not filling out paperwork or filing taxes, but shortcuts like these put everything at risk. It's easier to do things right the first time than to sort out a mess later.

- **Keep business and personal accounts separate.** Don't mingle work and personal funds; open a checking account specifically for the business. Then document everything that enters and leaves that account.

- **Keep costs low.** Do what you can to keep your overhead down. For example, don't spend $1,000 on a fancy Aeron chair when you can pick up a decent desk chair from Goodwill for five bucks. You'll be less stressed and have better odds of success if you don't have a lot of bills dragging you down.

- **Be willing to spend on training.** Buy the books and manuals you need and pay for classes. Training like this is a necessary business expense, not a luxury.

- **Keep good records.** Business will be slow at first, so it won't seem like a big deal that you keep receipts in a shoebox and don't have a filing system. But in time, you'll be flooded with paperwork. Get organized from the start to prevent future headaches.

 Note If you run a small business, take a look at Outright.com, a simple, free bookkeeping site. It's like Mint or Wesabe (page 50) for freelancers and small businesses.

- **Be confident.** When you start out, don't let your customers know you're nervous. They're lost, too, and hoping you'll guide them to the right product or service. So do research and become an expert. And if you make mistakes, learn from them.

- **Charge the going rate—or close to it.** If you start a house-cleaning service, don't go in with low-ball bids. If you're too cheap, people will think there's a reason for it. Charge the going rate, and raise your price as demand increases.

- **Have an exit strategy.** Know where you're going and why. Is your goal to sell your business? To have competent employees who can run things, leaving you to pursue other interests? Or is it just a lark, something you'll do for fun for a few years before dropping it altogether?

These are just the basics. There are tons of books out there with more detailed advice on starting and running a small business, and they're well worth reading if you want to make a go of it on your own. Remember: Millions of people have successfully quit their day jobs and pursued their dreams.

 Turning something you love into your full-time job may kill the fun. After all, work is work. If you decide to pursue your passion, take it slow. Start as a hobby business (page 115) and expand from there. If you reach a point where you don't enjoy what you do, back off a little to see if you can get the magic back.

Resources for Entrepreneurs

If you're curious about starting your own business, your best source of info is the people you know. Do you have an uncle who owns his own machine shop? A friend who does freelance web design? A coworker who does landscaping on the side? These folks have real-world experience. Take them to lunch and pick their brains—it may be the best $20 you ever spend.

Here are some online sources of information:

- **A List Apart** has a great article about starting a business (*http://tinyurl.com/starting-business*). The piece is aimed at artists and computer programmers, but its advice applies to nearly everyone.

- **The U.S. Small Business Administration** (*www.sba.gov*) offers info about writing a business plan, finding loans and grants, and getting local assistance.

- **SCORE** (*www.score.org*), the Service Core of Retired Executives, is a group of past and present business owners who act as mentors for young entrepreneurs.

- **The Business Owner's Toolkit** (*www.toolkit.com*) has more than 5,000 pages of free articles, tools, and forms to help small business owners get started. For $39 a year, you can get access to even more material.

You may also want to read a book or two on the subject:

- Pamela Slim's *Escape from Cubicle Nation* (Portfolio, 2009) gives advice about leaving a safe career to start your own business. Slim advocates a "life first, business second" philosophy: By setting clear, meaningful goals, you can develop a business that fits your lifestyle. (Slim has a blog at *www.escapefromcubiclenation.com*.)

- In *Career Renegade* (Broadway, 2009), Jonathan Fields explains how to turn your passion into a business. He includes lots of stories about people who've made a great living doing what they love. (You can read more from Fields at *www.careerrenegade.com*.)

- In *Go It Alone* (Harper, 2005), Bruce Judson argues that to succeed with a small business, you should focus on what you do best and automate or pay others to handle everything else. For example, if you're a good photographer, focus on taking great shots and hire someone to balance the books.

Outearning Spending

"You can't outearn dumb spending," financial author Greg Karp likes to say. Some people believe they can always earn more money to maintain their lifestyles—but their spending usually grows to match their income. (For some examples, see the box on page 13.) And you never know when the economy is going to take an unexpected turn, making it hard to find a job.

When you earn more, resist the temptation to *spend* more. If your spending increases with your earnings, you'll get stuck on the hedonic treadmill (page 11) and be at risk of a financial crisis if you lose your job. If, on the other hand, you keep your spending steady, you can use that increased cash flow to pay down debt or save for the future.

By spending smart (see Chapter 5), you can make the most of your income and enjoy life.

Money-Making Hobbies

Even if you're not interested in owning a business that you work at full time, a small-scale venture might be right for you. Why not build a business around one of your hobbies? You won't get rich by playing your violin at weddings or weaving baskets, but it never hurts to earn a little extra cash from things you'd do anyhow. This section suggests some key ways to make money from your hobbies.

Do what you love

Choose a hobby you enjoy, and *then* try to find a way to make money from it. Don't dive into a hobby simply because it might be profitable. You should do this thing because you love it; any income should be secondary. Keep it fun and it won't become a chore.

Example: I love to write. When I was struggling with debt, I read personal finance books, and then summarized what I'd learned on my website. Eventually, this grew into Get Rich Slowly. I've managed to make a career out of writing about personal finance, but I didn't start doing it for the money—I was passionate about the subject.

Be creative

If you don't know which hobby to pursue, think outside the box. What skills do you have that others don't? Define the term "hobby" broadly so you don't limit yourself. Find something that you can do that most others can't—and that people might be willing to pay for.

Example: One of my friends loves to travel, and he discovered that he can fund his adventures by writing about the places he visits. He makes money selling e-books, and gets paid to write for newspapers and magazines.

Don't expect too much

You probably won't get rich off your hobby. In fact, you likely won't even earn enough to quit your day job. But you might be able to earn enough to make the hobby self-sustaining, meaning you earn enough to cover the cost of new tools and equipment.

Example: My brother builds speakers and works with audio equipment for fun. He makes a little spending money doing speaker jobs for other people, but he's not interested in turning his hobby into a full-time business.

Don't underestimate yourself

When you truly love something, your experience can give you skills and knowledge that you may take for granted. But just because you know all about growing orchids doesn't mean everyone else does. If you're an expert on a subject, think of ways to share it with others—for a fee.

Example: If you're passionate about cycling and want to help others learn the sport, start a bike-fitting service or open a part-time bike repair shop. Doing these things may seem simple to you, but others will gladly pay for the help.

Market yourself

To earn an income, you need customers. Many people are uncomfortable promoting themselves, but you have to if you hope to earn money from your hobby: People need to know you're available before they can hire you.

Example: There's no shame in discussing your money-making hobby with friends, family, and neighbors. You don't need to be pushy; just bring it up naturally in conversation. Eventually word will get out about what you do, and people will call for your services.

Hone your skills

You know the old mantra: Practice, practice, practice. The more time and energy you devote to your hobby, the better you'll get at it, which will improve your chances of earning money.

Example: Love photography? If you take a hundred shots a day and read up on how to compose images, you can improve your skills quickly. You may never become a professional photographer, but you might be able to sell images to stock photo agencies (like iStockPhoto.com) or enter (and win) photography contests.

Choose carefully

Not every hobby is a good source of income. Some—like collecting—can actually be huge drains on your budget. And remember: You probably won't get rich off your side business, but you *can* improve your cash flow, which will help you get out of debt and build wealth that much quicker.

Your Money and Your Life

Cash for Cupcakes

Jessie Smith graduated from college with an art degree and no firm career plans. When the economy tanked in 2008, she began to wonder what she could do with her degree. "There were all these articles about women losing their jobs," she says. "I read an article about a grandma who started her own peanut brittle company, selling it at farmers markets." This gave Jessie an idea.

With encouragement from friends and family, she started Confectionery (*www. confectionerypdx.com*), her own cupcake business. Jessie bakes and decorates cupcakes and sells them at local stores and farmers markets. "They're pretty elaborate and creative," she says. "I get satisfaction out of that." This isn't how she *planned* to use her art degree, but she's having fun while learning new skills.

Starting a small business is a scary prospect, but Jessie figured that at age 24, she could afford to take a chance: "When you're young, *that's* the time to make mistakes."

Jessie doesn't have any employees, and it's her own money at risk. Despite some bumps along the way, she still came close to breaking even her first year. Now she's taking a business class to help her with the non-creative side of the cupcake trade, and she believes she'll do much better in the future. She's found an outlet for her creativity and enjoys what she does, which is just frosting on the cake.

Other Ways to Make Money

Your career will always be your main source of income—but that doesn't mean it has to be your *only* source. There are lots of other ways to dig up dollars (without resorting to a life of crime). The next few pages are full of tips for turning clutter into cash and making money in your spare time.

Selling Stuff

Americans pay tons of money to store Stuff (page 96). According to the Self Storage Association (yes, that's a real organization), in 1984 there were fewer than 300 million square feet of self-storage space. By the end of 2008, that number had grown to 2.35 *billion* square feet. And just imagine how much Stuff is tucked away in garages, attics, and basements. Instead of letting your Stuff gather dust, why not sell it and make a little money?

 Note Page 98 has tips for coping with clutter.

As long as you don't try to do it all at once, it's not hard to sell your used Stuff. To keep things manageable, follow these steps:

1. Sell your most valuable items on eBay.

2. Hold a yard sale with everything else.

3. Try to get rid of the remaining things on Craigslist.

4. Donate the rest to charity.

Depending on how much Stuff you have, this process can take weeks or months to finish. But when you're done, you'll have far less clutter around the house—and a fat wad of dough you can use to pay down debt or to save for that Hawaiian vacation.

Selling on eBay

If you want to turn your Stuff into cash, eBay—the world's largest auction website—should be your first stop. You can skip this step if you just want to get things out of your hair quickly, but if you want to earn real money, eBay is the best way to get top dollar for your valuable items.

There are tons of great books and websites that can help you master eBay—including **eBay Hacks** (O'Reilly, 2005)—but here are some basics to get you started:

- **Research each item you post.** Comb through completed eBay auctions to see what similar items fetch (and how often they sell). Also check other sources (like Amazon, Craigslist, and so on) to see what they charge for the item.

- **Start low.** Setting a low opening bid is a win-win situation: It costs you less and encourages more bids. The more popular you expect an item to be, the lower you should set your starting bid.

- **Timing is everything.** You can get top dollar for your Stuff by scheduling your auctions so that folks are more likely to see them. Try:

  - Ending your auction on a weekend between 7 p.m. and 10 p.m. Eastern Time.

  - Running a 10-day auction for maximum exposure.

  - Not having your listings end within 2 minutes of each other, especially if they're related items. This gives bidders a chance to chase more than one of your items.

- **Offer a money-back guarantee—with restrictions.** Make it clear that you'll refund the buyer's money only if he feels the item isn't as you described it, not if he simply changes his mind or made a mistake.

- **Charge reasonable shipping.** If you're selling a Beanie Baby for $3 but charging $10 for shipping, you're not going to get many bids. You might think it's clever to make a mint on shipping, but you'll just make buyers angry. Free shipping doesn't usually attract more bidders, but high shipping rates scare them away.

- **Write a thorough description.** Be honest: List the strengths and flaws of your item. Write things like "This book is in great shape, but somebody wrote notes in the margins." If you don't provide enough info for buyers to make informed decisions, you won't get many bids.

- **Post photos.** If condition is a concern (as it is for many collectibles), provide as many photos as possible.

- **Don't accept bids from headaches.** You don't have to take bids from people who might cause problems, like folks with negative feedback, people who haven't paid for items, or overseas bidders.

- **Answer questions.** You'll inevitably get questions about your items, and some of the questions will be stupid. Answer them anyhow. If you think other people might wonder the same thing, post your response publicly.

- **Be friendly.** An easy-going style will get you more bids than a business-like listing, so don't be afraid to make jokes and show enthusiasm.

 Note If you don't want to go through the hassle of listing stuff on eBay, then start with Craigslist (page 122).

If eBay doesn't appeal to you, there are lots of other ways to sell your Stuff online. Two of the most prominent are:

- **Half.com**, which is actually owned by eBay, but uses a different business model. You don't pay to *list* your items; you only owe the site money when your things sell. The downside is that you're limited to items with ISBNs or UPCs in certain categories: books, music, movies, and videogames. Learn more here: *http://tinyurl.com/half-sell*.

- **Amazon Marketplace** lets you sell your stuff on Amazon.com, the world's largest online retailer. Simply search Amazon for the item you want to sell (be sure it's exactly the same, though—sometimes you'll find many versions of the same product, like hardback and paperback editions of a book), and then click the "Sell Yours Here" button. Here's more info: *http://tinyurl.com/amzn-sell*.

Your biggest decision with Amazon and Half.com is how to price your item. If you have the lowest price, your things will certainly sell quickly, but you might have been able to get more for them. But if you set your price too high, you'll still be storing Stuff in the attic 3 years from now.

Holding a yard sale

After you've sold the good stuff online, it's time to hold a yard sale. As a yard-sale veteran—I've spent more than 20 years buying and selling—here's my advice for having fun and making money while getting rid of your Stuff:

- **Group sales work better.** If you can coordinate with your neighbors, you'll draw more traffic. When our neighborhood hosts a group sale, people come from all over; when I sell on my own, I'm lucky to get one tenth that many people. Place ads in the local paper and on Craigslist, and put up signs.

Tip A good yard-sale sign is easy to read from a distance. Use dark ink on a light background, and keep it simple; all you need is the date and location: "Huge Sale 6/30, 265 River Road." (An arrow helps, too.) Make sure the sign is rigid so the wind won't mangle it, and remember to take your signs down when the sale is over. For more signage tips, go to *http://tinyurl.com/ysq-signs*.

- **Be prepared.** Wear comfortable clothes and have water and snacks handy. Get plenty of one-dollar bills the day before so you can make change. Move things out early so you're ready to go when the sale is scheduled to start. (If you don't want to deal with early-bird shoppers, tell them to go away; don't let them push you around.)

- **Think like a customer.** Make your sale inviting and easy to browse: Are things clearly marked? Is there enough space to move around? If the garage feels dark and dreary, consider moving your tables to the driveway or the lawn. And have an extension cord on hand so folks can plug in any electrical gadgets you're selling to see how they work.

- **Showcase items to their advantage.** Place stuff that appeals to older folks on tables and stuff for kids on the ground. Put the things you want lots of people to see in the middle of the driveway, and the really eye-catching stuff near the road. If your lawn chairs aren't selling, maybe it's because they're folded up and leaning against the wall of the garage; unfold them and set them on the lawn. If nobody's buying your boxed-up books, place them on a bookshelf so they're easier to browse.

- **Promote expensive items.** Selling big-ticket items takes a bit of extra effort. If you're trying to sell a digital camera, for example, gather all the bits and pieces and put them together, including the original packaging (if you have it). Print the current online pricing from eBay or Amazon and place it next to your item so folks can see what a good deal you're offering.

- **Price things carefully.** Most items are easy to price, but some will give you trouble. You don't want to give *away* your perfectly good DVD player, but you want the price low enough that people will be interested. And be warned: Some stuff won't sell at any price. (You should just give that encyclopedia set to your nephew.)

 Note Some things are notoriously tough to unload at a yard sale, like adult clothes. You may have better luck selling them through a consignment shop. For more on how to do this, check out *http://tinyurl.com/DSconsign*.

- **Label things well.** No matter how well labeled your Stuff is, people will still ask how much you want for the potholder with the $2 price tag on it. Label anyhow. If something "works great," write that on the label and be ready to demonstrate it.

- **Be friendly.** You don't need to chat with everyone, but greet customers and answer questions. Entertain kids so their parents can shop.

- **Don't bad-mouth your items.** Clearly you wouldn't be selling your items if they were perfect and you couldn't bear to part with them. But rather than emphasizing why you don't want the items ("That book is awful"; "That movie is boring"; "That game isn't very challenging"), emphasize the positives: "That book is really popular"; "That movie won three Oscars"; "That game is fun for kids."

- **Be willing to bargain.** Early in the day, you want to get as much as you can for each item. Most people will still buy Aunt Lucy's soup tureen at $5 even after they offer you $3. (If they're bargaining, it's because they want the item.) Don't be completely rigid, but don't give your Stuff away either. Later in the day, be more open to negotiating.

- **Keep a ledger.** It's easy—and useful—to keep a written record of what you sell. For each item, jot down a brief description, how much your sold it for, and—if you're having a multi-person yard sale—who gets the money.

- ***Don't*** **use a cash box.** Carry your money with you at all times so you're not a target for casual thieves or professional swindlers who run distraction con games. Use an apron, fanny pack, or something similar.

Running a yard sale isn't rocket science. If you put a little effort into creating a pleasant environment where it's easy to browse for hidden treasures, you'll make a lot more money than you would by just stacking stuff in your driveway.

 Tip For lots more about running a successful yard sale, check out *www.yardsalequeen.com*.

Posting items on Craigslist

The final step in selling Stuff is to list it on *www.Craigslist.org*, a *free* classified-ad site. Craigslist doesn't reach as many people as eBay because it's limited to your local area, but that means you don't have to deal with shipping. Also, Craigslist doesn't have any built-in protections; people can and do get scammed, so be careful. Despite these caveats, Craigslist is a great way to get cold, hard cash for your dusty old Stuff.

Though posting an ad on Craigslist is fairly straightforward, there are things you can do to increase your chances of success:

- **Write detailed descriptions.** Provide all the info—like size, color, style, and so on—that buyers need to make a decision.

- **Be honest.** Don't try to fool anyone. If you say something is "like new" and a potential buyer shows up to discover it's well-worn, you won't make the sale—and you'll have a cranky customer on your hands.

- **Post photos.** You don't *have* to include photos in your ad, but you'll have better luck if you do. Even if you write well, you can't describe that old dining room table as well as a picture can show it.

- **Ask a reasonable price.** If you're not sure how much to ask, check Craigslist and eBay to see how much similar items fetch. And remember: No matter how much an item cost you, you won't get near what you paid for it.

- **Be patient.** You'll get lots of responses, but few people will follow through. Don't let it bother you—that's just how Craigslist works. Be grateful for the folks who do follow up.

- **Stand firm.** Don't let buyers talk you into alternate forms of payment. For example, if you're asking $250 for something, don't accept a trade for it instead. Folks who want to trade are sometimes trying to pull a fast one.

 Tip If you're new to the site, check out Dayana Yochim's article on how to speak Craigslist: *http://tinyurl.com/MFcraigslist*.

Donating to Charity

After you've sold your expensive items on eBay, held a yard sale, and sold things on Craigslist, you'll still have Stuff left over. Fortunately, there are better ways to get rid of it than throwing it in the trash.

Try giving your Stuff to charity: Donate it to a local church or school, or take it to a thrift shop. And ask your friends and coworkers if they know of any specialized charities. For example, your town may have an organization like Free Geek (*www.freegeek.org*), a Portland-based nonprofit that accepts computers and refurbishes them for local schools and charities.

If you can't find a charity that wants your Stuff, check out Freecycle (*www. freecycle.org*), a grassroots nonprofit made up of thousands of people who give and get items for free. Their goal is to reduce waste by re-using items that others no longer want or need. Best of all, membership is free.

Tip Any time you make a donation, keep a detailed record of what you donated where. If you itemize enough deductions on your tax return, you can pay less to Uncle Sam.

Earning Extra Cash in Your Spare Time

Maybe you don't have a productive hobby or an attic full of Stuff to sell, but that doesn't mean you can't make a little money on the side. Here are a handful of ways to add to your cash flow:

Research studies

You can earn quick cash by participating in medical research and marketing studies. I once earned $120 for spending an hour inside an MRI scanner while answering questions about money. Other folks have earned $150 for giving opinions on food packaging, $50 to record 40 minutes of audio for a speech-recognition program—and even $35 for watching porn!

Colleges and companies are always looking for people to join their experiments and focus groups. To find studies in your area, check Craigslist.org's "miscellaneous jobs" section or scope out college newspapers and bulletin boards. Here's a short video from MSN Money that describes one study: *http://tinyurl.com/MSNmoneystudies*.

Tutoring

Are you good at math? A piano prodigy? A computer whiz? Consider offering your services as a private tutor. For more info, check out *http://tinyurl.com/GRStutoring* and *http://tinyurl.com/st-tutor*.

Mystery shopping

Market-research companies use mystery shoppers to gather info on products and services. These people get paid a nominal fee to pose as regular customers, and then report on their experiences. Mystery shopping won't replace your day job, but you can have a good time while earning a bit of extra money. Here are sources for more info:

- Be sure to read the FTC's consumer alert on mystery shopping: *http://tinyurl.com/FTCmystery-shop*. (Summary: Watch out for scams; you don't have to pay to become a mystery shopper.)

- For the lowdown on mystery shoppers and how to become one, visit the Mystery Shopping Providers Association at *www.mysteryshop.org*.

- Here's a first-hand account of life as a mystery shopper: *http://tinyurl. com/freedmanMS*. (The box below has more about the author, Donna Freedman.)

- One popular hangout for mystery shoppers is *www.volition.com/ mystery.html*.

Your Money and Your Life

Making Ends Meet with Odd Jobs

Donna Freedman has a history of odd jobs. She's found creative ways to make money since she was young, and at 52 she still draws income from a variety of sources. Since moving to Seattle in 2004, she's babysat, dogsat, participated in medical research studies, mystery-shopped, done light housework, run an Internet message board, and been an apartment manager.

"Simply put, I needed the money," Donna says. "I was at that point a freelance writer and, starting in September 2005, a full-time student. Neither of those gigs guarantees a lot of income, if you know what I mean. Any extra $10 or $20 I could pick up was a tremendous help."

Donna's most memorable gig was earning $35 for watching a short porn film in a study on female sexual response. The biggest boost to her budget has been her apartment management job, which for a long time meant she didn't have to pay rent. She now pays some rent to the new owners, but it's less than other tenants pay—plus she gets a monthly salary *and* an hourly wage for doing chores around the complex.

"I've scaled back on the odd-jobbery since getting a regular writing gig at MSN Money, but I haven't given it up entirely," Donna says. Since resolving to walk every day for exercise, for example, she's thought about doing a stint as a dog-walker. "I also plan to pick up more mystery-shopping gigs when I graduate."

You can read more about Donna's adventures in her "Living with Less" column at MSN Money: *http://tinyurl.com/DFreedman*.

Renting out a spare room

If you have space in your basement or garage, consider renting it out. If you choose your tenants carefully, this can be a win-win situation: You give them a cheap, safe place to live and you make a bit of extra money. (Plus it may help with your tax bill!) But before you do this, be sure to check your local laws and homeowners insurance policy to make sure it's allowed. Here's a Get Rich Slowly article where readers shared their tips on renting spare rooms: *http://tinyurl.com/GRSrental*.

Unclaimed property

The National Association of Unclaimed Property Administrators is a non-profit organization that assists in "reuniting owners with their property". The group sponsors the site *www.missingmoney.com*, which lets you search unclaimed property records from participating states.

Common types of unclaimed property include bank accounts and safe deposit boxes; stocks, mutual funds, bonds, and dividends; uncashed checks and wages; insurance policies, certificates of deposit, and trust funds; and utility deposits and escrow accounts.

The Missing Money database includes 40 states and one Canadian province (Alberta). For other unclaimed property resources, check out the U.S. government's "Government May Owe You Money" page (*http://tinyurl.com/GovtOwes*) or contact your state's unclaimed property office.

Blogging

Let's get one thing straight: Blogging won't make you rich. But if you have something to say that people want to hear, you can put $50 or $500 a month in your pocket. (And some lucky folks are able to make blogging a full-time gig.)

Blogs don't have to be intimidating—my *mother* blogs. Sites like *www.blogger.com* and *www.wordpress.org* make setting one up a breeze. Pick a topic you're passionate about, start writing, and share the blog with folks you know. If you're able to build an audience—which might take a year or two—add a bit of tasteful advertising through Google Adsense (*www.adsense.com*) or Blogads (*www.blogads.com*) and you'll have some extra pocket money.

Other ideas

None of those options sound appealing? Let your imagination run wild: Do yard work for the neighbors (just like when you were a kid). Collect cans and bottles for the deposit. Babysit or petsit. Haul stuff. (I once met a man who earned $250 a week using his van to haul stuff for people he met on Craigslist!) Get a paper route.

There are tons of ways to make extra money in your spare time. But in order to make them work, you've got to be willing to put in some effort. So instead of sitting around watching TV or playing *World of Warcraft*, get out there and make some money!

A Pep Talk

After reading this chapter, some people will come up with all kinds of reasons they can't make more money. They'll think, "That's easy for you to say, but I can't because…" To be successful, you have to overcome this sort of negative thinking.

The truth is, there are no shortcuts. Despite some companies' promises, you won't get rich quickly stuffing envelopes or peddling vitamin pills. If you want to earn more, you have to put in time and effort.

Every aspect of personal finance has its naysayers (see page 35). Some people believe that being frugal is the same as being cheap. Others think that building wealth means you're a greedy capitalist. Of these limiting beliefs, the most common is, "I can't make more money." Lots of folks think people with high-paying jobs have something they lack, or that those people are lucky. There's no question that luck and talent play a role, but by far the most important factor in career success is perseverance.

Henry Ford supposedly said, "Whether you believe you can or can't, you're probably right." If you don't think you can spend a year working 60-hour weeks to earn enough to pay off your debt, then you'll probably never reach that goal. But if you truly believe that you can make a go of it, you'll likely succeed.

So get out there and do the work—and stick with it when others won't.

7 Banking for Fun and Profit

"A penny saved is a penny earned." —*Benjamin Franklin*

Banking is the cornerstone of our financial lives, yet few people give it much thought. If you're like most folks, you'll shop around for a good deal on toilet paper, but you pick a bank simply because it's close to you, your parents banked there, or they're giving out free coffee mugs. But choosing the right bank and the right accounts can make your life easier and help you save (and possibly earn) some moolah.

In this chapter, you'll learn how to find a bank and accounts that match your lifestyle. You'll also get tips for reducing fees and making the most of your accounts.

Choosing a Bank

Finding ways to increase your income can be exciting (see Chapter 6). You can even have fun looking for ways to cut your everyday expenses (Chapter 5), especially when you see the results in your bank account. But selecting the bank account itself? Boring, boring, boring. At least that's the conventional view. Actually, you *can* have fun banking.

Consider two things when choosing a financial institution: the bank itself and the accounts it offers. Banks are tools for building positive cash flow, and bank accounts can help guide you toward your financial goals (some are better suited for the job than others). This section covers the different types of banks out there, and the next section (page 135) explains the various kinds of accounts you can choose from.

Types of Banks

People use the word "bank" to mean lots of different things, including commercial banks, retail banks, and investment banks (which are a different kind of bank entirely). When deciding where to open basic accounts like checking and savings, you only need to worry about three broad categories of banks: traditional banks, credit unions, and online banks. Keep reading to learn about each option.

Traditional banks

When most people think of a bank, they imagine a huge company with hundreds (or thousands) of branches spread across the country. Because these large banks have locations everywhere, having an account with one is convenient. And big banks generally offer a wider variety of products and services than smaller banks: They're one-stop shopping centers for your financial needs. Big banks have their place, but you have other options.

Lots of small, local banks have only a handful of branches (sometimes only one branch). These institutions don't offer the same convenience as the big boys, but they often make up for it in lower costs and better service. Small banks have other benefits, too. Many are active in their communities, and some are built on religious or political philosophies that appeal to certain customers. *Community development banks,* for example, are designed to serve residents and spur economic development in low- to moderate-income areas.

Note For more on community development banks, visit *www.communityinvest.org*, which lets you search for organizations that share your values.

If you travel a lot and need access to branches across the country, a big bank may be right for you. On the other hand, if you stick close to home and there's a local bank with great service and values similar to yours, it may be your best bet. But be sure to check out your other options, explained next.

Credit unions

Unlike banks, credit unions are not-for-profit institutions. Because of that, they usually have better interest rates and lower fees than traditional banks. According to the National Credit Union Association (NCUA)—which is probably a bit biased—credit unions offer better rates on nearly every product, from credit cards to car loans to mortgages to savings accounts.

 Note Don't assume that a small bank or credit union will give you a less-polished experience than a bigger organization. When I switched to a local, four-branch credit union, I found it had better online features than the huge national bank I'd been using for years!

Another difference is that credit unions are ***member owned***. In other words, if you have an account there, you're one of the owners. Members elect the board of directors, which sets interest rates and makes other important decisions.

Also, credit unions are more selective than banks—you can't just join any ol' one. Each credit union limits membership to a specific region, job, or association. For example, some are only for teachers and their families, and others limit membership to people living in specific counties. So make sure you can actually join your local credit union before getting your heart set on opening an account there. Use the Credit Union Locator (*http://tinyurl.com/ CU-locator*) to find one near you.

 Tip Your money is safe in a credit union. It's insured by the NCUA in much the same way the FDIC insures bank deposits (see the box on page 132).

Credit unions typically have strong ties to the communities they serve. They also tend to cooperate with each other instead of compete. In fact, many provide "shared branching," which means that if you bank at a credit union in Delaware, you may be able to make deposits, withdrawals, and loan payments at an unrelated credit union in Montana. It's as if they're all members of one gigantic banking network. (For more on shared branching, check out *www.cuservicecenter.com*.)

If there's a credit union in your area that you qualify to join, it's definitely worth considering. Just be sure to check out the types of accounts (page 135) and interest rates it offers.

Frequently Asked Question

How Safe Is My Money?

You've probably heard the phrase "member FDIC" before, but what does that actually *mean*?

During the Great Depression, the U.S. government created the Federal Deposit Insurance Corporation in response to all the bank failures that were happening. The FDIC's job is to watch banks to make sure they're treating customers well, and to insure customer deposits so that even if your bank goes belly up, your money is safe.

The FDIC insures up to $250,000 per *depositor* per bank, but you can have more than this insured at a single bank if you have accounts that fall into different categories of legal ownership. For example, you can have an individual account insured for $250,000 and a joint account (with your spouse, say) insured for that amount, too. For more info, talk to your bank or check out the FDIC's website, *www.fdic.gov*, which includes a deposit insurance estimator.

Bear in mind that FDIC insurance covers only checking, savings, money market, and CD accounts (all of which you'll learn about later in this chapter). And note that the insurance limit is scheduled to drop to $100,000 per depositor on January 1, 2014.

As long as you keep your money in an FDIC-insured bank, you should be fine. If you're worried about your bank's health, do a little research using tools like the BauerFinancial star ratings (*http://tinyurl.com/BCstar*) or BankRate's Safe & Sound ratings (*http://tinyurl.com/BRsafe*).

Online banks

Online banks offer the same sorts of products and services as traditional banks. The big difference is that online banks don't have storefronts, so you can't walk in and talk to a teller. That means you have to make all your transactions online, by phone, or via snail mail. But for many people, these drawbacks aren't drawbacks at all—they're advantages.

In its July 2009 issue, the *Consumer Reports Money Adviser* stated, "Online banking, despite a rocky start, is becoming the rule rather than the exception." The newsletter cites research by Forrester Associates that predicts that 76% of American households with Internet access will bank online by 2011.

If you're considering an online bank, keep two things in mind: First, though many traditional banks (like Bank of America and Wells Fargo) have a growing online presence, they generally offer lower interest rates and have higher fees than online-only banks like ING Direct and HSBC Direct. And second, the biggest thing that holds people back from banking online is security concerns. But *Consumer Reports Money Adviser* claims that online banking may actually be *safer* than traditional banking because there's less of a paper trail and your transactions are digitally encrypted.

Here are some online banks to consider:

- **Ally Bank:** *www.ally.com* or 1-877-247-2559
- **Capital One:** *www.capitalone.com* or 1-866-871-7932
- **Citibank:** *www.citibank.com* or 1-800-374-9700
- **EverBank:** *www.everbank.com* or 1-888-882-3837
- **HSBC Direct:** *www.hsbcdirect.com* or 1-888-404-4050
- **ING Direct:** *www.ingdirect.com* or 1-800-ING-DIRECT

For a more complete list, check out MoneyRates (*www.money-rates.com*) or BankRate (*www.bankrate.com*). At Get Rich Slowly, I've compiled a list of online banks that offer high interest rates and good security: *http://tinyurl.com/GRSbanks*.

It's easy to try an online bank—you're not stuck with the first bank you choose. Sign up for an account at one, give it a spin for a few weeks, and if it doesn't meet your needs, then move on to something else. Take the time to find a bank that works for you.

The Right Bank for You

I opened my first bank account the day I started college. I had two options: a bank that offered free checking and a bank that was handing out Frisbees. I chose the Frisbee, as did many of my classmates. The bank knew college kids couldn't resist free toys.

My new checking account came with a $5 monthly service charge. I didn't think much about it; after all, my parents had always paid a monthly service charge. No big deal, right?

I paid that "no big deal" for more than *15* years, even after the bank upped the charge to $8 a month. I asked them to waive it a couple of times, but they wouldn't. Eventually I wised up and switched to a credit union that didn't charge a monthly fee—but not before I'd paid that first bank about *$1,500* for the "privilege" of banking with them. And all because I wanted a "free" Frisbee.

I'm not the only sucker out there. Banks give away all sorts of stuff to bring in new customers: iPods, gift cards—you name it. But as I learned the hard way, you should never choose a bank just because it's giving something away. Instead, pick a bank based on things that matter, like:

- **Convenience.** How convenient is the bank? What are its hours? Where are its branches? How easy is it to find an ATM?

- **Fees.** What sorts of fees does the bank charge? What's its policy on overdrafts? Does it offer free checking? Free online billpay? Free access to canceled checks?

- **Service.** How's the customer service? Ask your friends and family, and check for reviews online.

- **Internet banking.** Is the website easy to use? You may have to hunt around online to get info on this or go into a branch and ask someone to give you a demo.

- **Rates.** What kinds of interest rates does it offer on savings accounts and CDs? (If you'll soon be shopping for a mortgage or other loan, check those rates, too.)

- **Values.** What about the intangibles? For example, many folks are willing to sacrifice a few percentage points or pay extra fees to put their money in a community development bank (page 130). Make sure the bank's philosophy matches yours.

And remember: You're not stuck with a bank forever. Shop around. Don't stay with a bank simply because it's the one you've always had if other banks are offering better rates or lower fees. There's no reason to settle for crappy service at a crappy bank.

 Tip If you serve (or have served) in the U.S. military, be sure to check out USAA (*www. usaa.com*), a sort of financial clearinghouse for veterans. USAA has excellent customer service and offers banking, insurance, and investment products at competitive rates.

After you've figured out what kind of bank would work best for you, there's one other important factor to consider: What kinds of accounts the institution offers. The next few pages explain what to look for.

Finding Accounts That Meet Your Needs

The other half of the banking equation is accounts. Even if you find what seems like the best bank in the world—one with convenient locations, long hours, and a wonderful website—if its account options don't meet your needs, you're better off somewhere else. This section gives you an overview of the most common offerings and explains the pros and cons of each.

Types of Accounts

Picking a bank account is like choosing the right tool for a job: Sure, you *can* pound a nail into the wall with a screwdriver if that's all you have, but you'll get the work done faster and more precisely if you use a hammer. The same is true with money: Find the right account and you'll get better results. The next four sections cover common types of accounts so you can pick the best ones to help you reach your goals.

Checking accounts

Most people use their checking accounts as the hubs of their financial lives. This is where they stash their paychecks and pay their bills. Nobody expects much more than that from checking accounts. But believe it or not, under certain circumstances, checking accounts can actually offer *better* interest rates than savings accounts.

Many small community banks and credit unions offer *rewards checking accounts*, which they provide in partnership with a company called BancVue (*www.bancvue.com*). Different banks have different names for rewards checking accounts, but they all share similar features. These accounts offer high interest rates—*if* you meet certain requirements. You have to:

- Get your monthly statement online—not via snail mail.
- Log into your account at least once a month.
- Make a certain number of debit-card purchases each month (usually around 12—and ATM withdrawals don't count).
- Make at least one electronic transaction per month, like an automatic payment to your electric company.

If you use your debit card often, a rewards checking account makes a lot of sense. The biggest catch is that the high interest rate only applies to a certain portion of the money in your account. (At some banks, this amount is $10,000; at others, it's $100,000.) Any money above that cap earns only a tiny return.

You can read more about these accounts at My Money Blog (*http://tinyurl.com/MMBchecking*), or check out the huge list of such accounts at *http://tinyurl.com/HYchecking*.

 Note Banks pay interest on many accounts, but they don't do it out of the kindness of their hearts. It's good business. The bank takes your money and lends it out to other folks at higher interest rates, or invests it to earn better returns. In exchange for using your money, the bank pays you interest—but much less than they expect to make themselves.

Savings accounts

You use your checking account for day-to-day stuff, but your savings account helps you meet your long-term goals. It's also the best place to tuck your emergency fund (page 59). Because you'll eventually end up with a ton of money there, the number-one feature to look for in a savings account is a high interest rate.

A lot of folks have their checking and savings accounts at the same bank. But you're usually better off with your checking account at a local bank and your savings account at an online bank because:

- Traditional banks generally offer a pittance on their savings accounts (my credit union's "high-yield" savings account is currently paying 0.10% interest). Online banks can offer higher rates because they tend to have lower operating costs.

- It's easy to connect your checking account to an online savings account, but it's slightly tougher to transfer money from an online account to your checking account (it usually takes a couple of days for the money to move from one back to the other). This is generally a good thing because it keeps you from spending the money on impulse—you can't simply pull your money from savings to checking and spend it that same day.

Online saving isn't your only option. Some traditional banks actually offer decent interest rates, so check rates in your neighborhood. When you do, don't forget to ask about unadvertised specials; they might offer great deals you won't know about otherwise.

Be sure to keep an eye on your savings account's interest rate. Rates fluctuate from time to time, and an account that once had a high rate may eventually offer next to nothing. It usually doesn't make sense to chase after higher rates every time your bank makes an adjustment, but you don't want to get stuck in an account paying 0.25% when others are paying 2.5%!

Money market accounts

Money market accounts are basically souped-up savings accounts that sport higher interest rates and higher minimum balances. My credit union, for example, requires me to have at least $10,000 in my money market account, though not all banks have minimums this high. With some money market accounts, you can write a few checks every month, too.

Because money market accounts have higher minimum balances, banks have more leeway to use the funds in your account (see the Note on page 136), so they're able to pay more interest. Other than that, there's not a lot of difference between money market accounts and regular savings accounts. Still, it's important to know the term because it's one you'll hear often.

Certificates of Deposit

Certificates of Deposit (CDs) are *time deposits*: You give your money to a bank and promise not to touch it for a specific amount of time. A CD is basically a loan that you make to your bank, which can invest the money however it wants during period you agreed to. In general, the longer you let the bank keep your money, the higher the interest rate you get.

Unlike a savings account, once you put money into a CD, the interest rate doesn't change. If you open a 12-month CD at 3.50%, say, and then interest rates drop to 1.00% (as they did in 2008–2009), you still earn 3.50% over the whole year.

The catch is that CDs are less *liquid* than other accounts, meaning you can't move money in and out of them any ol' time without paying penalties. If you take your money out of a CD before it *matures* (that is, before the agreed upon amount of time), you'll be docked interest. In some cases, you may even lose part of your principal.

 Unlike savings accounts, CDs end—or mature—after a set period. What happens then depends on the arrangements you've made with the bank. Many CDs renew automatically, which may not be what you want. So make sure you know what will happen when yours mature.

Here's a screenshot showing info about an actual CD that I opened recently at ING Direct to set aside money for a trip to France and Italy:

The Anatomy of a Certificate of Deposit

Details for Trip to Europe
For information on adding or removing a joint owner for this account, click here.

Current Annual Percentage Yield: **1.75%**	Maturity Date: **Nov 12, 2010**
Term: **12 Months**	Maturity Value: **$ 14,244.99**
Initial Deposit: **$ 14,000.00**	Early Redemption Policy: **3 months interest**
Interest Earned to Date: **$0.67**	Today's Early Redemption Value: **$ 13,940.74**

Account Maintenance   Account History

View: 10 per page	History		⬇ Download
Date	**Description**	**Amount**	**Balance**
Nov 12, 2009	Certificate Deposit transferred from OSA XXXX1043	14,000.00	14,000.00

This CD started out at $14,000, earns 1.75% interest, and has a term (lifespan) of 12 months. If I decide to redeem this CD early, I'll sacrifice 3 months' interest, regardless of whether I've already earned that interest. In other words, if I had taken my money out of the CD during the second month, the bank would have taken part of my principal because I'd have only earned 2 months' interest at that point.

When my CD matures on November 12, 2010, I'll have $14,244.99—almost $250 more than I started with, which is enough to pay for quite a few nice meals in Europe! That's not a huge return, but your goal with CDs isn't to get rich—it's to earn a decent return in a safe account, and CDs are super safe. This account is a great way for me to earn a little extra money for my trip without worrying about losing money in the stock market. (There's more about risk in Chapter 12.)

Choosing Accounts

As you can see, certain accounts are better for certain situations, so you want to make sure you're using the right tool for each job. When you choose an account, ask yourself:

- **What do you need the account for?** Long-term savings? Business? Personal? Everyday use?

- **How much will you keep in the account?** Remember that some accounts require minimum deposits to get the best interest rate. (To get the top rate with my credit union's money market account, I need to have *$50,000* in the account.)

- **How liquid does the money need to be?** If you need quick, easy access to your cash, choose accounts at a local, traditional bank. If you don't mind a small delay in getting to your dinero, an account with an online bank will work fine. And if you can let your money sit for months (or years) at a time, a CD might be your best option.

- **Do you need easy access to the money?** If you need frequent access to your account, make sure to open one with a bank that has ATMs all over the place. If you'd rather create a sort of barrier so it's tougher to spend your money, choose an account that isn't tied to an ATM card.

- **How important is online access?** Do you want to download your transactions to Quicken or Excel? Do you need online billpay? Some accounts (and banks) offer more advanced online features than others.

Your answers to these questions will direct your search: If you need constant access to your money, a CD isn't the best choice. If you intend to keep a high balance, look into a money market account. By putting in a little time and doing some research, you can pick the best accounts for your situation.

Making the Most of Your Accounts

You'll have more fun banking—and earn more money—if you do more than just accept the accounts you get by default. When you open an account, find out everything about it; read the fine print to learn what you can and can't do. And remember that accounts aren't just places to stash money—use them to pursue your goals! Here are some easy ways to make the most of your accounts.

Finding the Best Rates

If you're shopping for the best interest rates, check out online banks (page 132). In general, they offer better rates than traditional banks and credit unions.

Many websites have tables listing current interest rates. I keep one at Get Rich Slowly (*http://tinyurl.com/GRSrates*), and you can find others at sites like MoneyRates (*www.money-rates.com*) and BankRate (*www.bankrate.com*).

Keeping Your Accounts Optimized

If you use a traditional bank or a credit union, you should ask a teller once or twice a year if there are any improvements you could make to your accounts. Ask about:

- **Better interest rates.** Is there a similar account that might give you a better return?

- **Lower fees.** It's a shame to throw money away on service charges and other fees, so ask about free checking or to have fees reduced.

- **Automation.** Does the bank have a new website? Do they now offer free billpay? Can they help you set up a direct deposit of your paycheck?

- **Special offers.** Is the bank running any promotions?

Banks often introduce new products and services to meet customer demand. They're perfectly content, however, to let you keep your old low-interest, high-fee accounts. It's up to you to take the initiative to ask for better deals!

 Tip It can pay to develop a relationship with a banker. When she gets to know you and your circumstances, she can make suggestions based on your needs and goals. Such advice may not matter if you have only $100 in the bank, but it becomes more valuable as you grow older—and wealthier.

Getting Fees Waived

Banks make a lot of money from fees. According to a report in the *Financial Times*, U.S. banks were set to earn over $38 *billion* in overdraft fees alone in 2009. And there are plenty of other kinds of fees: stop payment fees, billpay fees, monthly service charges, returned check fees, and so on.

Banks get away with charging for this stuff because few people challenge them—folks just accept the fees as a matter of course. But it doesn't have to be that way. You may be able to get fees waived simply by asking. For best results:

- **Know what you want—and why.** Banks are more likely to waive fees if you give them reasons to. Point out things like how long you've been a customer, how you've never had trouble before, and that you generally have a lot of money in your accounts.

- **Ask in person.** You'll typically have better luck speaking to a real human being—face-to-face, if possible. It's easier to say "no" to an email than to a customer you see all the time.

- **Ask to speak with a manager** if the person you're dealing with can't help you.

- **Be polite.** Remember: You have the right to ask for lower fees, but you're not entitled to them. Be calm and considerate.

For more tips on asking for things, flip back to the box on page 77.

 Tip The **best** way to deal with bank fees is to avoid them in the first place. To do this, read all the paperwork about your account and all the new stuff the bank sends you in the mail so you know which services are free and which aren't. Keep reading for advice on avoiding overdraft fees.

Switching Banks

Moving your money to a new bank isn't hard, but a lot of people put it off because it seems like a chore. The biggest challenge is getting your automatic transactions stopped at the old bank and started at the new one. Here's how to switch:

1. Open an account at your new bank using some (but not all) of the cash from your current account.

2. Transfer any direct deposits or automatic payments to the new account. (It may take a couple of weeks for the remaining transactions and outstanding checks to clear, so don't close the old account yet.)

3. Start using your new account for day-to-day activities.

4. After a month or two, when you're sure that everything's set up correctly, close your old account.

That's all there is to it. Doesn't sound so bad, right? Every month you put off switching is another month you'll pay higher fees and earn less interest. If you've been procrastinating, take the plunge and start the process today.

Avoiding Overdraft Fees

If you live paycheck-to-paycheck and don't track your expenses, you'll eventually be charged overdraft fees. *Overdrafting* is when you write a check for more than you have in your bank account. The bank will usually honor the check, but will charge you for this "favor." Here are a handful of ways to deal with overdrafts:

- Some banks let you sign up for **overdraft protection**, which can involve linking your checking account to a second account (like a savings account), but usually takes the form of a small loan from the bank. Be careful: This option involves fees of its own.

- **Create a buffer** to prevent overdrafts. For example, mentally set a $100 minimum balance in your account. When you drop below this level, *stop spending*. (Some banks will let you sign up to receive email alerts when your accounts reach a certain balance; that way, they let you know when your account drops below $100 so you don't have to keep track yourself.)

- **Use the envelope budgeting system** (page 46) to make sure you don't overspend. Your bank is more than happy to let you overdraw at the supermarket, but when you use this system and have a fixed amount of cash, you *can't* spend more than you have.

- **Track your spending**. Don't just trust the balance at the ATM; keep a checkbook register or use Quicken so you know how much you *really* have. (See page 45 for more ways to track your spending.) Good recordkeeping may not cure all your financial woes, but it can help reduce the chances that you'll overdraw.

It seems convenient to track your spending using your bank's website, but remember that there may be checks or other transactions "in process" that don't show up online, so you might not actually have as much as the site tells you. (Even debit-card transactions can take a whole *week* to show up in your account.) It's *your* responsibility to know how much is in your account; don't simply rely on the bank.

 Tip Don't forget the number one way to avoid overdraft fees: Don't buy stuff you can't afford!

Targeted Savings Accounts

Most people work toward several financial goals at once, but keep their money clumped together in a single account. With that setup, it's easy to forget how much you've saved for each goal—and to borrow money from one goal to pay for something else.

In *The Six-Day Financial Makeover* (St. Martin's Press, 2006), Robert Pagliarini advocates targeted saving through what he calls purpose-driven investing:

> Purpose-Driven Investing [lets us think] of each of our goals as a separate "basket." Each of our baskets represents a single goal with a clear purpose that we can see and grow. What does this mean in the real world? It means that we have a single investment account for every goal.

If you want to try targeted saving, ask your bank or credit union if you can give your accounts nicknames. My credit union let me name my new savings account Nintendo Wii when I decided to save for that goal. And my accounts at the online bank ING Direct are named for the things I'm saving for, as you can see in the following image:

Account Type	Nickname	Account #	Balance	Available
Electric Orange	Checking		228.29	228.29
Orange Savings	Backpacking England 2011		4,046.18	4,046.18
Orange Savings	Mini Cooper Fund		5,928.14	5,928.14
Orange Savings	GRS Business Taxes		16,214.20	16,214.20
Orange Savings	Emergency Fund		10,201.81	10,201.81
Orange CD [Nov 12, 2010]	Trip to Europe 2010		14,000.00	14,000.00
		Total Deposits:	$50,618.62	$50,618.62

Though organizing your accounts this way might seem trivial, it can actually be a powerful motivator. Targeted saving lets you see how you're progressing toward each goal and helps you set priorities.

 Targeted saving lets one person save for many goals. But what if you have *many* people who want to save for *one* goal? Check out SmartyPig (*www.smartypig.com*), which bills itself as a savings program for chasing goals. The site lets your friends and family members add money directly to your account so they can help you save for things like your wedding or a down payment on a house.

Building a CD Ladder

Just as you can use systematic investing (page 266) to reduce the risk that fluctuations in the stock market pose to your portfolio, you can use a *CD ladder* to reduce the risk that fluctuations in interest rates pose to your savings goals.

Say you have $5,000 in savings that you want to get a better interest rate on. To build a CD ladder, you'd open CDs with staggered maturation dates. For example, you might put:

- $1,000 in a 1-year CD
- $1,000 in a 2-year CD
- $1,000 in a 3-year CD
- $1,000 in a 4-year CD
- $1,000 in a 5-year CD

As each CD matures, you put your money right back into a *new* 5-year CD; this lets you keep the 1-year stagger, or *ladder*. This will help you keep your interest income relatively constant.

Protecting Yourself with Parallel CDs

With a CD, one of the biggest risks is that you'll need to pull your money out before it matures. When you do this, you pay a penalty. The site Five-CentNickel.com suggests that you can decrease this risk with *parallel CDs*: *http://tinyurl.com/parallel-CDs*.

Here's how it works: Let's say you have $5,000 you'd like to put into CDs. Instead of opening a single CD and putting that whole amount in it, you'd open multiple CDs, all with the *same* maturation date. You could open five CDs of $1,000 each, say, or open two with $1,000 and one with $3,000.

This gives you a buffer in case you need to get at the money early. If you need $500 for an emergency, for example, you can break just a single $1,000 CD. That way you don't pay a penalty on the rest of the money you have in CDs, and the penalty will be smaller than what you would have paid if you'd put the whole $5,000 in a single CD.

Get in the game

Think of all this money management as a game that has real financial payoffs. If you take the time to learn about the accounts your bank offers—and the accounts that *other* banks offer—you can actually have fun finding ways to make more money. (Even if optimizing your accounts isn't your idea of a good time, it really is important. You don't want to end up paying $1,500 for a "free" Frisbee!)

After you've got your bank accounts whipped into shape, it's time to optimize another part of your financial life: your credit cards. The next chapter shows you how.

Pay Yourself First

If you're living paycheck to paycheck, saving may seem impossible. You have to pay for things like rent, a car payment, groceries, and maybe even student loans. You'd *like* to save, but at the end of the month, there's no money left to set aside. And that's the problem: Most people try to save something out of what's left over instead of saving *first*.

One of the best ways to build wealth is to set aside a portion of your income for savings *before* you pay your bills, buy groceries, or do anything else with your money. Here are three reasons to pay yourself first:

- **It makes you the priority.** You're telling yourself that *you* are more important than the electric company or the landlord. Think of the money you put into savings as a down payment on your future.

- **It encourages sound financial habits.** Most people spend their money in the following order: bills, fun, savings. But if you bump savings to the front of that list, you can set money aside before you come up with reasons to spend it. That way, since the money is no longer in your checking account to tempt you, you end up spending less.

- **It builds a cash buffer you can use later in life.** Regular contributions to a savings account are an excellent way to build a nest egg. You can then use the money to deal with emergencies, buy a home, or spend during retirement.

To develop a saving habit, make the process as painless as possible. Automating is a great way to do that: Try opening a high-interest savings account at an online bank like the ones listed on page 133. Then set up automatic transfers into this account, either directly from your paycheck or from your regular bank account. That way you get used to not having that money stay in your checking account; eventually, you'll hardly notice it's missing. (Even better, deposit your entire paycheck to your savings account and only transfer what you need to checking.)

How much should you put into savings when paying yourself first? Financial gurus say you should save *at least* 10% of your income. That's a great goal, though it can be tough to find that much at first. But almost everyone can save at least 1% of their income. Start there, and then increase that percentage as quickly as you can. Another tactic to try: Plan to set aside a part of your next raise for saving. As you make more money, *save* more so you don't end up on the hedonic treadmill (page 11).

For more tips on paying yourself first, visit The Digerati Life: *http://tinyurl.com/TDL-pyf*.

8 Using Credit Wisely

*"Credit cards are great for convenience, but terrible for borrowing. Either cut them up, if you can't pay on time; or—if you **can** pay on time—make your credit cards pay **you**."*
—*Andrew Tobias*

You already know that using credit cards carelessly can lead to debt. But did you know that people tend to spend more when they pay with credit? (See the box on page 150.) That's one of the many reasons it's so important to think before you whip out the plastic.

Credit cards aren't evil, but they can be dangerous. Just as you'd treat a chainsaw with respect, you need to be careful with credit to avoid hurting yourself. And if you use them wisely, credit cards can actually give you a financial edge.

This chapter will show you how to choose a credit card and use it without getting burned. You'll also learn how to manage your credit report and find out what your credit score is—and how to boost it.

Credit Cards

First, the basics: When you buy something with a credit card, you're taking out a small loan from the card issuer—Bank of America, Capital One, or your local credit union—and you owe the issuer that amount. If you pay your balance in full every month, the card basically gives you an interest-free, short-term loan. But if you carry a balance from one month to the next, you'll end up paying high interest rates and fees on top of the cost of Stuff you buy.

 There's a difference between a *credit card company* and a *card issuer*. The card issuer is the bank that you're borrowing money from; credit card companies—like Visa and MasterCard—are the go-betweens that take care of handling most of the paperwork. Some credit card companies, like American Express, are also card issuers, but Visa and MasterCard are not.

How many Americans carry balances and how much does the average cardholder owe? There's a lot of conflicting info out there, but one reliable source is the Federal Reserve, the organization whose policies influence the short-term interest rates banks charge to lend money to each other (which, in turn, influence the interest rates *you* pay for loans and credit cards).

Every three years, the Fed publishes its Survey of Consumer Finances (*http://tinyurl.com/fed-SCF*), which paints a picture of the average American's financial habits. The latest study, from 2007, found that 73% of American families have at least one credit card. Of those families, about 60% carry a balance, which means about 44% of Americans have credit card debt. And of those who carry a balance, the median amount owed is $3,000. (That is, half owe more than $3,000 and half owe less.)

So, while most people have no credit card debt, lots of people do. In fact, nearly a quarter of all Americans owe more than $3,000 on their credit cards. To avoid joining these folks—or to escape their ranks—you have to be careful when using credit. Let's start by looking at why you'd want to use a credit card in the first place.

Note Though credit cards and debit cards are similar, they're not the same. Debit cards are tied directly to a bank account; credit cards let you borrow money from the issuer. Using debit instead of credit can keep you from overspending, but credit cards offer more protection if your card is lost or stolen. Lastly, credit cards affect your credit score (which you'll learn about on page 161), but debit cards don't.

Why Use a Credit Card?

You don't *have* to use credit cards. Though the Survey of Consumer Finances (mentioned in the previous section) shows that 73% of families have credit cards, roughly one quarter of American adults don't carry plastic. So if you're worried about your self-discipline, the smart choice is to not use credit cards at all. (The box on page 158 has the story of someone who's gone this route, and you can read about more such folks at *http://tinyurl.com/no-ccards*.) That said, legitimate reasons to use credit cards include:

- **Convenience.** It's easier to carry around a single piece of plastic than to deal with cash and checks. And a lot of people like the automatic recordkeeping that comes with using a card (especially online expense tracking).

- **Protection.** Many cards will extend the warranties on the things you buy, and some offer insurance against theft. That's why most of us would rather have someone steal our credit card than a wallet full of cash—you rarely lose money if somebody else uses your card. (Credit card companies can charge you up to $50, but most won't hold you liable for any fraudulent charges.)

- **Building credit.** As you'll learn in a moment, your credit score has a huge impact on your personal finances. Using credit cards carefully helps you improve your credit score so you can get the best rates on things like mortgages and other loans.

- **Rewards.** Some credit cards offer cash back on things you buy. Others offer frequent-flyer miles or gift certificates.

But all these benefits are meaningless if you don't use credit cards responsibly: Miss a payment or carry a balance and you've negated your cashback bonus for months (or years), *and* you've hurt your credit score. Pay your full balance on time every month and credit cards can be a valuable addition to your financial toolbox.

The Pain of Paying

There's evidence that people spend more when using credit instead of cash. For example, a study in the September 2008 issue of the *Journal of Experimental Psychology: Applied* (*http://tinyurl.com/APA-spend*) found that paying with cash leads to "an immediate pain of paying". But "any payment made that makes the outflow of money less vivid, and thus less painful"—like using a credit card—"reduces the psychological barrier to spend." Another study found that people remember cash expenses better than those made with credit.

So it's not just you: In general, it looks like most people who use credit cards end up shelling out more when they pay with plastic than with cash. For more on this subject, see *http://tinyurl.com/GRS-credit-spending*.

Choosing a Card

There are hundreds of different credit cards out there, and they all claim they're offering a good deal. So how can you tell which one is best for you?

The biggest factor to consider is whether you carry a balance on your cards. If you typically carry a balance—or think you might in the future—focus on cards with low interest rates. On the other hand, if you pay your balance in full every month, look for a card with no annual fee, a solid rewards program, and at least a 21-day grace period.

 The *grace period* is the time between when you buy something and when you have to pay interest on it. Your grace period runs from the end of the billing cycle (usually the day the bill is mailed) until the day the bill is due. You're not charged interest during this time. Thanks to the Credit CARD Act of 2009, this is at least 21 days on cards that have a grace period (not all of them do). But if you carried a balance the previous month, there's *no* grace period: Whenever you buy something new, you're charged interest on it immediately.

In either case, keep the following in mind:

- **Take time to do research.** Your goal is to find the card that best fits your situation, so don't just sign up for the first offer that comes in the mail. You can research cards at:
    - **CardRatings.com,** which has a searchable database of credit cards, a blog with tips and news, and a forum where folks can write reviews of the cards they use.

- **IndexCreditCards.com,** which lists over 1,200 different cards and offers tips for using them wisely.

- **BankRate.com,** which has a bunch of online calculators to help you choose the best card for you.

- **FatWallet.com,** which has a great "What credit card should I get?" discussion at *http://tinyurl.com/FW-credit*.

- **Check with your credit union.** If you belong to a credit union (page 131), you may be able to get a great deal on a card. A 2009 study from Pew Charitable Trusts (*http://tinyurl.com/PCT-credit*) found that "credit unions offered significantly lower advertised rates compared to bank credit cards, with penalty fees that were half the cost of comparable bank fees and fewer dangers associated with 'unfair or deceptive' practices." In other words, credit unions rock.

- **If you're after a rewards card, choose one that offers something you value.** Some give you frequent-flyer miles, others points. If these appeal to you, great. But there's no sense in earning stuff you'll never use, so don't forget cash rewards. Cash is versatile and, unlike frequent-flyer miles, never expires.

- **Watch out for extra fees.** Some fancy cards will give you all sorts of perks—for a price. You're usually better off with a no-fee card than paying $20 or $50 (or more!) every year for features you hardly use.

- **Look for more than just a low interest rate.** Though it sounds like gibberish, a credit card's "method of computing the balance for purchases" is important. Look for cards that calculate your interest using either "average daily balance" or "adjusted balance."

 Tip Tired of getting credit-card offers in the mail? You can stop them by calling 1-888-5-OPTOUT or visiting OptOutPrescreen.com. This method, endorsed by the Federal Trade Commission (FTC), is the best way to stop such offers.

- **Don't be a sucker.** Don't sign up for a card just to get a free t-shirt, Frisbee, or airline ticket. And don't choose a card just because it offers a sign-up bonus or gives you a discount at your favorite store.

- **Don't overdo it.** There's no reason to carry a dozen cards. The fewer cards you have, the less there is to worry about. Start with one. If you discover you need another card, get it. But don't just load up your wallet with plastic for the heck of it.

Once you decide on a card, be sure you understand its limitations. Remember: Your goal is to pick a useful tool. You're not looking for a one-time bonus, but rather a long-term relationship you can live with.

Using Credit Without Getting Burned

In order to use a credit card without getting burned, you can't let it change your spending habits. (This is easier said than done—see the box on page 150.) Remember: A credit card isn't a license to spend—it's just a different way to pay.

In Chapter 4, you learned how a negative cash flow leads to debt and unhappiness. For many folks, credit cards make it far too easy to overspend and wind up in debt. Here's the most important thing to remember: *If you're using credit cards to spend more than you earn, you're using them wrong.*

Lots of people pay for things with credit because they don't have the money to pay cash, but that's a *really* bad idea that'll likely get you into debt. To change how you use your credit card, think of it as a debit card: Don't buy anything with it unless you already have cash in the bank to pay for it. And don't let your credit card influence your shopping decisions. You should decide to buy something first, and then decide how to pay for it; don't tell yourself, "I have a credit card, so I can buy this." (Like Mom always said, just because you *can* do something doesn't mean you *should*.)

 Note A credit card isn't an emergency fund. You shouldn't be holding onto plastic "just in case something bad happens." That's what your *actual* emergency fund is for. For more on saving for a rainy day, see page 59.

Here are some other ways to use credit cards effectively:

- **Read the fine print.** Read the legal stuff that's on the application and comes with your card, and that's in any future mailings. Yes, this can be tedious, but it can help you avoid headaches and help you discover hidden features (see the box on page 152). If you don't understand something, call customer service and ask them to explain it. (For help reading the legalese, check out Wells Fargo's credit card glossary: *http://tinyurl.com/cc-glossary.*)

- **Review your statement every month.** Due dates, fees, and interest rates can change, so keep an eye on those notices that come in the mail. And double-checking the list of transactions can help you spot fraud. Many people (including me) check their statements online several times a month. By paying attention, you can prevent small annoyances like extra fees or unauthorized charges from becoming big hassles.

- **Don't be afraid to speak up.** If you notice something strange on your bill, want to dispute a charge (page 155), or want a rate reduction, call customer service.

- **Be wary of special offers.** On my desk, I have an American Express mailing about a "free" appointment book. It's not really free, of course. If I take the bait, I'm on the hook for almost 50 bucks a year! Also be wary of "courtesy checks" and offers to skip a payment. (You may want to ask your card issuer to simply stop sending you checks.) Be suspicious of other products the company tries to push, like insurance, fraud protection, and so on. These usually aren't bargains—you can find better deals elsewhere.

- **Pay your bill on time and in full every month.** This is the #1 way to keep credit cards under control. The Credit CARD Act of 2009 says card issuers have to send bills at least 21 days before the due date. This gives you plenty of time to send a check. But it's best to take care of business as soon as possible, so set up automatic payments or pay your bills as they arrive. (And remember that you're responsible for paying your bill every month, even if you never receive the statement.)

- **Set up "expense notifications" from your credit card's website.** Many card issuers offer free tools that tip you off to how your card is being used. For instance, you may be able to set things up so you get an email anytime your card is charged more than $50 or $100. This can help you spot a stolen card quickly.

If you're not yet in credit card debt, don't start. Credit cards are *not* a source of free money—quite the opposite in fact: they can end up being the source of super-high-interest loans—so don't rely on them to support a lifestyle you can't afford. Remember: Don't resort to using a credit card just because you can't pay cash for something—use a card because you *can* pay cash.

Credit Where It's Due

Jim Wang, who writes about money at *www.bargaineering.com*, is a great example of someone who has his credit cards under control, instead of letting them control him.

Wang loves credit cards. "I use credit cards for the cash-back rewards," he says. He has some cards that give 5% cash back on certain purchases. "Credit cards also make things easier from a money-management perspective. All my spending records are in one place."

He has a wallet full of credit cards. "I have eight or nine cards, but I only have two that I really use," he explains. "The others are just cards I keep open for credit score reasons or for special cases." (Flip to page 161 for info on credit scores.)

Wang says the key to profiting from credit cards is to pay your balance every month. He's been using credit cards for 11 years and has never paid a finance charge. He's never paid a late fee, either, though he's come close. "There have been times my payments were a couple days late, but every time I've been able to call and have them remove the late fee and the finance charges. Everything's been fine."

For more on savvy use of credit cards, pick up a copy of *How You Can Profit from Credit Cards* (FT Press, 2008) by Curtis Arnold.

Disputing Charges

Mistakes happen. Once in a while, a restaurant will charge you twice for the same meal or an online bookstore will bill you for somebody else's purchase. When you notice something goofy on your credit card statement, it's important to act quickly to correct the problem. Here's how:

- **Get it in writing.** To make things easier in case you have problems, always save receipts and warranties, and ask for written confirmation of promises like delivery dates.

- **Start at the source.** First, try to solve the problem by contacting the merchant that charged the card. Explain why you think the charge is wrong and ask them to reverse it. If that doesn't work, go to the next step.

- **File a dispute with your card issuer.** As soon as possible, send a written complaint to the issuer's "billing inquiries" address (not the address where you send your payments). Include info about your account, an explanation of the problem, and copies of any receipts. The FTC has a detailed description of this process at *http://tinyurl.com/ftc-fcba*. (Many card issuers have online dispute-resolution forms, which may be more convenient than filing a dispute by mail.)

- **Take your complaint elsewhere.** If you're unhappy with how things turn out, contact agencies like your state's attorney general's office or the local Better Business Bureau.

 These steps are for disputing improper charges, not for fighting over shoddy merchandise. Your credit card may offer some sort of protection if your new computer is a lemon, but you'll need to read your card agreement to know your rights. Save the dispute process outlined above for billing errors.

How and When to Cancel a Card

If you have trouble with compulsive spending (page 65), it's best to cancel your credit card accounts. Don't just cut up the cards—*cancel* them. This will buy you time to learn to manage credit responsibly without an ever-present temptation to spend.

Even if you don't have trouble managing credit, you still may want to close an account from time to time. Whatever your reasons, be aware that canceling a credit card may ding your credit score (*http://tinyurl.com/cc-close*). (Page 161 has more about credit scores.)

Part of your credit score is based on how much of your available credit you actually use (this is called your *utilization ratio*). When you close an unused card, this ratio jumps because you're using more of your available credit; and when the ratio jumps, your credit score goes down. Also note that the longer you've had an account, the more you'll affect your credit score by closing it.

Despite this warning, there are several arguments for closing unused accounts. Doing so prevents you from abusing credit, reduces the risk of identity theft, and makes bookkeeping easier.

Whether these factors outweigh the potential damage to your credit score is for you to decide. When I was struggling with debt, I canceled my accounts, and I'm glad I did. It gave me time to learn about money without the temptation to spend. Now that I can manage my finances responsibly, I carry just one personal credit card.

Note If you think you'll take out a major loan (like a car loan or a mortgage) in the next year, don't risk dinging your credit score by canceling credit card accounts. If you're worried you'll be tempted to spend if the accounts are open, try freezing the cards in a block of ice (really!) or putting them in a safe deposit box.

Canceling a credit card is easy, but if you decide to do it, do it right. Here are a couple of things to keep in mind:

- **Close one account at a time, even if you want to close several accounts.** Start by canceling cards that charge you fees. Also, it's better to cancel new cards before old ones. Finally, consider keeping cards that offer good rewards programs.

- **Before you cancel a card, pay off the balance or transfer it elsewhere.** Never try to cancel a card that you still owe money on. If you do, you might end up paying nasty fees and high interest rates.

When you're ready to cancel a card, follow these simple steps:

1. **Call your credit card company.** Check with customer service to be sure your balance is zero before you start the process. After you ask to cancel your card, the sales rep will try to talk you out of it; be prepared to stand your ground. Take notes about things like the time you called and who you spoke to.

2. **Send written confirmation.** Using the notes from your phone call, write a letter and send it to the card issuer. Here's a sample credit card cancelation letter: *http://tinyurl.com/dolans-letter*.

3. **Watch your credit report.** After you receive written confirmation that your card has been canceled, it may take several weeks for the change to show up on your credit report (page 158). It's *your* responsibility to make sure the report is accurate, so keep tabs on it.

4. **Once you're certain the account is closed, cut up your card.** Hurrah!

Should you cancel your cards? Only you can make that call. Do what makes sense for you and your situation. If you think it's important to keep a high credit score and you're sure you won't abuse them, then keep the accounts open. But it's a mistake to keep your credit cards if having them will lead you deeper into debt.

No Credit Needed

Mike Iannantuano is 29 and has never had a major credit card. He once briefly opened a department store card about 10 years ago, but closed it soon after. He's been credit card free ever since.

"I don't really like the idea of credit cards. I'm wary of them," Mike says. "I have a debit card with a MasterCard logo that I've been able to use anywhere I needed credit."

What about renting cars? Getting a hotel room? "I haven't had a problem," he says. When a rental car company asks for a credit card, he uses his debit card instead. They place a hold on his account for $300 to $500 in case something goes wrong, but they release the hold a few days after he returns the car. The situation is similar when he stays at a hotel. (For info about the holds that specific companies will place on your account, check their websites.)

And what about getting loans and a mortgage? "I haven't had problems getting loans," Mike says. "I have student loans, two car loans—one paid off, one current—through my credit union, and I have a mortgage through Wells Fargo. My credit union gave me their best rates both times." He wonders, though, if a lack of credit cards might have hurt the rate on his mortgage: "My mortgage rate was decent considering my age and other factors, but it could definitely have been better."

Mike has no regrets about being credit card free, and he doesn't feel like he's missing anything. "I haven't really had any issues from not having a credit card. I can't spend what I don't have, which is how I like to operate."

For a look at other folks who get by just fine without credit cards, check out this article from *Money* magazine: *http://tinyurl.com/no-cards*.

Your Credit Report

As you move through life, you leave a trail of transactions: You take out a mortgage, buy a new car, and use your credit cards. Every month, your creditors—the companies you owe money to—send info about your recent activities to a variety of credit reporting agencies (also called credit bureaus). Each agency collects this info into a file called a *credit report*.

This report is a history of how well you've managed your credit. It contains info about where you've lived, how much you've borrowed, and whether you tend to pay your bills on time. It also indicates whether you've ever filed for bankruptcy.

The credit bureaus—Equifax (*www.equifax.com*), Experian (*www.experian. com*), and TransUnion (*www.transunion.com*)—sell your credit report to other businesses so they can decide whether to lend you money, sell you insurance, rent you a place to live, or give you a job.

Credit reports may be boring, but they're vitally important because they're the basis of your *credit score,* which you'll learn all about starting on page 161. Because they can play such a huge role in your finances, you should do what you can to keep your credit strong. You should also check your report a couple of times a year to make sure there aren't any errors and to protect against identity theft. The next section explains how.

 According to a 2004 U.S. Public Interest Research Groups report, 79% of credit reports contain an error of some kind, and 25% contain *serious* errors.

Getting a Free Credit Report

Happily, you don't need to pay to see your credit report. The Fair Credit Reporting Act says that each of the major credit bureaus has to let you view your credit report for free once per year. They do this through AnnualCreditReport. com, a site set up specifically for requesting these reports. This is the official, government-approved, free credit report site.

If you want, you can get reports from all three companies at once. Or you can stagger your requests, pulling one report every 4 months from a different credit bureau. You can get your report by calling 1-877-322-8228, going to *www.AnnualCreditReport.com*, or filling out AnnualCreditReport.com's report request form (*http://tinyurl.com/mailreq*), and then mailing it to Annual Credit Report Request Service, P.O. Box 105281, Atlanta, GA 30348-5281.

 If you plan to check your report online, be wary of impostor sites. Be absolutely certain you're on AnnualCreditReport.com. Another site—FreeCreditReport.com— lets you look at your credit report free for 7 days, but then it automatically enrolls you in a $15/month credit-monitoring service. Steer clear.

To get your report, you'll need to provide some basic info, including your Social Security number. You may also need to answer some questions about your current accounts, like how much your monthly mortgage payment is.

When you pull your credit report, don't be overwhelmed—it's not as scary as it looks. First, check your basic info (address, birthday, and so on) to be sure it's correct. Next, look at each of the credit accounts listed in the report to be sure they match your records. Finally, check the inquiries (listed under "requests for credit history") to be sure nothing fishy is going on such as credit checks from banks in eastern Europe. These could be signs that somebody's managed to swipe your credit card info.

 Note AnnualCreditReport.com lets you see your credit report, *not* your credit score—there's a difference (see page 160).

If everything looks good, shred your report or file it someplace safe. If you spot errors, take the time to clean things up. The Federal Trade Commission publishes a 6-page guide to disputing credit report errors (*http://tinyurl.com/FTC-corrections*), but all you really need to do is:

1. **Notify the creditor.** Contact the company that reported the incorrect info in your credit report. In writing, explain why you think they're wrong. Provide copies of any paperwork you have to prove your case. Most companies (especially credit card issuers) have a specific phone number and/or address you can use to file these kinds of disputes.

2. **Notify the credit agency.** Contact the credit bureau in writing and explain what you think is wrong (the FTC guide mentioned above includes a sample letter). Again, if you have documentation to support your case, include it; send copies, not originals.

Be sure to write down the name and employee ID of anyone you deal with. This may seem excessive, but it could save your bacon down the road.

 Tip Here's a step-by-step guide to getting your free credit report: *http://tinyurl.com/GRS-crguide*.

Your Credit Score

While your credit *report* collects all sorts of info about your debt history, your credit *score* is a single number that summarizes all that data.

Credit scoring has been around for decades in various forms, but only became widely used during the 1980s when a firm called Fair Isaac (now known as FICO) developed a new type of credit score, called a *FICO score*. The mortgage industry adopted FICO scores in the mid-1990s, and now lots of other industries use them, too.

A FICO score takes bits from your personal credit report and compares them to similar data from millions of other people. FICO (the company) uses complex secret formulas to crunch all this info into a single number, which can range from 300 to 850. This number gives lenders a good idea of how likely you are to pay them back, and they use it to decide how much to lend you, what interest rates to charge, and what terms to set.

 Note Though the FICO score is the most widely used credit score, it's not the *only* one out there. Other companies provide competing scores, and FICO (the company) offers a variety of other, specialized scores that measure things like how likely you are to declare bankruptcy, close an account, and so on. You can read more about your "secret" credit scores at MSN Money: *http://tinyurl.com/secret-scores*.

"A bad or even mediocre credit score can easily cost you tens of thousands and even hundreds of thousands of dollars in your lifetime," Liz Pulliam Weston writes in *Your Credit Score* (FT Press, 2009), which is full of info about how credit scores work. "You don't even have to have tons of credit problems to pay a price. Sometimes all it takes is a single missed payment to knock more than 100 points off your credit score and put you in a lender's high-risk category."

A high credit score will get you the best interest rates on credit cards and loans, including mortgages. With a low score, you'll pay higher fees and interest rates. The following table shows how much you might have paid for two types of loans in November 2009, depending on your credit score:

The cost of lousy credit (numbers as of November 23, 2009)

	36-month $10,000 auto loan		
Credit score	**650**	**700**	**800**
Interest rate	13.35%	7.55%	5.94%
Monthly payment	$338.63	$311.30	$303.96
Total interest	$2,190.78	$1,206.84	$942.44

	30-year fixed $200,000 mortgage		
Credit score	**650**	**700**	**800**
Interest rate	5.59%	4.77%	4.55%
Monthly payment	$1,147.40	$1,046.07	$1,019.44
Total interest	$213,064.50	$176,584.89	$166.998.48

Bad credit can be a downward spiral: Your money mistakes lead to bad credit, which costs you more money and leads to more debt, which gives you worse credit…and so on. But your credit history doesn't just affect your ability to borrow money. Nowadays it's used by insurance companies, landlords, and even employers:

- Some insurance companies use a specific credit score (known simply as your *insurance score*)—combined with other info—as a gauge of how likely you are to file a claim. A lower score can lead to higher insurance premiums. You can read more at *http://tinyurl.com/iscore*.

- When you try to rent a place to live, your prospective landlord may run a credit check (*http://tinyurl.com/lscore*). If your credit score is low, she may see you as a high-risk tenant and ask for a bigger security deposit or simply reject your application.

- Current and potential employers can pull your credit report if you give them written permission (*http://tinyurl.com/wscore*). This is especially true for jobs where security is important: To some employers, a good credit record shows you're less likely to steal from the company, take bribes, or reveal sensitive information.

As you can see, your credit score can have a very real impact on your life, affecting everything from where you live and work to how much the credit card company charges you for interest. But where does your credit score come from? Let's take a look.

The Anatomy of a Credit Score

According to FICO, the company that developed credit scores, certain factors can predict how likely you are to repay the money you borrow. Your credit score tracks 22 specific pieces of info from five broad categories:

- **Payment history** (35% of your FICO score): Do you pay bills on time? If you pay late, how late? How long has it been since you missed a payment? How many times have you had problems? The more responsible you've been, the higher your score.

- **Amounts owed** (30%): How much credit do you currently have? And of that credit, how much do you actually use? How many of your accounts have balances? The less of your available credit you use, the better your score.

- **Credit age** (15%): How long have your accounts been open? How long has it been since you used them? The longer you've had accounts, the better your score.

- **Account mix** (10%): How many different types of credit accounts do you have? (The two main kinds are *installment debt* like a car loan or a mortgage, and *revolving debt* like credit cards.) How many do you have of each type? Your FICO score will be higher if you use a mix of different kinds of credit.

- **New credit** (10%): Have you opened new credit accounts recently? How many? Opening new accounts may ding your score, especially if you open a lot at once.

 For some people—like young adults who don't have a lengthy credit history—the importance of each category may be somewhat different.

The site myFICO.com has a detailed list of what goes into a credit score (*http://tinyurl.com/FICO-pie*), but the actual formula is a secret. Because FICO makes its money selling credit scores, they're hush-hush about how the numbers are calculated. However, the company shares some basic stats. According to myFICO.com, the median credit score in the U.S. is 723, meaning half the population has a credit score of 723 or above, and half has a score of 723 or below.

 For more info, download the PDF "Understanding Your FICO Score" from myFICO.com: *http://tinyurl.com/FICO-pdf*.

How to Get Your Credit Score

While it's easy to get your credit *report* for free, learning your credit score takes a bit more work. Sometimes banks or lenders will let you see your score when you apply for credit, but you generally have to pay to get that info. Here are a few sites that can help you get a sense of your score:

- **myFICO** (*www.myfico.com*) is the official site of the company that developed FICO scores. It's jam-packed with useful info and offers several different services that let you monitor your credit score (for a fee). You can get free trials of some of these services, so you can check your score once and then cancel before you get billed anything. You can also pay a one-time fee of $16 to see your score.

- **Credit Karma** (*www.creditkarma.com*) lets you see your TransUnion credit score for free. Using the data in your credit report, Credit Karma anonymously compares you to other folks who use the site and offers tips on how to improve your credit rating.

- **Quizzle** (*www.quizzle.com*) gives you free access to your Experian credit score. This site doesn't have Credit Karma's cool credit-comparison features, but it offers a variety of other financial tools and tips.

- **Credit Report Card** (*http://tinyurl.com/CRCtool*) gives you a quick, free snapshot of your credit health. It doesn't provide an actual credit score, but instead gives you a grade (A+, C, F, or whatever) based on how the different parts of your credit score (described on page 163) compare to the general public.

Keep in mind that there's no such thing as a single, absolute credit score. Your score will vary depending on where you get it. For example, a FICO score based on your TransUnion credit record may be 755, while your Equifax score is 787. That's because each credit bureau has different info about you and score providers may tweak the formulas to emphasize different things.

Boosting Your Score

Simply knowing your credit score doesn't do you a lot of good. But if you're not happy with your score, you *can* take steps to improve it:

- **Pay off your debt.** According to credit expert Liz Pulliam Weston, "The most powerful thing you can do to improve your credit score is to reduce your credit utilization." FICO reports that about one in seven people who carry credit cards are using over 80% of their credit limit. "Below 30% is good," says Weston. "Below 10% is better." Repaying your debt helps your pocketbook *and* your credit score. (See Chapter 4 for more on reducing debt.)

- **Pay on time.** According to Weston, if your FICO score is 780, a single late payment can drop it 100 points. If your score is 680, a late payment can cut it 70 points. (For more info, see *http://tinyurl.com/kill-scores*.) If you miss a payment, don't panic: Do what you can to get current and stay current.

- **Only open new accounts you need.** Don't open a store charge account just for kicks. New accounts are only a small part of your total score, but they do have an effect. So keep new accounts to a minimum, especially if you're planning a big purchase like buying a house.

- **Don't close old accounts.** It's okay to cut up your cards or to freeze them in a block of ice, but to maximize your score, keep the accounts open. If you have to close an account or two, close newer accounts before older ones. For more on the pros and cons of canceling credit cards, see page 156.

 Tip If you don't use a credit card for several months, your card issuer can close your account, which can ding your credit score. To avoid this, make an occasional purchase with the card so the account seems active. One way to do this without risking temptation is to autopay your utility bills (see page 86).

- **Keep tabs on your credit report.** Even if you do everything right, your credit score can take a hit from identity theft and other forms of fraud. Even simple errors can hurt your score. So check your credit report regularly (page 159) and correct any problems you find.

A word of advice: Don't obsess over your credit score. Sure, it's important, but ultimately it's a number for lenders, not for you. A less-than-perfect credit score isn't the end of the world. If you struggle with compulsive spending, it's far better to cancel your accounts and take the hit to your credit score than to risk getting buried deeper in debt. The bottom line: Be smart with money and your score will be fine.

Final Thoughts on Credit

The credit card industry earns billions of dollars every year because they've made it easy for folks to spend more than they should and because people don't understand the rules of the game. Remember: Your credit card company is *not* your friend; they're hoping you screw up—that's how they make their money! In fact, the industry's term for somebody who pays bills *on time* is "deadbeat." (Nice, huh?)

But millions of people have found that if they play by the rules, credit cards make their lives a little easier. Your cards will never make you rich, but used wisely they can free you to focus on the things that matter most in your life, and earn you a few rewards in the process.

Here are the things to take away from this chapter: Use your credit card as a tool, not a toy; keep tabs on your credit report; and don't obsess over your credit score. And remember: If using credit cards gives you a negative cash flow (page 54), they're hurting you, not helping you.

9 Sweating the Big Stuff

"Count the dollars, not the pennies." —Elizabeth Warren

While it's important to save money on everyday stuff (see Chapter 5), it's even more important to save on big purchases. By making smart choices on big-ticket items, you can save *thousands* of dollars in one blow.

In the next few chapters, you'll learn how to save on big stuff like insurance, housing, and transportation. This chapter gets you started by looking at money-saving tactics for buying a new or used car and booking vacations.

Counting the Dollars

In Chapter 1, you learned that to be happy, you should focus on the most important things in your life before you worry about the little stuff (see the box on page 20). Turns out the same is true of your finances.

In *All Your Worth*, Elizabeth Warren and Amelia Tyagi write, "Savvy money managers don't spend a lot of time looking for ways to save a few pennies. They charge right ahead to the big-ticket items, looking to make high-impact changes in the shortest period of time. They don't sweat the small stuff."

As I mentioned in Chapter 5, by making a few small changes to my daily habits, I reduced my spending—and boosted my cash flow—by almost $200 a month. But as powerful as frugality can be, it's saving on the big stuff that'll *really* improve your cash flow.

You want to make sure you don't negate your daily scrimping and saving by making silly choices on big things that'll burden you for years. It's great that you fuel up at the cheapest gas station in town, say—but if you're driving a $63,000 Hummer H2 that gets 10 miles to the gallon, that small economy doesn't make much of a difference.

Obviously, you only get a few chances in life to save big on stuff like a home or a car. Because you so rarely make financial decisions involving tens (or hundreds) of thousands of dollars, it's extra important to be smart when these choices come along. The next chapter looks at ways to save money on housing. In this chapter, we'll focus on other big-ticket items like cars and travel.

 Tip To learn ways to save money on furniture and appliances, head to this book's Missing CD page at *www.missingmanuals.com*.

Buying a Car

First things first: A car is *not* an investment. In fact, it may be one of the dumbest purchases you'll ever make. Many financial experts say this, but almost nobody listens because Americans love their cars.

The average new car loses 20% of its value in the first year you own it, 15% in the second year, 13% in the third year, and 12% in the fourth. So a brand-new $30,000 Ford Mustang will only be worth $24,000 next year—and in 5 years, it'll be worth just $10,500. By the fifth year, the average car has lost a whopping **65%** of its value. Can you think of anything else you'd buy new for $30,000 that loses value that quickly?

 Tip To see how much your car is likely to lose in value, check out this vehicle depreciation calculator: *http://tinyurl.com/depreciation-calc*.

Financially, the best car-buying decision is almost always not to buy one. If you made your decision purely based on depreciation, it'd make more sense to walk, take the bus, or try to coax a little more life out of your current car than buying a new one. Basically, you're better off doing whatever you can to put off buying a new car. (As you'll see on page 177, buying a decent used car can take some of the bite out of depreciation.)

But even knowing all that, most of us aren't ready to give up our vehicles. For better or worse, we live in a car-centric culture: We want to be able to drive where we want, when we want. If you can't shake the new-car itch, you can at least save money at the dealership by being smart.

 Tip In *Stop Acting Rich* (Wiley, 2009), Thomas Stanley writes, "There is no significant correlation between the make of motor vehicle you drive and your level of happiness with life." So buy a car for transportation—not as a status symbol.

While many honest, hard-working car salespeople do their best to provide their customers with great service at a fair price, there are also plenty who use slimy high-pressure tactics to make you part with as much money as possible. The next few pages will arm you with the info you need to resist such tactics and get yourself a great deal on your new ride.

The Wrong Way to Buy a Car

Recently, I saw that a local dealer had a used Mini Cooper on the lot, so I stopped to take a look. I took a test drive and told the salesman how much I liked the car's sportiness and handling. I admitted that I'd been saving for 2 years to buy a Mini, and now had enough to pay this car's sticker price ($17,000).

When we got back to the showroom, we negotiated. I talked the salesman down to $15,000. I was patting myself on the back when the "closer"— a more experienced, higher-pressure salesman—sat down at the table. Armed with the info I'd told the first guy—that I had $17,000 to spend, was willing to pay at least $15,000, and really liked the car—he spent an hour talking me up to $15,600. I could (and should) have walked away, but I'd become emotionally invested: I *wanted* to drive that car home.

In the end, I paid $15,600—and I traded in my old car for much less than it was worth. That's exactly the wrong way to buy a car, yet nearly everyone does the same thing. We get emotionally attached to a vehicle and convince ourselves we have to buy *today*, so the dealer gets to call the shots. Fortunately, there are smarter ways to buy.

 Tip It's important to keep your emotions out of a negotiation. In his book *You Can Negotiate Anything* (Bantam, 1982), Herb Cohen writes, "When you feel you have to have something, you always pay top dollar. You put yourself in a position where the other party can manipulate you with ease."

The Right Way to Buy a Car

Over a decade ago, my wife decided to buy a new car. She wanted a Honda Civic but didn't care much about anything else. Together, we drafted a letter that read something like this:

> Dear Car Dealer: We're in the market for a new Honda Civic. We don't care what color it is, but it needs to have features X, Y, and Z. We have $5,000 for a down payment and would like to drive the car home on Saturday afternoon. We're sending this letter to all the Honda dealers in the area. If you give us the lowest price, we'll buy from you.

We faxed the letter to a dozen Honda dealers in nearby cities. Half of them didn't bother to reply, and three tried to convince us to visit them today because they couldn't quote a price over the phone. But three of the dealers gave us prices, and two actually bid for our business.

 Tip See the box on page 176 for more on competitive bidding.

In the end, my wife got the car she wanted for a little more than *dealer invoice* (how much the dealer paid for the car—in theory, anyway). Rather than trade in her old car, we sold it ourselves for a bit more than we thought it was worth. Nearly 15 years later, my wife is still driving that Civic, which she paid off long ago.

That was smart car shopping. Even if a fax blitz isn't your style, the next few sections are chock full of advice that can help you stay in control of the car-buying process, whether you're in the market for a new or used vehicle.

 Note There's nothing in this book about leasing a car because, financially, leasing is almost always a bad idea. You're probably better off buying a new car than leasing—and that's saying something! The only advantage to a lease is lower monthly payments, but your overall long-term costs are greater—and you have nothing to show for it at the end of the lease. For more on leasing vs. buying, check out *http://tinyurl.com/buy-vs-lease*.

Buying New

Most people dread buying a new car: They hate the games, the high-pressure sales tactics, and the confusing pricing. But with a little bit of research and a whole lot of patience, you can put yourself in the driver's seat during negotiations.

Money matters

The first step in buying a car is to figure out the finances. It's best to pay cash if you can. If you can afford to do that, have the money in your bank account ready to go before you head to the dealership.

Most people, however, have to take out a loan. If you're one of these folks, be smart about how much you borrow. When you know how much room you have in your budget for a car payment (see Chapter 3), it's easier to manage your expectations so you don't drive off with a car you can't afford. If you need to take out a loan, take care of that in advance through your bank or credit union so you don't put yourself at the mercy of dealer financing, which is almost never a good deal.

On the Money

Saying Goodbye to Car Payments

Despite what you might think, you're not doomed to have a car payment for the rest of your life. In Chapter 7, you learned the importance of paying yourself first to save for retirement (page 145). You can apply the same principle to saving for a car.

According to the National Automobile Dealers Association, the average price of a new car is just over $28,000. Let's say you put $8,000 down to buy a car at that price, and you finance the remaining $20,000 for 4 years at 9% interest, meaning your payments will be just under $500 per month. At the end of those 4 years, you'll have paid almost $32,000 for a car that's now worth $14,000. That's $18,000 vanished into thin air!

There is a better way, one recommended by financial gurus like Dave Ramsey and Suze Orman. Instead of financing a new car, take that $8,000 and use it to buy a high-quality used car. Then, instead of paying $500 a month to the finance company, set the money aside in a named bank account specifically for your next car (see page 142). That way you're paying yourself rather than the car company.

At the end of a year, your used car will have lost 15% or so of its value, making it worth around $6,800. You can keep driving it and saving for a new car, or take the $6,000 you now have in the bank, combine it with the used car's value, and trade in for a car worth $12,800. And if you keep saving, the next year you can trade in that second car for one worth $17,000. In theory, after 4 years of this you'll have paid out $32,000—just as if you'd bought that new car at 9% interest—but you'll be driving a car worth $23,000 instead of $14,000.

Pretty cool, yeah? Instead of paying interest to a finance company for a vehicle that's losing value, you're paying yourself and gradually upgrading your car every year. For more about this clever way of budgeting your way to a new vehicle without a car payment, watch Dave Ramsey's "Drive Free, Retire Rich" presentation: http://tinyurl.com/drivefree.

Do your homework

Before you set foot on a car lot, figure out which makes and models you're interested in. It's best to give yourself at least three options, because if you set your heart on just one vehicle, you're more likely to become emotionally involved with the deal, which puts you at a huge disadvantage.

 Tip Once you've narrowed your choices down to a handful of models, you can thin the field further by using Edmunds.com's true-cost-to-own calculator: *http://tinyurl.com/edmundsTCO*. It lets you compare the ownership costs of new and used vehicles. Enter a car's make, model, year, and trim style, and it tells you how much it costs to run that vehicle for a year.

Know exactly which cars you're considering and why, and be familiar with the packages and options. The more info you have, the more bargaining leverage you've got. (And doing your homework may reveal that buying used is a better option for you. If that's the case, flip to page 177.)

Take your time

The more time you have to shop, the better deal you can get. If you need a car *today*, the dealer has no reason to lower the price. A whole weekend is good; two weekends are better. And with an entire month, you should be able to get a great deal.

If you feel rushed at any time, the best thing you can do is stop. Leave the lot. Go home. Take a breather. When you feel hurried, the dealer gains the advantage.

Go for a test drive

Okay, so this tip is a no-brainer. But it's easy to get excited when you're shopping for a new car and forget that the point of a test drive is to do more than just find out whether you feel cool behind the wheel of a particular model. You want to see how the car does under normal conditions. If you do mostly freeway driving, be sure to take the car on the interstate. If you live in a hilly area, take it up some hills.

Here are some other things to keep in mind: How does the car handle? Is it comfortable? Do you feel safe? Trust your gut. If something bugs you about the car in the first few minutes, it'll just get worse with time. And ask the salesperson any questions that come up during the drive.

To keep all your ducks in a row, you may want to print out the *Consumer Reports* test-drive checklist (*http://tinyurl.com/CR-testdrive*) and have a friend help you fill it out while you drive.

 Note The test drive is a double-edged sword. First, you need to make sure you're driving the model you want; if you drive a model with options that aren't important, you may fall in love with those features. Also, many dealers consider the test drive the salesperson's best friend: It gives them time to build rapport with you, to learn your strengths and weaknesses. Test drives are important, but don't let them distract you from your mission: getting a great deal.

Research prices

After you've taken a few test drives, you'll probably find a car that's a good fit, but don't buy it yet. Go home and research how much you should pay. Here are some sites to try:

- **Edmunds.com** lets you compare the suggested retail price with the dealer invoice price and what other people in your area are actually paying.

- **Autobytel.com** offers info similar to Edmunds.com and gives you a chance to get competitive bids from dealers near you.

- **Consumer Reports** has a popular new-car pricing service (*http://tinyurl. com/CR-carprice*). For $14, you can get a report that includes the dealer invoice price and all possible options, a list of dealer rebates, a theoretical rock-bottom price, and negotiating tips.

You can also find out if the manufacturer is offering any rebates or incentives to lower the cost of the car by hopping onto Autopedia.com: *http:// tinyurl.com/AP-rebates*. Armed with your pricing info, it's time to make a deal.

 Tip If a dealer doesn't have a car with the exact package you're looking for, don't be talked into paying extra for the things you don't want or need. Find a car that has the right options, even if it means waiting a little longer.

Make a deal

Find a dealer who has the car you want with the options you want. (And if you expect to have an ongoing relationship with the dealership—for service, maybe—make sure you trust the dealer overall.) After you test-drive the car, it's time to start haggling. Here are some things to keep in mind while you're discussing the price:

- **Don't start negotiations from the sticker price.** Because you've done your research, you know roughly what the dealer paid for the car, so use that as your starting point.

- **Be sure you're talking about the drive-it-off-the-lot price.** The salespeople will try hard to negotiate around a monthly payment amount; ignore that. Because you took care of the money beforehand (page 171), you don't care about the monthly payment. All that matters is the price you're going to pay to drive the car home. (Seriously, this is a *huge* trap to avoid: Whatever you do, don't get caught up in discussing monthly payments.)

- **Don't negotiate more than one thing at once.** Dealers love to negotiate lots of things at the same time—purchase price, monthly payments, trade-in value, and so on—because that gives them a chance to give a little in one area while making a killing in another. Insist on taking care of one thing at a time.

- **Stay in control.** Remember that you're in charge. You're the one buying the car—don't let somebody *sell* one to you. The salesman will do everything he can to get you to buy this car today. He wants you to feel pressured. But because you're not emotionally attached to this car and because you've given yourself plenty of time, you don't have to buy today. Don't let the dealer make you feel like a jerk for taking time to think things over.

 Tip It can help to go car shopping with a partner so that, if you get too wrapped up in the situation, the other person can play the "bad cop" and pull you away.

- **Be willing to walk away.** Salespeople can be sneaky snakes, and are apt to introduce new fees or terms into the deal anytime. The most powerful weapon you have in your car-buying arsenal is your legs; don't be afraid to use them to head for the door.

Negotiate Everything

Americans generally don't like to haggle, but negotiating is an important skill—that can have a huge impact on your financial life.

In Chapter 6, you learned how negotiating your salary could have a lasting effect on your income. In *You Can Negotiate Anything*, Herb Cohen argues that, to negotiate effectively, you need to control three crucial variables:

- **Power** is the ability to get things done. You can gain power in a negotiation by generating competition (having three contractors bid to re-roof your house, for example). Other tactics are to use persistence, precedence ("This is how I've always done it"), empathy (understanding the other side), perceived legitimacy (*"Consumer Reports* says this model isn't as good as others"), and silence (not saying anything at all will often cause the other side to continue negotiating, as if you'd made a counter-offer).

- **Time** also plays a role—the side with the most time has the advantage. No matter how rushed you are, keep your cool. Don't ignore deadlines, but don't follow them blindly either.

- **Information** is the final variable: The more you know, the better off you are, so do your research *before* you start haggling. And during negotiations, act on whatever new info comes to light: Has this model been discontinued? Does it have a scratch? Did the store order too many? Use this knowledge to adjust your offer.

For more about how everyday people use negotiation skills in real life, check out this article from the *Washington Post*: http://tinyurl.com/wp-haggle.

Close the deal

Now that you've agreed on a sales price, the final step is to sign the paperwork. But before you do, the dealer will try to sell you a few more things. Ignore anything they offer after you agree on the sales price. Sure, you could buy a service contract or floor mats or underbody coating or an extended warranty from the dealer. But these are almost always a bad deal.

If you really want underbody coating, buy it somewhere else for less. If you want an extended warranty, buy it online at places like WarrantyDirect.com, or from your bank or credit union. Better yet, open a new named bank account called "car repairs" (see page 142) and pay yourself instead of lining somebody else's pockets.

Whatever you do, ***don't sign anything until the very end***. And don't sign anything you don't understand: If it seems strange, it probably is. Ask questions and don't be afraid to pull out at the last minute.

Note For an entertaining look at what goes on behind the scenes at dealerships, set aside a couple hours to read "Confessions of a Car Salesman" at Edmunds.com: *http://tinyurl.com/car-confessions*. It's funny and will help you get a better deal.

On the Money

Competitive Bidding

The tips in this chapter can help you get a good price on a new car, but you can do even better without visiting a dealership at all!

In his presentation "How to Buy a New Car Without Getting Screwed" (*http://tinyurl. com/newcar-howto*), Rob Gruhl argues that the way to get the best price on a new car is *competitive bidding*, pitting dealerships against each other: "Call eight to 10 dealerships and tell them, 'I'm really interested in buying this car today. Can you give me a price? I'm doing competitive bidding.' They'll say, 'We don't do competitive bidding.' And you'll say, 'If you give me the best price, I'll come down and buy it from you *today*.'" At that point, most dealers will give you a price.

When you're getting bids from dealers, make sure they're quoting you the price for the same car with the same options, and that you're getting the drive-it-off-the-lot price. Once you have bids from as many dealers as possible, contact them again to share the best offer you received and see if they can match it. When you have the best price, ask the winning dealership to put it in writing, and then go down and pick up your car. (If anything goes wrong during the process, leave.)

If you like the idea of competitive bidding, but need a little help, check out FightingChance.com, where you can pay $40 to get pricing info for the car you're looking at, car-buying tips, and instructions for executing a "fax attack" similar to the one my wife and I used when buying her Civic (see page 170). Or check out this free car-buying guide at The Motley Fool: *http://tinyurl.com/MF-carfax*.

Take delivery

Congratulations! You got yourself a great deal on a new car. Now all that's left is to get the keys and drive it home.

In all the excitement, it's easy to forget things like double-checking that the owner's manual is in the glove box or that there's gas in the tank. To make sure you don't miss anything, download this free new-car checklist from *Consumer Reports*: *http://tinyurl.com/CR-newcar*.

Sell your old car separately

If you want to get the most for your old car, don't trade it in. By the time you've spent hours negotiating the price of your new car, you're ready to be finished. The dealer knows this and will try to take advantage of your exhaustion to give you a raw deal on your trade-in.

Even though it takes more time and effort, you're far better off selling your old car yourself (see page 178). At the very least, don't mention that you have a car to trade in while you're negotiating the price of the new car.

Buying Used

You can save thousands of dollars by choosing a car that's just 2 or 3 years old instead of buying a new one. Though they continue to lose about 12–15% of their value every year, used cars have already taken their biggest depreciation hit (the one that happens when they leave the dealership—see page 168), and they cost less to insure.

Some people aren't willing to buy used because they're afraid of getting stuck with a lemon. This concern is understandable (it's happened to both me and my wife), but you can reduce the risk by being a smart shopper. If you feel more comfortable buying from a dealer than a private party, consider a certified used car. These may cost a little more than other used vehicles, but they come with a warranty (and possibly other features) that can give you peace of mind. But be careful: "certified" has become a marketing buzzword. Make sure the car is certified by the *manufacturer*—anything else is meaningless.

In many ways, the process of buying a used car (especially from a dealer) is the same as buying a new car, but there are a few extra things to keep in mind:

- **Research reliability.** In addition to figuring out how you're going to pay (page 171), do some research to find out whether the models you're interested in are dependable. *Consumer Reports* publishes reliability records every year. (Your public library should have a copy of the most recent car-buying issue.)

 Note To get official, government advice on the legal ins and outs of buying a used car, check out this FTC guide: *http://tinyurl.com/FTC-usedcar*.

- **Know the vehicle's value.** Check prices at Kelley Blue Book (*www.kbb.com*), Edmunds.com, NADA Guides (*www.nadaguides.com*), and the *Consumer Reports* Used Car Service (*http://tinyurl.com/CR-usedcar*).

- **Ask questions.** Whether you're buying from a dealer or a private party, find out as much as you can about the car. How many owners has it had? Has it ever been in an accident? Are all the maintenance records available? What sort of gas mileage does it get? Why is it for sale?

 Tip For $35, you can get the Carfax (*www.carfax.com*) vehicle history report, which tells you if the car has been in any accidents, how many owners it's had, and so on. (Better yet, if you're buying from a dealer, ask them to pull the report for you—there's a good chance they already have it on file.)

- **Inspect the car thoroughly.** Check the interior, exterior, tires, tailpipe, and engine. When you test drive it, pay attention to the handling and acceleration, and listen for strange noises.

- **Take the vehicle to an independent mechanic.** For $100–$150, a mechanic can tell you if the car has any major problems.

- **Make an offer.** Start below what you think the car is worth (minus the cost of any repairs it needs) and work up from there.

- **Trust your gut.** If something bugs you about the deal, call it off.

 Tip If you *really* want to save money, consider owning a *beater*—an older used car that's near the end of its life. Beater Review (*www.beaterreview.com*) can help you find great cars for under $5,000.

Selling a Car

To avoid hassle and haggling, many folks simply trade in their old vehicles at the dealership. It's quick and easy—but costly. Dealers often make significantly more on your trade-in than they do selling you a new car! To get a fair price for your old car, you're better off selling it yourself. Before you do, remember to:

- **Prep your vehicle.** Make sure everything works. Consider having a mechanic check the car and issue a report about its condition. And clean the car (inside and out) until it shines.

- **Research the market.** Spend a few weeks reading used-car ads in the newspaper and on Craigslist.org to see what people are asking for similar vehicles. And use the Kelley Blue Book or NADA Guides sites (page 178) to get more info.

- **Set a competitive price.** Figure out what you think your car is worth—being honest about its condition and value—then add a little to the price for wiggle room during negotiations. Decide what your rock-bottom price is.

- **Gather your records.** Put together a folder with all your car's maintenance records. If you had a mechanic inspect the car, include his report. Consider getting a vehicle report from Carfax.com to help set the buyer's mind at ease. And have a bill-of-sale document ready to go. (What you need for a bill of sale depends on where you live, so check your state's DMV website for details.)

- **Write an ad that sells.** Mention features, improvements, and any recent upgrades, like new tires or battery. Have you always parked it in a garage? Say so. Do you have all the maintenance records? Mention that, too. And if you're posting an ad online, include as many photos as you can.

- **Spread the word.** Get as much exposure for your ad as possible. The more demand you can generate, the more money you'll make. Online, try Craigslist.org, Autotrader.com, and Cars.com. Run your ad in a newspaper over the weekend when it'll reach the largest audience.

- **Be prepared to answer questions.** People will call or email to ask for detailed info. Be ready to provide it by keeping a list of key facts near the phone.

- **Show your car to interested buyers.** If you're nervous about dealing with people, get a friend to help. You're selling yourself as well as the car, so make a good impression. Let the buyer test-drive it, but be sure to ask for a valid driver's license first. Go along for the ride, or ask for some sort of collateral (their car keys or wallet, say). If your car has any major defects, be honest about them. Offer to let the buyer take the car to a mechanic of their choice, even if you've already taken it to yours.

- **Negotiate a price.** A good price is fair to both parties. Having done your research, you know what your car is worth, so be confident and stand strong when somebody tries to lowball you. Remember your rock-bottom price, but if you get an offer that's only a couple hundred dollars below this figure, consider accepting it.

- **Make the sale.** Get cash or a cashier's check, and then complete the bill of sale to transfer ownership. Be certain that the paperwork includes a statement to this effect: "This vehicle is sold as is. Buyer assumes all liability and guarantees the vehicle will be registered in their name immediately."

- **Take care of the details.** After the sale, cancel your insurance policy for the car and complete any necessary DMV paperwork.

Most buyers are honest people who are happy to work with a private party instead of a dealership. But there are scammers out there, so if anything about the transaction makes you nervous, call it off. For advice on spotting fraud, check out this article: *www.carbuyingtips.com/fraud.htm*.

Your Money and Your Life

Finding a Trustworthy Mechanic

There are a lot of greaseball auto mechanics out there who try to fleece the unsuspecting, but there are plenty of good guys, too. It's best to find a good mechanic *before* your car needs a major repair. You can save a lot of money (and gain peace of mind) by finding a mechanic you trust.

Though price is important, don't make it the *only* factor in your choice. Ask your friends and family for recommendations. When you meet somebody who has a car similar to yours, ask her where she gets it serviced.

Many Get Rich Slowly readers swear by the *Car Talk* Mechanics Files (*http://tinyurl. com/cartalk-mechanic*), a database of over 16,000 mechanics recommended by folks around the country. Just enter your Zip code and the type of car you own to see a list of shops in your area that includes ratings and reviews.

Before you take your car to a shop, check with the Better Business Bureau (*www. bbb.org*) to see if it has any complaints on file. Also be sure the mechanic is certified by the National Institute for Automotive Service Excellence (*www.ase.com*). Once you find a candidate, take your car in for its next oil change. If you get a good vibe, use the shop for future service and repairs. If something bugs you about the shop, go elsewhere.

Even after you find a good shop, always check your bill and be willing to ask questions. It's your right to know what you were charged and why. If a mechanic knows you're going to watch the bill, he's less likely to try pulling a fast one.

Once you have a mechanic you like, go out of your way to let him know you appreciate his services: Send him a thank-you note, take him donuts, and recommend him to your friends.

Reducing Your Cost of Ownership

Buying a car is one thing, but it also costs a pretty penny to use and maintain your vehicle. The American Automobile Association (AAA) estimates that the average car costs just over 54 cents per mile to operate; that includes fuel, routine maintenance, insurance, registration, and the cost of buying the vehicle (with finance charges).

You already learned how to pay less for a car in the first place, but there are other tricks you can use to keep your costs down. The simplest one is to drive the car longer. Here's a real-life example: As I was writing this chapter, I got an email from a Get Rich Slowly reader named Chris, who wrote, "I have a 1997 Geo Metro. I bought it 10 years ago with 60,000 miles. It now has 180,000 miles. I paid $1,800 for it, and pay $220 a year in insurance. This has been the best investment of my life! I even have a bumper sticker that says 'My other car is a Roth IRA.'" By milking more miles from his car, Chris can use the money he saves for more important things.

The next two sections cover the other main expenses you can save on: maintenance and gas.

Lowering maintenance costs

Proper upkeep can save you big bucks over the life of your car. A 2007 article from *Consumer Reports* found that driving your car to death (keeping it for 200,000 miles or more) can let you save enough money to buy a new car—but only if you take good care of your current vehicle and diligently set aside funds for the new one.

A well-maintained car is safer *and* cheaper to run. To save money on maintenance, remember to:

- **Read the manual.** This one's obvious, but how many people actually do it? Reading the manual can teach you how to operate your car safely and efficiently. Be sure to check out the manufacturer's recommended maintenance schedule—and do your best to follow it.

- **Change the oil regularly.** Changing your oil every 3,000 miles is essentially a scam, a marketing ploy from the quick-lube industry. You *might* need oil changes that often if you drive lots of miles under rough conditions, but for most vehicles, it's okay to change the oil every 5,000 miles or 6 months (whichever comes first). Check the manual or ask your mechanic what's best for your car.

- **Keep your tires full.** If your tires are under-inflated, your car won't handle as well or get the best mileage. If they're over-inflated, they're more likely to get damaged, your ride will be rougher, and you'll have a tougher time stopping when it's wet out.

- **Park in the garage, if you have one.** (If necessary, get rid of all the Stuff that's hogging the space—see page 96.) Letting your car live in-doors is easier on the paint job *and* helps prolong the life of your battery, starter, and motor oil.

- **Deal with trouble before it starts.** If you notice strange sounds or vibrations, look into them right away so they don't turn into pricey repairs.

Saving on gas

Gas is the thing you buy most frequently for your car, which gives you lots of chances to save on it. Here are some ways to save at the pump:

- **Get a fuel-efficient car.** This one's obvious, but the numbers are still pretty eye-opening. As an extreme example, a Hummer H2 uses about *five times* as much gas as a Toyota Prius. If you can't replace your cur-rent car right now, keep fuel economy in mind the next time you're in the market for a vehicle. FuelEconomy.gov has an online calculator (*http://tinyurl.com/gascalc*) that lets you compare the cost difference between two vehicles based on their mileage per gallon.

- **Take good care of your car.** "The best way to get the most from a tank of gas is to follow the vehicle manufacturer's service schedule," advises *Consumer Reports*. That means checking and replacing the air filter at regular intervals, keeping the tires properly inflated, and using the recommended grade of motor oil.

- **Drive sensibly.** Edmunds.com found that the best way to improve fuel efficiency was to accelerate slowly and brake over long distances. Here are some other tips:

  - **Drive at a constant, moderate pace.** Cruise control can help with this.

  - **Don't speed.** According to FuelEconomy.gov, each 5 MPH you drive over 60 adds about 25 cents per gallon to your fuel costs.

  - **Avoid idling.** *Hypermilers*—people obsessed with getting the best fuel economy—recommend turning off your engine if you stop for more than 10 seconds. Even if you're not that hardcore, try to commute when traffic is lighter and plan routes with as few traffic signals as possible to spend less time idling.

  - **Consolidate trips.** If you can, buy groceries, take your clothes to the dry-cleaner, and then drop little Johnny at soccer practice all in one trip.

- **Save at the pump.** If it's convenient to buy gas at a cheaper place, do it; if not, don't. It usually doesn't make sense to go more than a mile out of your way to find cheaper gas. For example, on a 10-gallon fill-up, saving five cents a gallon only nets you 50 cents.

  If you plan ahead, you can find cheap gas using GasBuddy.com, which lets people enter current prices at service stations in their neighborhoods. Just type in your Zip code to find gas prices near you. (If you don't get results, that's because nobody has entered prices for your area in the past 72 hours.)

If you want to track your fuel economy, check out Fuelly (*www.fuelly.com*), a site that lets you record your vehicle's gas mileage and compare data with other drivers. When you enter info about each fill-up, Fuelly computes your average miles per gallon, cost per tank, and more. There's also a version of the site you can use with mobile gadgets like iPhones.

Car-Free Living

The best way to save money on a car is to not own one. Each year, AAA publishes an estimate of driving costs (*http://tinyurl.com/driving-costs*). They figure the average American spends about $9,369 each year to own a car. That works out to over $25 a day, or $750 per month. Imagine what else you could do with that money if you ditched your car!

Not everyone has the option of going car-free. But for millions of people in cities like New York, Boston, Atlanta, and Los Angeles, giving up a vehicle is a viable option. In Chicago, for example, you can buy a week-long pass for unlimited subway and bus trips for only $24—that's just $96 per month.

Though many people like the idea of going car-free, it can be tough to actually make the leap. Still, with rising gas prices, more folks are looking for ways to live well without wheels. Most people who give up their vehicles aren't radical, anti-car environmentalists; they've simply decided they'd rather use their time and money in different ways. (For an example, see the story of Chris Guillebeau on page 15.)

Even if you keep your car, just driving less can save you money. And it may seem old-fashioned, but don't forget walking and biking as ways to get around (and burn a few calories). Or check out the public transportation in your area. If those options won't cut it, look into getting a scooter (you can read about one Get Rich Slowly reader's scooter-based lifestyle at *http://tinyurl.com/GRS-scooter*.) Or check out car-sharing organizations like Zipcar (*www.zipcar.com*).

 If the idea of a car-free lifestyle intrigues you, pick up a copy of **How to Live Well Without Owning a Car** (Ten Speed Press, 2006) by Chris Balish. It includes tips for getting to work without a car, as well as some hints on what do with all the money you'll save!

Finding Deals on Vacation and Travel

As you learned in Chapter 1, experiences are more likely to make you happy than Stuff. Traveling can create lasting memories, but it can also be expensive: airfare, hotels, restaurants—the costs add up quickly. But you don't need to stay in a luxury hotel to have a good time on vacation. You can travel on the cheap, volunteer, or even stay home.

The best way to keep travel costs down is to set a budget so you know exactly how much you can spend. But because you buy so many little things while on vacation, it's easy to lose track. To keep things in check, use a spending log: Every time you pay for something, write it down. At the end of each day, tally the totals to be sure you're still on budget. You might also want to use envelope budgeting (page 46): Withdraw cash and divide it into envelopes for each day. Once the cash is gone, stop spending until the next day. (Visit Get Rich Slowly to read more about how to track travel expenses and stick to a vacation budget: *http://tinyurl.com/vacation-budget*.)

If you're planning a trip overseas, take exchange rates into consideration. For example, if you're choosing between Paris and London right now, you'll get the most bang for your buck in merry old England. (Exchange rates change constantly, so check around before you travel.)

 Tip How far will your dollar go? Use Tripbase.com's travel-cost calculator (*http://tinyurl. com/trip-calculator*) to get a rough idea.

If you're trying to pick a place to vacation in the U.S., keep cost of living in mind. Look for areas where you can stretch your dollar. You can have just as much fun in Minneapolis as you can in New York for a lot less money.

 Tip To get more money-saving ideas , follow the adventures of Matt Gross, the Frugal Traveler: *http://frugaltraveler.blogs.nytimes.com/*. Gross travels around the country— and the world—describing how he saves on hotels, food, and entertainment.

Here are some more tips for making your vacations fun and affordable:

- **Save up and pay cash.** Enough said.
- **Plan ahead.** While you can sometimes find great last-minute bargains, you're usually better off making travel plans as early as possible. Before you leave, make a list of sightseeing priorities. Use the Web to find free and inexpensive attractions.

If you're traveling to Europe, be sure to take advice from Rick Steves (*www.ricksteves.com*). His website, books, and TV show are packed with info on how to make Europe fun and affordable. I'm a huge fan of his packing philosophy: *http://tinyurl.com/RS-packing*.

- **Travel light.** Experienced travelers always give this advice, but rookies seldom heed it. Even if you're staying in the same hotel for 3 weeks, packing light can prevent headaches. For example, don't bother taking stuff you can buy there, like shampoo.

- **Settle for less.** If you want luxurious meals and accommodations, you'll pay luxury prices. You can still have a wonderful experience traveling second or third class. Yes, this may mean stepping outside your comfort zone, but you'll save money and have a more memorable trip. My wife and I honeymooned in Victoria, British Columbia, for instance. Because our budget was tight, we stayed at a $40-a-night dive outside the city so we could afford to splurge on exploring the island.

- **Carry a guidebook.** A travel guide is worth its weight in gold. You'll pay $20–$30 for a good one, but ultimately the book will save you money. It can give you the inside scoop on the best days to visit museums and tell you about free events.

 Should you buy travel insurance? According to **Consumer Reports**, the answer is usually no (*http://tinyurl.com/CR-travel-insurance*), though it **might** make sense if you're in poor health and traveling overseas. If you do opt for insurance, check out the comparison site InsureMyTrip.com.

- **Look for discounts.** If you're traveling in the U.S., order a copy of the Entertainment Book for your destination city from Entertainment.com. It includes coupons, passes, and discounts for a variety of restaurants, hotels, and attractions. Also consider getting a National Parks Pass (*www.nps.gov/fees_passes.htm*) or a AAA membership (*www.aaa.com*).

- **Be flexible.** Don't be a slave to your itinerary. Some places will be more interesting than you expected and others less, so give yourself the freedom to adjust your schedule accordingly.

- **Eat cheap.** You'll want to eat out at least a few times, but for many meals, you can save money by picking up food at a grocery store. Stock up on your first day and eat light-and-easy meals throughout your trip. You'll find this especially handy on days when you're rushed.

- **Manage your money.** Know which payment method is best for each situation. For example, Visa charges a 1% overseas usage fee regardless of whether you use a credit card or a debit card. And some cards charge more than others to make withdrawals from foreign or out-of-network ATMs. Before you travel, find out your accounts' policies.

 Tip If you're going overseas, remember to let your bank and credit card companies know you'll be gone so they don't freeze your accounts for unusual charges. Also, be sure to make two copies of important documents (like your passport, credit cards, and driver license); leave one copy with somebody you trust, and take the other with you.

- **Steer clear of souvenirs.** Souvenirs are almost always Stuff—you bring them home and they turn into clutter. If you want a keepsake, choose something practical. When we toured Ireland, for example, I bought a wool sweater; whenever I wear it, I remember our trip.

Like so much of personal finance, saving on travel comes down to two things: doing it yourself and going against the flow. When you take self-guided tours, prepare your own meals, and arrange your own travel, you make your vacation dollars last longer. And by avoiding tourist traps, traveling during the off-season, and staying in modest hotels, you can save even more.

Travel for the Adventurous

If you're a little daring and have the time, you can use *slow travel* to escape the tourist traps and get a deeper look at a culture—while saving money, to boot. With slow travel, you avoid hotels and instead base your trip around longer stays in hostels, apartments, rental homes, or other creative accommodations. By staying put for a week or more, you can gradually explore the local culture. In many cases, you'll prepare your own food or share a table with your hosts.

There are two ways to ease into slow travel:

- **Consider a vacation rental, furnished home, or apartment that you can rent for a week or longer.** These kinds of places are often less expensive and more comfortable than hotels. Renting a home in another city gives you space and flexibility. For more info, check out Vacation Rentals by Owner (*www.vrbo.com*), which connects homeowners with travelers. For each available rental, you can view photos, read about its features, and look at renter reviews. Another option is to swap homes with other vacationers; check out HomeLink (*www.homelinkint.org*) and HomeExchange (*www.homeexchange.com*) to learn more.

- **For an even cheaper place to stay, look into hostels.** Hostels provide travelers with a bed (usually in a dorm-like setting), shared bathroom, and often a kitchen for cooking your own meals. In big cities like New York or London, hostels can run up to $35 per night—still just a fraction of the cost for a hotel. In smaller cities, they can be as cheap as $10 per night. Though hostels are more commonly used by younger folks, most welcome travelers of all ages. For more info, visit Hostelling International USA (*www.hiusa.org*).

You can learn all about slow travel at *www.slowtrav.com* and *www.sloweurope.com*. The following two sections cover two more slow-travel techniques: hospitality exchanges and volunteer tourism.

 Note Professional traveler Nora Dunn has a brilliant piece at IWillTeachYoutoBeRich.com that describes how to travel the world full-time for less than $14,000 per year: *http://tinyurl.com/dunn-travel*. If you've ever dreamed of touring the world, this is a must-read article.

Hospitality exchanges

If you like meeting new people, a *hospitality exchange* is a great way to save money. These exchanges connect folks who have extra room in their homes with travelers who need places to stay. Costs are minimal, and you get an excellent introduction to another culture—even if it's just in the next state!

CouchSurfing (*www.couchsurfing.org*) is a free hospitality-exchange network with over a million members worldwide. When you join, you fill out a profile. You can then volunteer to host—by offering a spare couch or bed to travelers—or request to "surf" in somebody else's home. Couch-surfing lets you save money and make new friends in the cities you visit. (Here's a real-life overview of the couch-surfing experience: *http://tinyurl.com/GRS-couchsurfing*.)

You'll find similar communities at The Hospitality Club (*http://hospitalityclub.org*), Airbnb (*http://airbnb.com*), and Servas (*http://usservas.org/*), which has been around for over 60 years. (Note that you have to pay to join Servas.)

 Tip Hi Everywhere! (*http://hieverywhere.com*) is a free site that helps you find (or be) a volunteer tour guide. You tell the site when and where you plan to travel, and if a local guide is available, she can sign up to show you around the city.

Volunteer tourism

Some folks want to go beyond sightseeing and get a real feel for the culture, and volunteer tourism is a great way to do just that. Groups like Volunteer Adventures (*http://volunteeradventures.com*), Volunteers for Peace (*http://vfp.org*), and Se7en (*http://the7interchange.com/*) connect people with organizations that need help around the world.

While it's rewarding, volunteering can still be expensive. If you need to keep costs down, consider a work exchange. The site Workaway.info helps travelers see more of the countries they visit while giving something back to the local community. You put in a few hours of hard work each day in exchange for meals and somewhere to sleep. In the process, you experience the local culture, save money, and maybe even learn a new language. The box below has a real-life example.

Your Money and Your Life

A Volunteer Vacation

John is a retired shop teacher from Portland, Oregon. At 73, he spends his summers fishing in Alaska and his winters in New Zealand (where it's summer that time of year).

John lives on his own fishing boat while in Alaska, and keeps his costs low in New Zealand by "WWOOFing it." World Wide Opportunities on Organic Farms—or WWOOF, for short—connects volunteers like John with hosts who need help on their farms.

John stays on each farm for about 3 weeks doing carpentry, gardening, and yard work. This sort of volunteering helps him escape the tourist mindset: "The real benefit of WWOOFing is being in the culture. When I'm there, I get to do all the things the locals do. It really puts you in touch with the rhythm of things."

WWOOF lets you travel the world without spending a fortune. Though John spends 3 months in New Zealand every year moving from farm to farm, his only real cost is the round-trip plane ticket. "You do your work in exchange for room and board," he explains. "I probably don't spend any more than $200 total while I'm actually there."

To learn more about WWOOF visit *http://wwoof.org*, where you can read about the group's philosophy and learn how to volunteer your talents for a few days or weeks—or even years.

Travel Tools

You used to have to rely on a travel agent to help you find the best deals, but nowadays you can often track down good prices on airfare, tours, and lodging from the comfort of your own computer. There are number of robust websites to help travelers save money on their adventures.

You're probably familiar with the online travel agencies like Orbitz.com, Expedia.com, Travelocity.com, and Priceline.com. But there's another group of lesser-known sites called *aggregators*—they go out, find the best deals from a variety of sources (including the online travel agencies), and gather that info all in one place. This saves you from having to dig around on dozens of different sites yourself.

Kayak.com, Momondo.com, Mobissimo.com, and Skyscanner.net are all good fare aggregators (though Kayak is by far the most popular). You can't book anything through them, but they help you search for the cheapest flights, hotel rooms, and rental cars, and then point you to the places where you *can* make reservations.

The problem with big aggregation sites like the ones listed above is that they don't include many small, budget airlines. For that, you need a site like WhichBudget.com, a favorite among international travelers. WhichBudget can tell you which budget airlines fly specific routes. This is especially useful if you can't find a larger airline to get you where you want to go. Budget Flight Finder (*www.budgetflightfinder.com*) offers a similar service.

The web is filled with other tools you can use to get better deals on travel, including:

- **Travelzoo.com,** which bills itself as the largest publisher of travel deals on the Internet. At the site, you can sign up for a weekly email list of the top 20 travel deals on the web.

 Tip My wife swears by TripAdvisor.com. This site won't help you find the best deals, but it can help you find the best *values*. TripAdvisor members rate and review hotels, restaurants, and destinations. Using this feedback, you can find out which places are overpriced—and which offer the best bang for your buck.

- **Airfare Watchdog** (*www.airfarewatchdog.com*) sends you daily or weekly email updates about travel between destinations you choose. If, for example, you want to travel from Pittsburgh to visit your cousins in Phoenix, you can ask Airfare Watchdog to keep you updated on ticket prices. The site also features its top 50 fares of the day.

- If you're in school, **Student Universe** (*www.studentuniverse.com*) often has the best deals on airfare. (These offers apply to college students *and* faculty.) The site also helps you research hotels, rental cars, and more. **EF College Break** (*www.efcollegebreak.com*) is another great resource for students, providing affordable tours of other countries.

- If you want to take a cruise, **VacationsToGo.com** is a must-visit site. When the cruise lines can't fill their ships, they discount the unsold cabins and sell them through this website. You'll find the best bargains during a cruise's slow season—and usually in the last 90 days before departure. You may also want to take a look at **CruiseCompete.com**, which lets travel agencies blindly bid for your business.

- Tired of getting stuck in the worst seat on the plane? **SeatGuru.com** contains a library of layouts for over 700 different planes, as well as info on where to find power outlets, overhead TVs, and bathrooms. SeatGuru won't save you money, but it can certainly make your trips more comfortable.

- **Yapta.com** (short for Your Amazing Personal Travel Assistant) can help you find flights, track fares, and get alerts when a fare drops into your price range. Yapta also acts as a sort of PriceProtectr.com (page 96) for travel: Enter your flight confirmation number, and Yapta tracks ticket prices. If the price drops below what you paid for it, Yapta sends you an alert so you can take advantage of the better price.

Savvy travelers suggest using these web-based tools to find the flights and hotels you want—but then purchasing tickets or accommodations directly from the source. The tools will help you find the best deal, but you'll usually save even more by booking directly with the hotel or airline.

Hometown Vacations

When was the last time you vacationed in your city? I've lived in and around Portland, Oregon all my life, but never really viewed it through the eyes of a tourist. A couple of years ago, I spent a day doing touristy stuff with a friend from L.A. I had a great time, and learned more about my city in those few hours than ever before.

A hometown vacation—a *staycation*—can be both frugal and fun. As the site Finance for a Freelance Life notes in the article at *http://tinyurl.com/MM-staycations*, there are lots of advantages to hometown tourism: You save big on accommodations, since you don't pay for any. You also save on gas and travel expenses, and by packing meals from home. Perhaps best of all, vacationing in your hometown lets you stay in your comfort zone; you can use your knowledge of the area to pick cheap attractions.

But you don't *have* to pinch pennies during a staycation. You'll still save money even if you stay in a nice hotel, dine in fancy restaurants, see a show, and take a couple of tours. Because you don't pay any travel costs and you're familiar with the area, your vacation dollars go much further in your own city.

Regardless of how much you choose to spend, here are some tips for enjoying a vacation close to home:

- **Set a budget.** Whether you opt to take the frugal approach or splurge, create a spending plan and stick to it, just like you would on a regular vacation.

- **Grab a guidebook.** Tourist guides contain great info about cheap eats, cool spots, and local history. You can find guidebooks at local bookstores or better yet, borrow one from your public library. If you're a member of AAA, pick one up for free at the local office.

- **Book a tour.** Tours can be a fun way to get to know a city's history and trivia—even if you've lived there all your life. For example, Portland offers walking tours of local microbreweries. What's your city known for?

- **Be adventurous.** Be bold and try new things. If you live near a river, go kayaking. If you live near the mountains, go hiking or skiing.

- **Chat it up.** Talk with the actual tourists. Ask them what they like about the city. Get recommendations for cheap or fun spots to visit. Answer their questions. Talking with tourists is an excellent way to see your surroundings with new eyes.

- **Be unreachable.** Pretend you're vacationing out of town, even if you're still at home: Ignore the phone and don't check email. After all, a vacation is a time to relax and forget the cares of the workaday world—whether you're on a Caribbean cruise or simply walking down Main Street.

- **Swap houses.** Have some like-minded friends? Swap houses for a week (or a weekend). This cheap change of scenery can make you feel like you're in a completely different city. It may also give you insight into neighborhoods you haven't explored.

- **Mix things up.** When you've lived in the same city for 5, 10, or 40 years, you tend to have favorite routes, places, and things to do. A staycation is a chance to explore. While preparing for your vacation, keep a list of things you'd like to see and do. Ask your friends where they take out-of-town visitors. Use the events guide in your local paper to research activities.

Tip In their book *America's Cheapest Family*, Steve and Annette Economides suggest using a staycation for a mix of work and play. They write that, in addition to saving money, there's another benefit to taking a hometown vacation: "Completing a home improvement project during a week of vacation may sound illogical, but it can really be a stress reliever."

You can probably have a better time in your own city than you would somewhere hundreds of miles away—and for much, much less.

Cash Is King

Did you notice something about the recommendations in this chapter? In each case, the best way to save money *on* big things is to save money *for* them. When you use cash instead of credit to pay for a car or vacation, you can save hundreds (or even thousands) of dollars. All the money you would have otherwise paid in interest goes directly to boosting your cash flow, making it easier to save for retirement—and to pay cash again in the future. So planning ahead and saving for expenses isn't just a great way to get organized—it actually saves money.

In the next chapter, you'll learn ways to save on the biggest expense of all: housing.

10 House and Home

"*A house is made of brick and mortar, but home is made by the people who live there.*"
—*M.K. Soni*

Housing is by far the largest expense in most people's budgets. According to the U.S. government's 2008 Consumer Expenditure Survey, the average American family spends $1,747.83 on housing and related expenses every month. That's more than they spend on food, clothing, healthcare, and entertainment put together. So if you want a quick way to improve your financial health, housing is the place to look.

So far, you've read about a lot of different ways to save money: You know how to spend less on groceries, trim your transportation budget, and use credit wisely. Everyday thrift can boost your cash flow, helping you to get out of debt and save money. But even all those changes **combined** don't have the power to affect your budget like what you spend on housing.

This chapter will give you the facts you need to make smart housing decisions.

The Eternal Question: Rent or Buy?

Deciding whether to rent or buy is a complicated financial and emotional decision. Real-estate agents like to say, "Renting is like throwing your money away." On its surface, this advice seems to make sense, so it gets repeated a lot in popular culture. But in a 2008 issue of *Newsweek* (*http://tinyurl.com/nw-rentok*), Robert Shiller, a professor of economics at Yale University, wrote, "The popular argument that renting is equivalent to throwing money down the drain is really fallacious."

In some cases, it *does* make financial sense to buy a home. But in other situations, renting is the better choice. And often, there's not a lot of difference between the two, especially if you're smart and keep costs low. The decision usually comes down to personal preference. Let's take a brief look at the pros and cons of each.

Here are the advantages of owning your home:

- **Stability.** When you take out a mortgage, you know what your payments will be for years to come. There's no landlord to change the rules, and you don't need to worry about being kicked out at a moment's notice.

- **Equity.** As you make your mortgage payments, and as the property's value increases, you build *equity*, which is the difference between what you owe on your house and what you could sell it for. In other words, it's how much value you have stored in your home. For example, if your house is worth $225,000 and you owe $175,000, you've got $50,000 in equity.

- **Freedom.** You can do what you want with your home and yard, like plant a garden, paint the ceiling purple, or install a wet bar in the basement.

On the other hand, the advantages of renting include:

- **Flexibility.** With a rental, you don't have a long-term commitment. You can move on short notice, whether to get away from bad neighbors or to take advantage of lower rents elsewhere. There's also a wider range of rental options than homes for sale. It's difficult to buy a tiny house, for example, but you can easily find one- or two-room rentals.

- **Lower costs.** In the June 2007 issue of *Kiplinger's Personal Finance* (*http://tinyurl.com/kip0607*), editor Knight Kiplinger wrote, "It often costs less to rent. The annual cost of owning a property, be it a house or a condo, is usually greater than the cost of renting, after taxes." True, you don't build equity when you rent, but you're not burdened with taxes, insurance, and maintenance costs either. You can use the money you save to travel or buy stocks.

- **Lack of responsibility.** When you rent, somebody else does the yard work and repairs the leaky showerhead. (Of course, this can be a disadvantage if your landlord is slow to respond to problems.) All you do is stick to the terms of your lease or rental agreement and someone else takes care of the rest.

Both sides of the rent vs. buy argument can trot out numbers and statistics to prove why they're right and the other side is wrong. The bottom line is that the decision isn't just a financial one, so it's hard to generalize. Yes, renting can save you money and it comes with far fewer hassles than owning. But owning your home can give you non-financial benefits.

The best way to decide is to think about your goals and figure out what makes sense for you. Ask yourself these questions:

- **How long will you stay in one place?** The longer you plan to stay put, the more sense it makes to buy a home. Buying lets you recover your costs and build equity.

- **How do costs compare?** Find a good rent-vs.-buy calculator and crunch the numbers. The *New York Times* has a nifty web-based calculator (*http://tinyurl.com/NYT-rbcalc*) that can help you compare costs for renting vs. owning. The site lets you plug in numbers for your situation, and then shows you how long it would take to break even with buying.

- **How would you spend the savings?** When renting is cheaper, you can use the money you save to pursue other goals. Sure, you could spend the cash on purses and videogames, but you'll be better off in the long run if you use it to fund your retirement (see Chapter 13), budget for a new car—or even save for a down payment on a house.

- **How do you feel about homeownership?** For some, owning a home is a piece of the American Dream. For others, the chores and maintenance are a nightmare. Your feelings about homeownership are just as important as the financial stuff.

 Note Here's an excellent article from the *New York Times* (*http://tinyurl.com/NYT-buying*) that explains why the author—a long-time renter—decided to buy a home. It does a good job of laying out the pros and cons of each choice.

If you decide to buy, do it for the right reasons: because it fits your goals and will make you happy. *Don't* do it because you think it's a good investment. A mortgage is *not* a retirement plan—it won't make you rich. Instead, think of it as an investment in a certain lifestyle. If homeownership is a lifestyle you want and can afford, then buy; if not, rent.

Tips for Renters

One advantage to renting over buying is you have a lot more options, so make the most of it. Be choosy; don't settle for the first thing you see.

Pick a neighborhood close to work or school, and one with stores and entertainment options. If exercise is important to you, find a spot that gives you access to spaces for biking or running. By finding a rental in a walkable neighborhood, or next to a bus or train line, you can save tons by not owning a car (see page 184).

 Tip To find out how walkable an address is, check out WalkScore.com, which calculates how close it is to things like restaurants, libraries, and grocery stores.

Don't rent a place if it's going to cost so much you can't afford to have a social life or meet your financial goals. A good rule of thumb is to limit your monthly rent to no more that 25% of your pre-tax pay. You can use the Rentometer (*www.rentometer.com*) to find affordable rentals in your area.

 Tip If you have the time and inclination, you can save money by taking a gig as an apartment manager. Yes, you'll have to deal with locked-out tenants and leaky faucets, but you'll get free (or at least reduced) rent. The box on page 125 has an example of someone who does this.

Before you sign a lease or rental agreement, tour the unit you'll live in. This may seem like common sense, but you'd be surprised at how many people rent places sight unseen. If you can, visit the unit at various times of the day, and maybe once over the weekend. A neighborhood that's quiet on a weekday morning may be party central on Friday nights.

Believe it or not, you can often negotiate on rent before you sign the paperwork. Wait until you and the landlord seem to have made a connection. (Here's a list of tips for knocking the socks off your next landlord: *http://tinyurl.com/GRS-renttips*.) Once he likes you, it's okay to ask whether he can do things like include the cost of your Internet service in the price or let you have a dog: "Well, it's a great place, but I don't know. You don't allow pets. My next stop is with somebody who'll let me keep a dog. Is there anything you could do to help?" (See the box on page 175 for tips on negotiating.)

Remember to read (and understand) the contract before you sign it. Pay special attention to costs and dates, and don't be afraid to ask questions: What does it take to get your security deposit back? How much notice do you have to give before moving out or when does the lease end? Negotiate any details you don't like.

Be sure to document everything—even before you move in. To prevent future misunderstandings, record a video tour or take photos of the unit before you fill it with your stuff. If your landlord is there for the tour, that's even better.

Once you move in, live up to your end of the deal. The best way to stay on your landlord's good side is to pay the rent on time. If your check will be late, contact your landlord right away and explain the situation. Offer to pay as much as you can immediately, and give a firm date by which you'll pay the rest.

 Tip Don't forget to get renters insurance. Renters are 50% more likely to be burglarized than homeowners, and just as subject to fires and floods. Your landlord has insurance on the property and the things he owns—but not on *your* stuff. Plus, renters insurance protects you from liability lawsuits in case somebody gets hurt in your home and sues you. For about 10 bucks a month, renters insurance can give you peace of mind. (For more info, head to *http://tinyurl.com/GRS-renters*.)

When you're renting, it's vital to have good communication with your landlord to prevent misunderstandings, so don't rent from someone who's slow to return your calls and emails. To avoid disputes, put everything in writing—and ask your landlord to do the same. Try to stay on your landlord's good side; it can pay off in lots of ways. If he likes you, he'll be more likely to reduce rent if you ask, respond quickly to your maintenance requests, and maybe make other concessions.

If you have roommates, choose them carefully. Everyone on the lease or rental agreement is responsible for living by the rules. If your roommate leaves with no warning, you *still* have to pay the rent in full. (Here's some advice on what to do if you're frugal but your roommates aren't: *http://tinyurl.com/GRS-roommates*.)

Before you move out, find out exactly what you have to do to get your deposit back. (You and your landlord may have different definitions of "clean.") Just as you toured and photographed or videotaped the apartment with your landlord before moving in, do so again for the move-out inspection.

If you run into a sticky situation while renting (or after you move out), check your local laws. The U.S. Department of Housing and Urban Development has collected links about tenant rights for every state here: *http:// tinyurl.com/tenant-laws*. RentLaw.com is another good resource.

 Tip Spend some time researching tenancy laws in your state by picking up a book like *Renters' Rights* (Nolo, 2002) by Janet Portman and Marcia Stewart. A few hours spent reading can save you a lot of grief.

Buying a Home

Generally, once you've saved 20% for a down payment *and* you can afford monthly mortgage payments, you're ready to start looking for a home. Yes, you *can* buy a home with a smaller down payment, but it'll cost you in the long run. You'll need to carry private mortgage insurance (page 214), you'll pay more interest, and you could put yourself in a position where you can't afford to sell your home! For more info, check out the Mortgage Professor's down-payment calculator: *http://tinyurl.com/MP-dpcalc*.

If you think you're ready to buy a house, take a few months to do a trial run. In *The Money Book for the Young, Fabulous & Broke* (Riverhead, 2007), Suze Orman says that you should "play house before you buy a house." Here's how:

1. Figure out how much you think you can afford to pay for a home every month, including mortgage and maintenance. This might be $1,750, for example.

2. Subtract the amount you're currently paying for rent. If your rent is $1,000 per month, you'd subtract this from the $1,750 to get $750 per month.

3. Open a new, named savings account (see page 142). On the first day of each of the next *6 months*, stick $750 into this account.

If you can't make this work financially, Orman says you need to wait: "If you miss one payment, or if you are consistently late in making the payments, you are not ready to buy a home. If you can handle the extra payments, then you've got the thumbs-up to start looking for a home to buy." But before you start looking, you need to know how much you can spend.

How Much House Can You Afford?

Housing is the largest expense in most families' budgets. But how much is too much to spend on shelter?

Economists have used decades of financial stats to create computer models that predict how much people can afford to spend on housing and debt. Traditionally, lenders have used what's called a *debt-to-income ratio* (or DTI ratio)—a measure of how much of your income goes toward debt every month—to estimate how much people can afford to borrow to pay for a home. To find this ratio, divide your monthly debt payments by your gross (pre-tax) income. For example, if you pay $300 toward debt every month on a $3,000 income, your DTI ratio is 10%. (The lower the number, the better.)

Banks and mortgage brokers look at two numbers when deciding how much to loan you:

- **Front-end DTI ratios** (sometimes called *housing expense ratios*), which include your total housing expenses: mortgage principal, interest, taxes, and insurance. These four factors are often called PITI. (Yes, the mortgage industry is filled with acronyms and abbreviations.)

- **Back-end DTI ratios** (also known as *total expense ratios*), which include all of the above plus other debt payments like auto loans, student loans, and credit cards.

When you apply for a mortgage, a computer checks to be sure the amount of debt you want to take on falls within accepted ranges. This process is called *automated underwriting*. When the computer is finished, the loan application moves to *manual underwriting*, where an actual person uses industry-standard DTI ratios to decide whether to approve or deny the loan.

 Note The key thing to understand about DTI ratios is that they're used to estimate the *lender's* risk, not yours. That is, your mortgage company uses them to check whether they think you can make the payments—not whether you can *comfortably* make the payments. So if you want to be able to dine out and take vacations and pursue other financial goals, the DTI ratio you use in your calculations should be lower than the one your lender uses.

During the 1970s (before credit-card debt became common), DTI wasn't split between front-end and back-end. There was only one ratio, and it was 25%. If your mortgage, taxes, and insurance costs were less than 25% of your income, people assumed you could afford the payment. (This is still an excellent rule of thumb.)

Debt-to-income guidelines have relaxed over the years. When my wife and I bought our first home in 1994, our mortgage broker told us our front-end DTI ratio had to be 28% or less, meaning we couldn't pay any more than 28% of our gross income toward housing. The back-end DTI ratio was capped at 36%, which meant that our housing expenses *and* other debt payments combined couldn't be more than 36% of our income.

When we bought our new home in 2004, the accepted DTI ratios had grown by 5%. "That 28% figure is old," we were told. "Most people can go as high as 33%." The back-end ratio had been raised to 38%–41% in some cases. (During the housing bubble, some lenders went still higher, even above 50%!)

A 5% increase may not seem like a big deal, but when you're talking about a house payment, it's *huge.* If you're earning $60,000 per year, 5% is $3,000, or $250 a month. Many people have lost their homes because they took on mortgage payments that were just $250 more than they could afford each month.

Generally, banks are happy to lend you as much money as you want. (Within reason, of course, and if your credit is good.) The recent credit crisis has certainly made lenders more cautious, but they're still not going to stop you from digging a hole for yourself if that's what you want to do. In *The Automatic Millionaire Homeowner* (Broadway, 2008), David Bach writes:

> You should generally assume that the amount the bank or mortgage company is willing to loan you is more than you should borrow. [...] Don't fool around with this. Do the math. Be realistic about your situation. Don't pretend you're in better shape than you are.

Remember, nobody cares more about you than *you*. Your real-estate agent, mortgage broker, and bank all have a vested interest in encouraging you to buy as much house as possible—their incomes depend on it. Listen to what they have to say, but make your decisions based on what's best for you.

Homebuyers are often told to "buy as much house as you can afford." But the problem with following this advice is that you're left without a buffer. What if you lose your job? Or what if you're forced to sell your home, but housing prices have dropped? (Many Americans are facing this problem in the aftermath of the housing bubble.) Instead of buying as much house as you can afford, it makes more sense to buy as much house as you *need*, keeping conventional DTI ratios as ceilings. (The box on page 203 tells the story of a couple who bought more house than they ended up needing.)

Ultimately, it doesn't matter what the guidelines are. It all comes down to what you're comfortable paying. Just because conventional wisdom says you can afford a $1,650 housing payment on your $60,000 annual income doesn't mean you should do it.

Give yourself a margin for error. Instead of basing your home-buying bud-get on a 33% front-end DTI ratio, consider dropping that to 28% or, better yet, 25%. Another way to create a buffer is to base your estimates on your net (take-home) pay instead of your gross pay. You won't be able to afford as big of a mortgage, but you won't feel pinched by the payments, either.

Your Money and Your Life

Movin' on Down

When they got married, Sierra Black and her husband Martin bought a home near Boston, Massachusetts. "We found an old Victorian with gables and staircases and a finished attic." The 2,200 square-foot house was beautiful, and they loved it—but it was a nightmare to maintain that much space. "Buying that house meant buying a piece of the American Dream—but we both figured out pretty quickly that it wasn't *our* dream."

There was the $2,200 monthly mortgage payment and the $600 monthly cost of their combined commutes (which totaled 160 miles *every day*). Sierra tried to boost their cash flow by making the sorts of frugal choices described in Chapter 5, but she says, "It felt like I was bailing out a leaky boat with a teaspoon."

After 2 years of struggling to make ends meet, Sierra and Martin moved to a 1,500-square-foot colonial-style duplex closer to his office. "The new house feels small but not cramped," says Sierra. "We gave up a lot of square footage, but we didn't lose any functionality. It turns out we didn't need all that space."

They now pay about $1,600 each month for their mortgage. But that's not the only savings: "All of our utility bills are lower than they were," says Sierra, "and our com-muting costs are nonexistent." Martin used to drive 40 miles to work every day; now it's a four-block walk. And Sierra does a lot of her errands on foot. "The great thing about this is that it's saved a ton of money *and* a ton of time."

As Sierra and Martin have learned, it's not material things that bring happiness, but finding ways to align your spending with your values (see Chapter 2): "Every single day that goes by since we moved, we tell each other this is the best decision we ever made. This improved our quality of life *so much*."

Choosing a Home

Buying a home is an emotional process. It's probably the biggest financial decision you'll ever make, and there's a lot of pressure to get it right: You don't want to overpay, make any legal mistakes, or discover you've bought a house you hate. But you'll be happier in the long run—not to mention more financially secure—if you do your best to take emotions out of the process.

That's not to say that you should buy a house using detached, Spock-like logic; even with preparation, the decision will be emotional. But before you start looking, you can take steps to keep from spending too much. Let's look at three of the most important.

Getting pre-approved

Once you've figured out how much home **you** think you can afford (see page 201), it's time to talk to the banks. You need to know how much a mortgage company will loan you **before** you start shopping.

One option is to get **pre-qualified** for a loan. To do that, you give your basic financial info to a lender, who then does a quick calculation to give you a rough estimate of how much you can afford to spend on a house. Bear in mind that the bank isn't actually agreeing to loan you this amount; they're simply saying, "We think you can afford this much house—we'll work out the exact numbers later."

You're usually better off getting **pre-approved** for a loan instead. Pre-approval is more formal than pre-qualifying, and it takes days instead of minutes. The lender will pull your credit report, review your financial info, and check your employment history before giving you a pre-approval letter. This process may actually cost you money, but pre-approval gives you the confidence that you can actually afford the homes you're looking at, and gives sellers confidence that you'll be able to get a loan.

 Neither pre-qualification nor pre-approval is binding on you or the lender. If you buy a house, you're not required to use the bank you talked to, and they're not required to lend you money (but if you're pre-approved, they probably will).

Be careful: Even after the recent mortgage crisis, lenders can and do approve loans for more than people should borrow. Run the numbers yourself and be willing to put on the brakes. Don't spend $500,000 on a house just because a bank will lend you that much.

Making a list

While you're waiting for the pre-approval process to finish, put all your hopes and dreams down on paper. Having a list of wants and needs can help you avoid making an emotional buying decision.

First, list all the things your family wants in a house. This is a time to brainstorm, not be judgmental. Your aim here is to make a list of features in your **ideal** home. Do you want a laundry room? A large garage? A yard for the kids to play in? And what sort of neighborhood are you looking for?

Once you've made your list, prioritize it. Sort the things you want from most important to least important based on your family's goals. What makes you happy? Maybe you love to spend time outdoors gardening and entertaining, so a big yard is a necessity. But if your family spends a lot of time together watching TV, the size of the family room might be more important.

This list will help ground you when you think you've found the "perfect" house: It can remind you that you need a laundry room, and that you swore you didn't want a place where you'd have to remove asbestos ceiling tiles. As you search for homes, update your list as you discover new wants and needs.

On the Money

Does Size Matter?

A book on smart money management isn't the place to tell you what to look for when choosing a home. (So check out other great books on this subject, like *Buying a Home: The Missing Manual*.) But some parts of the decision can have a big impact on your bottom line. One of these is home size.

According to the U.S. Census Bureau, the average new home was 2,349 square feet in 2004, up from 1,695 square feet in 1974. During those 30 years, kitchen sizes doubled, ceilings rose more than a foot, and bedrooms grew by more than 50 square feet. But home sizes are ballooning even while our families are getting smaller: The average family had 3.1 people in 1974; it had shrunk to 2.6 people in 2004. (For the stats geeks out there, that means we've gone from having 547 square feet of home space per person to 903 square feet per person.)

But bigger isn't always better. The larger your house, the more it costs to buy, maintain, heat, light, paint, furnish, and repair. That's not to say you should live in a shack, but as you shop for a house, remember that size comes with a price. If you need the space, buy it. If you don't, you're better off saving your money for something else.

Shopping smart

Once you have your wish list and your pre-approval letter, it's time to start house hunting. Here's the last (and most important) way to outsmart yourself and help take emotion out of the buying process: ***Don't look at homes outside your price range***.

This seems simple, but it's not as easy as it sounds. Your real-estate agent will want to show you houses that are at the very top of your budget—or maybe cost a little bit beyond it. If she tries to push you out of your price range, politely refuse. If you don't look, you can't be tempted.

Stick to your budget and be patient. It can be tempting to snatch up the first good house that comes along because you're afraid of missing out. But the more you look, the better you'll know the market. You'll learn what features are typical for your area and be able to spot good deals.

Do what you can to prevent emotion from carrying you away. Set priorities, try not to compromise, and take your time. And remember that buying a home is a purchase, not an investment, so treat it like any other shopping decision: Do your research, shop for quality, negotiate a good price, and then keep it for a long time.

 Before you make an offer on a house, ask whether you'll have to join a **homeowners association** (HOA). Some people like them—some don't. If you like uniformity and standards, an HOA might be just your style. But be aware that HOAs usually charge a monthly fee, which could be a deal breaker if you can't afford it.

Picking a Mortgage

Once you've found a home and made an offer, it's time to select a mortgage. Happily, because you've been pre-approved and stayed within your budget (right?), financing shouldn't be too tough.

 The best thing you can do when shopping for a mortgage is to learn more about them. Start by spending a few hours reading the archives at The Mortgage Professor (*www.mtgprofessor.com*).

One easy way to research mortgage interest rates is to go online. Sites like BankRate.com, ShopRate.com, and Money-Rates.com can help you find the best rates from around the country. If you'd rather shop locally, your credit union or community bank is likely to have good rates, too. But perhaps the best way to find a good lender is to ask family and friends (*not* your real-estate agent). Personal recommendations offer color and nuance you can't get from a website.

 You may also want to check out the Up-Front Mortgage Brokers Association (*www.upfrontmortgagebrokers.org*), whose members pledge to be clear about their fees and give objective advice.

When shopping for a mortgage, consider these factors:

- **Good rates.** Many first-time homebuyers don't realize that even a small change in interest can make an enormous difference in their monthly mortgage payment—and in the total cost of the loan (see the table on page 208).

- **Low fees.** Find out what sorts of fees each lender charges. Closing costs (like those listed here: *http://tinyurl.com/FR-closing*) can have a big impact on the total cost of the mortgage, but many people ignore them, probably because the cost of the mortgage is so huge that these charges seem small by comparison. Be sure to get a *good-faith estimate* (*http://tinyurl.com/wiki-gfe*) whenever a lender or broker gives you a quote.

- **Gut feeling.** If the broker seems shady, find someone else.

Your goal is to find the lowest total cost for your loan. In most cases, this means focusing on the best interest rates, but if you expect to have your mortgage for only a couple of years, you might be better off paying a higher rate to get lower fees. Always run the numbers for your situation, using a mortgage-comparison calculator like this one from LendingTree: *http://tinyurl.com/LT-mtgcalc*.

Once you find a lender you think you can work with, ask lots of questions. When they "lock" your rate, how much time do you have to close the deal? What's the mortgage's *annual percentage rate* (APR)? (The APR doesn't just take into account the loan's interest rate; it factors in other fees and payments, too.) Are there any penalties if you pay the mortgage off early? And if you're dealing with a broker, how is he paid?

Remember that you'll get few chances in your life to have this kind of impact on your budget, so take the time to do things right. Four fundamental things reduce the cost of a mortgage:

- **Having a good credit score (see Chapter 8).** In the fallout of the mortgage crisis, qualifying for a loan can be tough. Lenders have tightened their standards so that their best rates are only available if you have solid credit.

- **Buying a cheaper house.** The lower the purchase price, the lower the mortgage. This is obvious but important (and a lot of people seem to forget it). It's the reason you need to set a budget *before* you start shopping for a house.

- **Making a bigger down payment.** The less you finance, the less you pay each month. And if you don't put 20% down, you'll have to pay for private mortgage insurance, which can cost you hundreds of dollars a year (see page 214).

- **Finding a better interest rate.** Interest rates have a *huge* impact on your monthly payments. As you can see in the following table, even one-half of a percent can make a difference of tens of thousands of dollars.

Monthly mortgage payments on a $250,000 loan

Interest Rate	Length of Loan				
	10 years	**15 years**	**20 years**	**25 years**	**30 years**
5.00%	$2,653	$1,978	$1,650	$1,463	$1,343
5.50%	$2,715	$2,046	$1,720	$1,538	$1,420
6.00%	$2,778	$2,110	$1,793	$1,613	$1,500
6.50%	$2,840	$2,180	$1,865	$1,690	$1,583
7.00%	$2,905	$2,248	$1,940	$1,768	$1,665
7.50%	$2,968	$2,318	$2,015	$1,848	$1,750
8.00%	$3,035	$2,390	$2,093	$1,930	$1,835
8.50%	$3,100	$2,463	$2,170	$2,015	$1,923

The table shows roughly how much you'd pay every month on a $250,000 mortgage (including principal and interest). For example, if you took out a 30-year loan at 6% interest, your payment would be about $1,500. But if you shopped around and found a 5.5% rate, you'd pay $1,420, saving $80 every month *for 30 years.* A difference like that really adds up over time.

 Tip Vertex42.com offers a free Excel spreadsheet that lets you calculate approximate home-ownership expenses, including your mortgage, taxes, and insurance, but also maintenance and improvements. Download it here: *http://tinyurl.com/home-calc.*

The type of mortgage you take out will depend on your goals and your financial situation. Most people opt for a mortgage with a fixed 15- or 30-year term. Here's some info that can help you decide which is best for you:

- Interest rates on **15-year mortgages** are lower than those on 30-year loans, but because the loan is only half as long, your monthly payments are higher. (See the table above to compare monthly payments.) If you can keep saving for retirement and other goals despite the higher monthly payments, a 15-year-loan is a great option because it'll save you a bundle in interest. But if it's going to crimp your cash flow, go with a 30-year mortgage instead.

- For most people, a **30-year, fixed-rate mortgage** is the best choice. The monthly payments are lower than with a 15-year loan, and you have greater flexibility. If you want to pay more than the minimum amount every month, you can (see page 215), but you don't *have* to. This gives you a kind of safety net: If you lose your job, say, it's easier to make the payments on a 30-year loan than a 15-year loan.

 Be wary of mortgage products like adjustable-rate and interest-only loans. These may seem attractive, but there are a lot of pitfalls involved. These types of loans are for "sophisticated" borrowers. (If you're not sure whether you're a sophisticated borrower, you're not.)

Closing the Deal

As you wait for the lender to approve your loan documents, there are a lot of other things to think about. Your top priority should be checking the background of the home you're about to buy. Your lender will require that the house be appraised, but you should go further. Once your offer is accepted:

- **Ask the seller to pull a CLUE report** (*http://tinyurl.com/clue-rpt*). The Comprehensive Loss Underwriting Exchange is a database the insurance industry uses to track insurance claims connected to people and property. A CLUE report tells you what sorts of claims were filed at the address during the past 7 years. You can't order this report yourself— only the person who owns the property can.

- **Get an independent inspection.** A good inspection will cost several hundred dollars, but it's worth every penny. Ask friends, family, and coworkers to recommend inspectors. *Don't* use an inspector recommended by the seller, broker, or real-estate agent; you want somebody who's thorough and tough, and whose livelihood isn't tied to others in the process. Tag along during the inspection and ask questions. (You may want to film the house at this time.) Don't panic if the inspector finds problems; instead, use them to negotiate.

- **Talk to the neighbors.** Ask about the house and the neighborhood. The seller may be reluctant to spill the beans on the garage conversion he did without a permit, but the old guy next door probably won't be.

- **Stay on top of things.** The home-buying process involves a lot of people, and they're usually juggling lots of other deals, too. Don't be afraid to be the squeaky wheel that needs a little grease. Your questions may drive people crazy, but that's okay. What's worse: To annoy the title-insurance company or to lose tens of thousands of dollars because you were too chicken to speak up?

- **Do a final walk-through.** On the day before you close the sale, ask to take one final pass through the house. Are the window treatments there? Are the light fixtures still the same? Have requested repairs been made? Your goal here isn't to do another home inspection or to find things to negotiate on, just to be sure everything's in the same condition as when you made the offer.

 Don't finance your closing costs into the mortgage. It might seem like a good idea, but it means you'll pay twice as much for them in the long run.

- **Ask to read the mortgage paperwork *before* closing.** (*Closing* is when you sit down and finalize the deal by signing all the necessary paperwork.) This is the most important item in this list. You're likely to sign more than 100 pages filled with legal gibberish—do you really want to read it for the first time at closing? What happens if you discover there's a penalty for prepaying the mortgage? Or that the contract specifies a term of 15 years instead of 30 years? If you don't read the contract, you have nobody to blame but yourself if something goes wrong. If you need to, have a lawyer review the paperwork. This is likely to be the biggest legal contract you ever sign, so take the time to get it right.

 If you don't already have a lawyer, consider hiring a real-estate attorney to review your mortgage paperwork. It'll cost you a few hundred bucks, but that's peanuts compared to the hundreds of thousands you're spending on your home. Besides, during this process, your lawyer will be the only other person actually in your corner representing your best interests.

Owning a Home

After all that research and hard work, you've finally got yourself a home—congratulations! Of course, your responsibilities don't end there.

When you rent a place to live, your only cost is the monthly rent payment (and maybe utilities). But when you own a home, the costs never seem to end. In addition to monthly mortgage payments, you have to pay property taxes, homeowners insurance, utilities, maintenance and repairs, redecorating, landscaping, and more.

Let's look at two of the most important expenses: maintenance and repairs and paying the mortgage.

 Tip For a look at the true cost of owning a home, read Cameron Huddleston's account at Kiplinger.com: *http://tinyurl.com/homecost*.

Saving Money through Regular Maintenance

Your house is like a living, breathing organism. As much as you try to keep things in working order, eventually something goes wrong—and usually at the worst possible time. Like that Christmas morning my wife and I woke to find our water heater had broken, flooding one end of the house. Happy holidays!

Just as daily exercise and a sensible diet keep your body healthy and help you avoid costly medical bills, regular home maintenance keeps normal wear-and-tear from developing into problems, and problems from turning into emergencies.

As a rule of thumb, every year you should set aside about 1% of your home's purchase price for maintenance and repairs. So if you bought a $300,000 home, figure about $3,000 for annual upkeep. Of course, this is just a guideline—some years you'll spend much more, and some years you'll spend nothing at all.

When we bought our new house in 2004, the home inspector told us that for every dollar we spent on maintenance, we'd avoid roughly $100 in future repairs. He wrote in his inspection report, "In my experience as a professional home inspector, I have looked at hundreds of homes in all age ranges, and I have seen thousands of dollars of damage to homes that could have been avoided by spending $5 to $10 and just a few minutes of work."

If you make a point of doing as much maintenance as possible yourself, you'll save money and develop confidence and know-how. It can be intimidating at first, but with time, you can learn how to do most common household repairs. Here are some things I've learned over 15 years of playing handyman:

- **Don't panic.** Stay calm and relaxed when making repairs. Rash actions can turn a small problem into a disaster.

- **Act quickly.** Take care of problems as soon as possible. I once put off repairing a leaky roof. Can you guess how that turned out during a rainy Oregon winter?

- **Use a reference.** Shelling out 20 bucks for a book like the *Reader's Digest Complete Do-It-Yourself Manual* (2005) can save you thousands of dollars over the years. And the Internet is a great place to find answers to common home maintenance questions, including downloadable videos and PDFs; just make sure to get your info from reputable websites.

- **Work methodically.** Be orderly. Follow instructions. Measure twice, cut once. When you take something apart, neatly set the pieces someplace safe (and label them if you don't think you'll be able to remember where they went). If you have a digital camera handy, take pictures of how things are assembled before you dismantle them.

- **Don't make assumptions.** Some of the most frustrating—and dangerous—do-it-yourself experiences happen when you *assume* things. For example, don't assume the power is off before you replace a light fixture; test the wires before you touch them. Don't assume a pipe is a certain diameter; measure it before you drive to the hardware store.

- **Pay attention.** You can never tell what piece of information might be important, so as you work, notice details. Are the electrical outlets you're replacing two pronged or three pronged? How big were the screws on that gizmo, anyhow?

- **Be safe.** Some tasks are dangerous, and things like electricity and chainsaws can kill you. Which brings us to the next item in this list.

- **Know when to call an expert.** Many nuisances around the home can be solved with patience, research, and elbow grease; don't be intimidated by replacing a light fixture or a garbage disposal. But be willing to call in a specialist for dangerous or complicated projects.

 Tip If you're interested in improving your DIY skills, take classes from your local community college or attend seminars at a home-improvement store.

Because routine maintenance is so vital, it can be helpful to draw up a checklist of annual chores. Here's one from the Mississippi State University Extension Service: *http://tinyurl.com/MS-homelist*. The National Center for Healthy Housing has a good list, too: *http://tinyurl.com/NCHH-homelist*. And for you old-school Internet fans, check out the Big List of Home Maintenance Tasks from alt.home.repair: *http://tinyurl.com/USENET-homelist*.

The Pros and Cons of Home-Equity Loans

One of the advantages of owning your home is that you can use the equity you build to meet other financial goals. Normally, this equity remains untapped, growing slowly with time. But there are a couple of ways to use your home's equity for other purposes:

- **A home-equity loan** (or HEL) is a second mortgage that generally has a fixed interest rate and a term of 10 to 15 years. Basically, it lets you borrow money from your bank using your home's equity as collateral.

- **A home-equity line of credit** (or HELOC) is also a second mortgage, but takes the form of a revolving credit account, much like a department store credit card. With one of these, you can borrow money repeatedly as long as you don't exceed the HELOC's upper limit. These loans generally have variable interest rates and a 10-year term.

Traditionally, people have used HELs and HELOCs to pay for home improvements, like remodels and additions. But you could also use them to pay medical bills, send the kids to college, or even pay off credit cards. (The recent credit crisis has put a damper on these sorts of loans; falling home values and stricter lending standards mean it's tougher to take out a second mortgage.)

Using home equity to pay off debt can be an appealing option: The interest rates on HELs and HELOCs are much lower than those on credit cards. And if you've got balances on several credit cards, it's likely that your combined card payments are higher than the single payment on a home-equity loan would be. Plus, in most cases, interest on a home-equity loan is tax deductible, just like mortgage interest.

Still, home-equity loans aren't magical cure-alls; they don't eliminate debt—they just shift it around. If you don't change the habits that led you into debt in the first place, you could end up in worse shape in the long run. And there are *serious* risks that come along with using home equity to pay down credit card debt: If something goes wrong, you could lose your house!

For more about how to tap your home's equity wisely, see *http://tinyurl.com/ MSN-equity*.

Making Mortgage Payments

Paying a mortgage is just like paying any other debt—except there's a lot more riding on it. If you don't pay your car loan, all you lose is a way to get around. But if you don't pay your mortgage, you could lose your home. So make it a priority to pay your mortgage on time and in full every month.

As you're making payments, there are a couple of things to keep in mind. First, you should get rid of private mortgage insurance as soon as possible. Second, decide whether accelerating your mortgage payments make sense for you. The next two sections have the details.

Private Mortgage Insurance

Lenders require *private mortgage insurance* (PMI) from homebuyers who take out loans for more than 80% of a property's value. So if you buy a house with a down payment of less than 20%, you'll probably have to carry PMI.

 Note If you can't afford a 20% down payment, you may be able to bypass PMI by taking out a second mortgage when you buy the house. This second loan—commonly called a *piggyback loan*—usually takes the form of a home-equity loan or a home-equity line of credit (see the box on page 213).

Though you can cancel PMI once you have 20% equity in your home (whether because home prices have increased or because you've made payments to the principal), lenders aren't required to automatically cancel PMI until you've repaid 22% of the loan. That means you need to stay on top of things so you don't keep paying for PMI any longer than you have to.

To find out whether you're paying PMI, check your most recent mortgage statement. If you are, do whatever you can to cancel it as soon as possible. Make extra mortgage payments. If home values in your area have risen, have your house re-appraised. (But note that not all lenders will drop PMI based on a new appraisal; some require you to refinance.) When you have at least 20% equity in your house, contact your lender and ask to have the PMI removed. Doing so could save you thousands of dollars.

 Tip For more on PMI, check out this article at OmniNerd.com: *http://tinyurl.com/pmi-on*.

Should you prepay your mortgage?

You can save tens of thousands of dollars by paying your mortgage off early. But is it a smart move? You won't find a definitive answer in this book or anywhere else. Ask a dozen different financial experts and you'll get a dozen different answers—literally: *http://tinyurl.com/invest-prepay*.

Why ***wouldn't*** you pay off your mortgage early? There are actually several sensible reasons you might choose to hang onto that debt:

- If you prepay in good times, there's no easy way to get that money back during bad times. The only way to "undo" prepayments is to take out a second mortgage.

- When you have a mortgage, inflation is your friend: In 30 years, your $2,000 monthly payment will seem like a $500 payment.

- No matter how much you prepay, the bank doesn't give you a break— you still have to make payments each month until the mortgage is completely paid off, even if you get sick or lose your job.

- There's an ***opportunity cost*** to prepaying your mortgage: When you send in an extra payment, you can't use that money elsewhere—such as investing in the stock market, which might give you a better return.

Despite these compelling arguments, millions of Americans prepay their mortgages. Their reasons make sense, too:

- Prepaying gives you a guaranteed return on your investment equal to whatever your mortgage rate is. That's because any time you pay down debt, you earn a return equal to the interest rate you're being charged. So if your home loan has a 6% interest rate, then paying extra on that debt is like ***earning*** 6% in a savings account. You'd be hard-pressed to find other places to earn a guaranteed 6% return!

- Prepaying gives you a safety net. While you'll still have a mortgage payment until you've paid off the loan, when you do pay it off, you'll have a huge cushion because your monthly expenses will drop by $1,000, $2,000, or even $3,000. Just think of what you could do with that cash flow!

- People who've paid off their homes feel a ***huge*** sense of relief (see *http://tinyurl.com/GRS-nomortgage*). It's freeing to not have a mortgage holding you down.

Few people would argue that prepaying your mortgage is a bad move, but there are some who don't think it's the ***best*** move. Is prepayment right for you? If you plan to stay in your home for a long time, it may be. The choice depends on your financial goals and what will make you happy.

When should you refinance your mortgage? When you can recover the costs in a reasonable amount of time, typically just a few years. The standard advice *used to* be to consider refinancing if interest rates dropped by 2%. But closing costs are lower now, and it often makes sense to refinance sooner. You'll need to run the numbers based on your own situation using a refinance calculator like the one here: *http://tinyurl.com/refi-calc*.

Strategies for prepaying your mortgage

If you've weighted the pros and cons of prepaying your mortgage and decide to go for it, there are several ways to approach it. You could:

- **Make extra payments to your mortgage each month.** This will give you a guaranteed rate of return equal to your mortgage interest rate, and will reduce the amount of interest you pay over the life of the loan. But doing this makes it difficult to get at your money if you need it for something else.

- **Make lump-sum payments to your mortgage every year.** Instead of paying a little bit every month, you could put the money in a savings account during the year and make a single, large payment every 12 months.

 Whenever you pay extra money toward your mortgage—or any other loan, for that matter—always note that you want the extra applied to principal only, not interest. (Check with your mortgage company to find out exactly how they'd like you to indicate this.) If you don't, some lenders will apply your extra payment to interest, which is lame but legal.

- **Send half the monthly amount every 2 weeks.** This is perhaps the most common way to accelerate mortgage payments. If your monthly minimum payment is $2,000, for example, you'd send $1,000 every other week. By doing this, you'd pay $26,000 a year instead of $24,000. That may not sound like much of a difference, but this strategy could trim 7 years off your loan! (Use this calculator to see how much you could save: *http://tinyurl.com/BR-biweekly*.)

If you decide on this strategy, check with your lender to see how they handle bi-weekly payments. Some aren't set up to process them, so you might have to enroll in some sort of program. Search for a free program rather than a paid one—but take the paid program if that's all that's available.

- **Put money into some other investment,** like an indexed mutual fund (which you'll learn about in Chapter 12) until you have enough to pay off your mortgage. This will, in theory, provide the highest rate of return for your money. But as with any stock-market investment, there's an element of risk. If your goal is to pay off your mortgage, a bear market (like the one in 2008) will make you sweat.

You can accelerate your mortgage payment in other ways. My wife and I chose to make a flat $2,000 monthly payment, which was $582.10 more than the minimum payment. This gave us flexibility—if we had an emergency we could drop down to a regular payment. You can read more about our plan here: *http://tinyurl.com/GRS-prepay*.

If you decide to accelerate your mortgage payments, try to do it on your own. Banks often charge a fee to add this as a service, but you can usually do it yourself for free.

11 Death and Taxes

"In this world nothing can be said to be certain, except death and taxes."
—Benjamin Franklin

Taxes and insurance are topics so dull that even the keenest reader feels her eyes glaze over. But they're important—very important. With a basic understanding of taxes and insurance, you can make better decisions about other parts of your financial life and avoid costly mistakes.

This chapter won't give you all the answers—for that you should consult a professional financial adviser. But it **will** give you the basic info you need to deal with taxes and insurance effectively. It also provides a very brief overview of estate planning. Ignore this info at your peril!

An Introduction to Insurance

Insurance is a way to manage risk. As you go about your life, there's always a chance that you'll be in a car accident, twist your knee, or that your house will burn down. The risk of these accidents is small, but if one of them *were* to happen, the effects could be catastrophic. Without insurance, you'd have to come up with the money on your own to repair your car, have knee surgery, or rebuild your home.

Although these things happen to some people, they don't happen to everyone. With enough data, it's possible to know roughly how many people are likely to experience these events—and how much recovering from them will cost. Using this info, an insurance company can spread the risk among all its customers.

Here's an example: Imagine a school with 100 students. Every year for the past 25 years, one student has broken an arm in the schoolyard, resulting in about $5,000 in medical expenses. Without insurance, every family would have to save $5,000 to cope with the odds that their child would be the one with the broken arm. At the end of the year, 99 families would have paid nothing (and have $5,000 in savings), but one family would have paid $5,000 (and have nothing left).

With insurance, the families could join together to spread out the risk. If they created an insurance fund, all 100 families would pay $50 at the start of the school year. This $5,000 would then go to the family of the child with the broken arm.

By spreading the risk, each family only has to save $50 instead of $5,000. Yes, that $50 is gone if it's not *your* child who breaks an arm, but for most people, that's an acceptable trade. Instead of having to scrape together the full $5,000, they'd rather risk losing $50 for a chance to avoid $5,000 in medical bills.

But is it really fair to have every family pay $50 into the insurance fund? Some kids go to the library at lunch and read books while their classmates are climbing around on the jungle gym. The bookworms are much less likely to break an arm. And maybe the 25 years of data show that girls break their arms less often than boys. With enough info, the playground insurance fund could charge each family a different rate depending on how likely their child is to break an arm.

Insurance is a bit like gambling: You're betting a little money now because you think odds are good that you'll need a larger payout in the future. But there's one huge difference between gambling and insurance: Gamblers *seek* risk in an attempt to get more money; when you buy insurance, your goal is to *reduce* risk so you don't lose money.

In fact, gambling casinos and insurance companies make use of the same statistical laws, especially the Law of Large Numbers, which says that the more you have of something, the more likely the characteristics of that something will tend toward average. The more people who roll the dice, for instance, the better the casino can predict its earnings. And the more people in an insurance fund, the more accurately the insurance company can predict its losses.

Most of the time, using insurance to spread risk is a good thing. That's why most states require car insurance, and why smart folks keep homeowners insurance even after their mortgage is paid off. But insurance can be expensive, especially if you have too much or the wrong kinds. Let's look at some ways to keep your insurance costs down.

 Note Wikipedia has a great article about insurance and how it works: *http://tinyurl.com/ ins-wiki*. The history section is especially interesting.

General Insurance Tips

All insurance works pretty much the same way: You pay a *premium* (a set amount of money) to the insurance company, usually on some sort of schedule (monthly or yearly, for instance). In return, they issue you a *policy*, which is a contract that gives you certain *coverage*, or financial protection. When you suffer an insured *loss*, you file a *claim* and the company pays you a *benefit*.

Insurance is meant to protect against catastrophes, not day-to-day annoyances. You use insurance to protect yourself from things that aren't likely, but which would cause financial hardship if they did happen.

Your goal should be to have just the right amount of insurance. If you have too much, you're wasting money. For example, if you have a $50 deductible on your car insurance, you'll probably end up paying the insurance company more in monthly premiums than they'll ever pay you in benefits. (The following list explains deductibles.) Or if you're young, unmarried, and have tons of credit-card debt, life insurance usually isn't a good place to put your money.

On the other hand, if you're a 40-year-old small-business owner and father of three, life insurance could be an excellent way to hedge against the risk that you'll die tomorrow. Or if you're a millionaire who likes to drive fast, increasing the limits on your automobile liability coverage could save your fortune if you get sued for damage you cause.

The number one thing you can do to save on insurance is to **self-insure as much as you can afford** (see box on page 223). You can also save by reviewing your coverage from time to time, and following these suggestions:

- **Shop around.** To find better rates, harness the power of the Web. Visit the National Association of Insurance Commissioners (*www.naic.org*) and click the "states and jurisdictions" link to find your state's insurance department. From there, you can find info about your state's insurance laws and, in some cases, get quotes. You can also get quotes from multiple insurance carriers at sites like Insweb.com, Insurance.com, and Insure.com.

- **Buy only what you need.** Insurance agents are happy to sell you more coverage than your situation calls for. So do some research before you buy. Figure out how much and what kind of insurance you need, and don't let the agent talk you into more.

- **Raise your deductible.** The *deductible* is the amount you pay on a loss before the insurance company kicks in money. For instance, if your car suffers $400 in damage and you have a $250 deductible, you pay the first $250 and your insurance company pays the rest. It's up to you where to set the deductible, but the lower your deductible, the higher your monthly premiums. Ask yourself how much you can afford to pay if something goes wrong; more specifically, how much is *too* much? Set your deductible just below "too much."

- **Consolidate.** Insurance companies often give a discount if you have multiple policies with them. Plus, this saves you the hassle of having to pay more than one company.

- **Read your policy.** As with all legal contracts, it's important that you read your policy so you know what's covered and what isn't. Pay attention to policy changes that come in the mail. If you have questions, ask. And make it a habit to review your policies every so often to be sure you understand them (and to check whether anything has changed).

- **Don't duplicate coverage.** Know which policies provide which benefits. If you have a AAA membership, for example, you don't need towing insurance on your auto policy. And if your credit card doubles the warranties on the things you buy, don't pay for extended warranties.

- **File fewer claims.** Don't nickel-and-dime your insurance company. If you file claims for every little thing, they'll raise your rates. Insurance is meant to cover unexpected *big* losses, not every ding your car gets from shopping carts.

- **Take care of the things you insure.** One of the best forms of insurance is routine maintenance. A well-maintained car is less likely to have an accident due to mechanical failure. If you take care of your house, it'll weather the ravages of time. And if you exercise and eat right, you'll get cheaper life and health insurance.

These tips can help you save on most types of insurance. Still, not all insurance advice can be generalized; each type of insurance has its quirks. Let's look at specific ways to save on three common types of insurance: auto, home, and life.

Your Money and Your Life

The Best Insurance Is Self-Insurance

Warranties are a form of insurance: When something is under a warranty, the store or company you bought it from will fix or replace the item if it breaks or malfunctions during a specific period of time.

Warranties may seem like a good deal, but according to the *Washington Post* (*http://tinyurl.com/WP-unwarranted*), Americans paid $15 billion for warranties in 2004. Of every $100 spent on extended warranties, only $20 was paid out in claims. So when you buy an extended warranty, you're basically throwing away 80% of your money.

Fortunately, there's a better way to protect yourself—*and* lower your overall insurance costs: Instead of paying somebody else to insure your new TV, computer, or digital camera, pay yourself! Open a named savings account (see page 142) and call it something like Personal Insurance. Then funnel money into the account whenever you find a way to save on insurance elsewhere.

For example, use self-insurance to replace service contracts and extended warranties. Take the amount you would have paid the store and put it into this savings account instead. The best part of this plan is that if you don't end up needing the money you've set away for self-insurance to fix stuff, you can use it for other things; if you'd paid for an extended warranty, that money would be long gone.

Self-insurance isn't just a good strategy for appliances. Try raising the deductibles on your auto and home insurance policies. Then take the difference between your old premiums and your new premiums and put it into your self-insurance account every month. It won't take long for you to have more than enough to cover the deductible.

It's worth paying for insurance to protect against life's catastrophes. But for smaller stuff like appliances and minor car accidents, self-insurance is usually the way to go.

Car Insurance

You've had car insurance since you were old enough to drive, but how much do you really know about it? At its heart, your policy probably contains a few basic types of coverage:

- In most states, you at least need to have **liability insurance**, which covers the cost of any damage you do to other people or things with your car. (But note that liability insurance *doesn't* cover injuries to you or other people on your policy; for that, you need PIP insurance, which we'll cover in a moment.)

  Insurance companies quote liability coverage as a series of three numbers, like 50/200/25. The first number is how much, in thousands of dollars, the policy will pay for each person (besides you) injured in an accident ($50,000 in this example). The second number is the total that the policy covers for each accident ($200,000 here). And the last number tells how much property damage will be reimbursed ($25,000 in this case).

 Tip Many experts recommend carrying liability coverage equal to your *net worth*—the total value of everything you own. This can be expensive to do on individual policies. Instead, it may be more cost effective to buy an *umbrella policy*, which gives you extra liability coverage above what your home and auto policies provide.

- **Collision insurance**, as you can probably guess, covers damage to your car when it hits (or gets hit by) another vehicle or object. But because collisions aren't the only way your car can get banged up, **comprehensive insurance** covers damage from events other than collisions: floods, fire, theft, and so on. Collision and comprehensive coverage make more sense for newer vehicles, and are generally required if you're still making payments on your car. They're less necessary—and may actually be a waste of money—on older cars.

- **Personal injury protection (PIP) insurance** is sometimes called "no-fault" insurance, and is required in certain states. It covers medical costs (and possibly lost wages) if you're injured in an accident. It may also cover passengers and pedestrians.

- **Uninsured motorist insurance** covers you and your passengers if you're in an accident caused by a driver who doesn't have insurance. It also covers hit-and-run accidents.

Tip For more on the different types of auto insurance coverage, check out this handy page of definitions: *http://tinyurl.com/cins-def.*

Every year, you spend hundreds—maybe even thousands—on car insurance, and chances are, you're paying too much. The August 2008 issue of *Consumer Reports* estimated that the average family could save $65 per month by shopping around for car insurance. Here are some other ways to lower your costs:

- **Ditch towing coverage.** Towing—or "emergency roadside service," as it's sometimes called—is an easy cost to self-insure (see page 223). You likely pay $10–$30 a year for towing insurance, and one tow costs $100. (If you're in an accident, towing is usually covered under collision, but check with your insurance company to be sure.) Sometimes your car *will* break down, but if it's well maintained, that won't happen often.

Tip If the value of your car has dropped so low that a major repair would cost the same as replacing it, consider dropping your comprehensive and collision coverage. Then use your savings on premiums to boost your self-insurance fund (see page 223).

- **Plan ahead.** Check on insurance *before* you buy your next car. Insurance costs are based on how likely a vehicle is to be stolen, damaged, or to inflict damage, and how badly occupants tend to get injured in accidents. Repair and replacement costs are also factors. Many insurance companies list cars with lower insurance costs on their websites.

- **Watch your credit.** As mentioned in Chapter 8, most insurance companies now look at parts of your credit report to determine your premiums. They can't adjust rates on your current car if you pay on time and in full, but anytime you add a new vehicle, its premiums are affected by your credit.

Tip If your credit has improved since you bought your car, ask your insurance company to re-check your credit score and see if they'll lower your premium.

- **Don't pay monthly.** Insurance companies charge a few bucks each month for monthly billing. To avoid that fee, pay every 6 months or even once a year, if possible. If you have to pay monthly, use their autopay program, which costs less because they don't have to send you a paper bill unless your premium changes.

Though it'll always cost more to insure a new Corvette than a Corolla, one of the best ways to keep costs low is to keep your driving record clean. Insurance companies charge you based on how likely you are to file a claim—and accidents are the biggest source of claims. Some insurance companies offer discounts for taking safe-driving courses. Others give low-mileage discounts—the less you're on the road, the safer you are. So be sure to ask about all the discounts you qualify for.

Homeowners Insurance

Your home is probably the most valuable thing you own. Plus, it's filled with all of your Stuff. If your house burned down or got burgled, that would certainly qualify as a financial catastrophe—which is exactly what insurance is designed to avert. It's impossible to give a specific figure since everyone's situation is different, but you should carry enough insurance on your home to protect you in case of just such a disaster.

Homeowners insurance policies have three main parts:

- **Dwelling coverage** insures your home in case it's damaged or destroyed. You want a *guaranteed replacement cost* policy, which requires the insurance company to fully rebuild your home. (Other policy types may not offer enough coverage.) But you don't need a policy that covers the full resale value of your property, since that includes your land, which doesn't need to be insured.

- **Personal property coverage** insures the Stuff inside your house, like clothes and furniture, and usually also insures the personal property you have with you while you're away from home. Your insurance can be for either *actual cash value* (how much your things are currently worth) or *replacement cost* (how much it would cost to buy them new). The latter is your best bet: You should carry insurance that would pay you to replace your belongings, not pay you based on what the insurance company thinks they're worth.

 Tip To help settle claims in case of a disaster, keep a record of the things you own (including receipts for expensive items). Use your digital camera to create a photo (or video) inventory of your Stuff, and keep a written record somewhere safe or use an online tool like KnowYourStuff.org or StuffSafe.com.

Some people buy *floater policies* to cover things like jewelry and antiques. Before doing this, check your personal property coverage—you may already have enough insurance to cover these kinds of items. (In order to be covered, your policy may require you to notify your insurance company if you have over a certain amount.)

- **Liability coverage** protects you if somebody is hurt on your property and sues you. Most policies cover you off your property, as well. You should have at least as much coverage as your net worth, and some experts say you should have *twice* your net worth. If someone trips on your doorstep and breaks his collarbone, say, he just might follow through on his threat to sue you for everything you own.

Most homeowners policies contain other pieces, like insurance for loss of use (which covers you if you have to live elsewhere while your home is being repaired). It's important to review your policy every year or so to be sure you have the right amount of coverage. (If you want disaster insurance for earthquakes, floods, or hurricanes, you'll have to ask your insurance agent how to get it; it's usually not part of a standard homeowners policy.)

To lower the cost of homeowners insurance, follow the general insurance tips on page 221, and take steps to reduce the risk of fire and theft: Keep fire extinguishers in your home, install modern smoke detectors, and even consider adding an automatic sprinkler system. Put deadbolts on the doors, and, if you can afford it, install a burglar alarm. If you have an older home, modernize your electrical and plumbing systems. Once you've made safety improvements, contact your insurance company and ask them to review your policy.

 Tip For more money-saving ideas, check out this advice from the Insurance Information Institute: *http://tinyurl.com/homeins.*

Life Insurance

In Chapter 6, you learned that your job is your second most important financial asset right after your health. Your income provides food and shelter for your family, and helps fund future plans. But what would happen to your family financially if you died? If the loss of your income would be a catastrophe for them, you need life insurance.

Tip Life-insurance premiums have fallen dramatically over the past decade. If you bought a policy during the 1990s, it's worth checking prices again today. The August 2008 issue of *Consumer Reports* found the average person could save over $100 per month by "refinancing" their life insurance—buying a new, cheaper policy. If you do find cheaper insurance, don't cancel your existing policy until the new one is in place.

The two basic types of life insurance are:

- **Term insurance**, which gives you coverage for a set period of time (the *term*), like 5 years, 25 years, or whatever (you can choose from different terms). As with car or home insurance, you decide how much coverage you want (more on that in a minute), and then pay an annual premium. Unless you buy *level* term insurance, your premiums start out small and get higher as time passes. If you die during the term, the policy's beneficiaries (usually your family) receive an income-tax-free payout.

- **Cash-value insurance** (officially called *permanent insurance*), which is similar to term insurance but lasts your entire life, not just for a fixed term. Common types of cash-value insurance include *whole life, variable life,* and *universal life.* Each of these adds an investment component to the policy that accumulates a cash value, which you can borrow against, re-claim if you cancel the policy, or eventually use to pay premiums.

Cash-value insurance sounds like a better deal, right? It lasts your whole life instead of just for a few years, and the insurance company invests some of your premiums so you can use them later. Not so fast. When you purchase permanent insurance, you're most likely committing an insurance sin: buying coverage you don't need. Term life insurance is usually the best choice for a number of reasons.

First, most people don't actually need permanent life insurance. Your need for life insurance tends to fade as you grow older and your family is no longer dependant on your income. So if you take out a permanent policy, you may be paying for life insurance when you no longer need it.

Second, the investment part of a cash-value policy isn't usually a good deal. After all, you don't buy a savings account with your auto insurance policy, so why would you do so with your life insurance? Keep your insurance and investments separate. If you want to invest, there are better ways to do it. (See Chapters 12 and 13 for investing info.) Don't buy life insurance as an investment.

Lastly and most importantly, cash-value insurance is *much* more expensive than term—five to 20 times more expensive! You could probably buy 30 years' worth of term coverage (which is all you really need) for the same cost as buying 5 years' of a cash-value policy.

 Tip For $75, the Consumer Federation of America (*http://tinyurl.com/CF-Linsurance*) will evaluate a cash-value policy—one you already own or one you're thinking about buying—to find the "true" investment returns. This fee may seem high, but it's cheaper than paying for insurance you don't need.

That said, cash-value policies do make sense for some people. If you have a high income, will leave behind a multi-million-dollar estate, or own a small business, cash-value insurance might be worth a look—*if* you think you'll have it for 20 years or more. Whatever you do, don't ask an insurance salesman for advice; *of course* he'll tell you to buy it. Instead, find an independent financial adviser and ask her about your options.

The bottom line: For most people, the best choice is guaranteed renewable term life insurance. (*Guaranteed renewable* means that as long as you keep paying your premiums, the insurance company can't cancel your policy.)

 Tip Any time you make a major life change like getting married or divorced, don't forget to change the beneficiary on important legal documents like your life insurance policy, retirement accounts, and will.

How much life insurance do you need?

Not everyone needs life insurance. Like all insurance, it's designed to prevent financial catastrophes. So you only need it if other people—like your spouse and children—depend on your income. You need it less when you're older because your kids will be on their own and you won't have any debts (presumably, anyway).

Specifically, life insurance is valuable if you have kids living at home; have a spouse whose income alone couldn't support your family's lifestyle; have large debts (like a mortgage); are wealthy and might be subject to estate taxes; or own a business. If any of these describe your situation, then life insurance is a good idea. If none of them apply to you, then you don't really need it.

How much life insurance should you buy? Different experts give different answers. Some say your policy should cover five times your annual income, others say 10. And in *The Money Book for the Young, Fabulous & Broke*, Suze Orman recommends *20* times your annual income. The truth is there's no hard-and-fast rule.

 Tip For a little help coming up with a coverage amount, use this handy online calculator from the nonprofit LIFE Foundation: *http://tinyurl.com/lins-calc*.

Rather than base your life insurance coverage on your income, it makes more sense to base it on what your survivors will need to pay their expenses. Think about why you want the insurance in the first place: Is it to pay off the mortgage? To fund your spouse's retirement? To send the kids to college? Then get enough insurance to do that. You can comparison shop for insurance at sites like AccuQuote.com, DirectInsuranceServices.com, and SelectQuote.com.

 Note A brief word about *disability insurance*: You're *far* more likely to become disabled than to die prematurely, and the loss of income is just as real. Even if you're smart and pay yourself first by saving 10% of your income (see page 145), just 6 months' of unemployment can wipe out 5 years' of saving. So if you need your salary to live on, you should get disability insurance. This topic is beyond the scope of this book, but you can learn about choosing and buying disability insurance at *http://tinyurl.com/GRS-disability*.

What You Need to Know About Taxes

There's no way to cover the complexity that is U.S. tax law in just a few pages, and it would be foolish to try. Your accountant has spent *years* working with the tax code, and even she needs to use reference books. Instead, this section describes the basics of how income tax works and gives you some useful info on how to make smart tax moves.

How Income Tax Works

The basic federal income tax structure is pretty simple, but there are layers and layers of laws that make it complicated. At its core, the tax system involves the following steps:

1. At the end of the year, you tally your total income from taxable sources. (Some income, like that from child support, isn't taxable.)

2. You subtract certain allowable sums known as *adjustments*—like **IRA contributions** and **moving expenses**—to find your *adjusted gross income*, or AGI. (Your AGI, which is shown on line 37 of tax Form 1040, is a key number, and comes up again and again in tax discussions.)

 Tip The front page of Form 1040 lists adjustments; you can read more about them at *www.irs.gov/taxtopics/tc450.html*.

From your AGI, you subtract *deductions* (allowances for living expenses) and *exemptions* (deductions for you and your dependents) to find your *taxable income*. (The back page of Form 1040 lists deductions and exemptions.) You can claim either the standard deduction (a single number that increases every year to account for inflation—see *www.irs.gov/taxtopics/tc551.html*) or individual itemized deductions (like mortgage interest and charitable contributions—see *www.irs.gov/taxtopics/tc500.html*).

3. After you calculate your taxable income, you check to see how much tax you're liable for (the box on page 233 explains how tax rates work).

4. You can reduce your tax liability through certain *tax credits*, which you qualify for by doing things like adopting a child or buying your first home. (The government usually gives tax credits for actions it wants to encourage.)

5. The final step is to calculate how much you owe, if any. Because you pay taxes throughout the year (through paycheck withholding, for instance), you have to subtract what you've already paid from your tax liability. If you've paid more than your liability, you get a refund; if not, you owe the difference.

When you get hired for a job, you fill out a Form W-4, which tells your employer how much tax to withhold from your paychecks. In theory, the money withheld should be enough to cover your income-tax liability, but this isn't always the case.

Maybe you made a mistake on your W-4 or have other sources of income (like a side business or a *capital gain* from selling stocks). Or say you got a big bonus in one paycheck and your company withheld too much. Whatever the case, it's unlikely that, at the end of the year, you'll find that your employer took out *exactly* the right amount of taxes. If you paid too much, the government owes you a refund. If you paid too little, you owe the government the difference between what you should have paid and what you've already paid.

Nobody likes to pay taxes, and some people get upset when they find they have taxes due. But your tax bill shouldn't come as a surprise—you can (and should) keep track of your tax liability throughout the year. If you're blindsided by a big tax bill at the end of the year, it's because you didn't think ahead. Advance planning is the best way to avoid such tax trauma.

Tax-Trimming Tips

You don't have to like taxes, but you *do* have to pay them. Fortunately, there are a few ways to legally trim your tax bill. One is to take all the deductions (page 231) you're entitled to. The following sections explain other ways to pay Uncle Sam a little less.

 Tip The best way to arm yourself for dealing with taxes is to get educated. That doesn't mean you have to become a tax professional, but try to get a *basic* understanding of tax laws. Go to the library and borrow a book on preparing your own taxes, and spend a couple of hours reading it. This may be boring, but it'll pay off in the long run.

Know what you owe

To many people, taxes are a sort of black box: They don't know how taxes are calculated, so they have too much or too little withheld from their paychecks. Having too much withheld usually isn't a problem—it just means you get a big refund. But people can get awfully get upset when they owe more than they were expecting at the end of the year; they feel like the government is doing something sneaky and is tricking them out of their money.

You don't need to be surprised by what you owe come tax time. Most of the tax info is available at the start of the year—you just have to find it.

For instance, it's worth taking a little time to look at your tax situation at the beginning of the year so you can get your withholding amount right. To figure out how much your employer should withhold from each paycheck, you can use an online calculator like those at *http://tinyurl.com/IRS-calc* or *http://tinyurl.com/PCC-calc*. If you discover that your employer is withholding too much or too little, file a revised Form W-4 to adjust the amount.

 Tip You can download great, *free* income-tax planning spreadsheets from *www.taxvisor. com/taxes* (scroll to the bottom for download links), which help you estimate out how much you'll owe in taxes so you're not surprised at the end of the year.

Marginal Tax Rates

Not all of your income is taxed the same; as you earn more, you pay more taxes. Your *marginal tax rate* is what you're taxed on the last dollar you earned. Confused? Here's a concrete example.

For the 2009 tax year, these were the tax rates for single filers making up to $171,550:

Taxable Income	2009 Tax Rates
Up to $8,350	10%
$8,351–$33,950	15%
$33,951–$82,250	25%
$82,251–$171,550	28%

Based on this table, if Gillian is single and had a taxable income of $100,000 in 2009, her marginal tax rate is 28%. However, this doesn't mean that *all* of her income is taxed at 28%—only the amount over $82,250 is taxed at that level. The fancy way to say this is that Gillian's income is taxed *progressively* at each bracket up to her marginal rate. That sounds confusing, but it's actually not so bad once you know what it means. Here's the breakdown:

- The first $8,350 of Gillian's $100,000 income is taxed at 10% (see the table), so she owes $835 in taxes on that portion of her income.
- The next $25,600 of her income (the amount from $8,351 to $33,950) is taxed at 15%, meaning she owes $3,840 in taxes on it.
- The next $48,300 of her income (the amount from $33,951 to $82,250) is taxed at 25%, so she owes $12,075 in taxes on it.
- The final $17,750 of her income (the amount from $82,251 to $100,000) is taxed at 28%, so she owes $4,970 in taxes on it.

Because Gillian earns $100,000 of taxable income, she's said to be in the 28% *tax bracket* based on the percentage she's taxed on the last dollar she earns. But as you can see above, most of her income is actually taxed at lower rates. In fact, she ended up owing a total of $21,720 in taxes in 2009, which means her *effective tax rate* was only 21.72%. (And her rate could actually be lower if she had any deductions and exemptions—see page 231.)

This info may seem esoteric and unimportant, but understanding marginal tax rates can help you make decisions when investing or taking out a mortgage. Knowing about marginal rates can also help you understand why statements like, "If I take a second job, I won't benefit because it'll just push me into the next tax bracket" aren't true. As long as there's no 100% tax bracket, there's *always* a benefit to earning more money. To explore tax rates over time, check out this interactive calculator: *http://tinyurl.com/usa-taxes*.

Shift income and expenses

In some cases, you can save on taxes by shifting income from one year to the next. This doesn't work if you have a steady paycheck, but it can make a difference if you're self-employed or get paid irregularly. Say, for instance, you had more than usual income in 2009—enough to bump you up a tax bracket. In that case, if you were planning to sell some stocks, you might put it off until 2010 because you figure your marginal tax rate (see the box on page 233) will be lower then.

You can apply this same principle elsewhere on your taxes. For example, you can use some expenses for itemized deductions if they're high enough. If you have medical expenses that total more than 7.5% of your AGI (page 231) in a given year, for instance, you can deduct the amount that's over 7.5% of your AGI. To get above that amount, it can make sense to bunch medical expenses into a single year.

 Note While it's good to look for clever ways like this to reduce your taxes, never make life decisions based solely on the tax consequences. Don't put off heart surgery just to save on taxes, for instance.

Hire a pro

Some people are reluctant to hire others to do their taxes. If your taxes are really simple and you're good with numbers, then you may not need to hire a tax professional.

 Tip If you do your own taxes, you might be able to use Free File, a program that lets many U.S. taxpayers file their tax returns electronically at no cost. (For the 2009 tax year, you can only use Free File if you made less than $57,000.) For more info, check out *http://tinyurl.com/IRS-freefile*.

But even if you like doing your own taxes to save money or because you think it's kind of fun (some people do!), it still might be worth hiring a pro. Professional tax advisers include tax attorneys, certified public accountants, tax preparers, and enrolled agents. To learn more about the different kinds of tax professionals, see *http://tinyurl.com/taxfolks*.

I used to do my own taxes. Then one year, as an experiment, I paid an accountant to do my taxes *and* did them on my own. The accountant earned back far more than his fee by cutting my tax bill below what I thought was due. Now I pay him every year, and I'm happy to do so.

Tip If you decide to hire someone to do your taxes, give yourself plenty of time—don't wait until April 1st to start looking!

The more complicated your taxes are, the more likely you need a pro's help. And remember that things you do throughout the year (not just at tax time) can have an impact on your taxes. So don't try to manage your money in ways that are out of your league. This is especially important before you make any big transactions (like giving money to your cousin Jim or selling a business). If you're not careful, you can run up your tax bill quickly without knowing it. If you don't understand the tax implications of a particular money move, ask a financial adviser for advice.

Don't cheat

Whatever you do, never, ever cheat on your taxes—it's not worth it. Getting upset about owing money doesn't do any good; just pay your taxes and move on. Still, you should absolutely do what you can to pay only the amount you're legally obligated to pay. Take all of the deductions you're entitled to. And remember: If you owe a lot, it means you had a good year.

 Tip If you don't like how high your taxes are or how they're being spent, take it up with your local politicians, not your tax professional— and *definitely* not the IRS.

Other moves

One of the best tax moves you can make is to save for retirement by putting money into a 401(k) or an IRA. These accounts (which you'll explore in detail in Chapter 13) are tax advantaged, meaning either contributions or withdrawals are tax free, and the money in the accounts grows tax free.

If you itemize deductions, donating to charity is another smart tax tactic. For example, you can donate your old car instead of trading it in. That way you do some good in the world, avoid the hassle of dealing with a dealership, *and* get a tax break.

Finally, every year, visit the IRS website (*www.irs.gov*) or ask your tax professional to learn about any new tax credits or deductions you may qualify for. If you bought a home in 2009, for example, you may be eligible for an $8,000 first-time homebuyer's credit.

Avoiding Audits

It's one of the most dreaded phrases in the English language: "You're being audited." Each year, about 1% of American taxpayers get audited. When the IRS audits you, they review your tax return to confirm that everything is correct. Fortunately, if you have an average income and a normal tax return, you don't have much to worry about. (But the IRS always audits a certain number of people at random, so no one is *totally* safe.)

Most returns are processed by IRS computers programmed to watch for anything odd. An item that falls outside the norm may be "flagged" so that an IRS employee can review it to see if there's actually a need for an audit. Common ways to raise red flags with the IRS include:

- **Incomplete or sloppy returns.** Math errors and missing info make the IRS cranky. If the agency's computers can't make sense of what you file, they'll flag your return. And make sure all your info is the same on both your federal and state returns.

- **Unreported income.** This is a no-brainer: If you file a return but don't report all your income, you're headed for trouble. You have to report *all* your interest, dividends, and other income.

- **Abnormal income.** If your income is suspiciously low or high, you're five times more likely to be audited. And if your income changes drastically from year to year, that may raise a flag, too.

- **Lots of itemized deductions.** There's nothing wrong with claiming all the deductions you're entitled to, but be aware that if you have a lot, you're more likely to be audited.

- **Being self-employed.** Filing a Schedule C ("Profit or Loss from Business" form) doesn't guarantee you'll get audited, but the IRS doesn't like to see small business show losses year after year while you have a regular job (*http://tinyurl.com/ IRS-hobby*). Home offices are a huge red flag, as are unlikely business deductions (no, that Nintendo Wii is *not* a business expense).

Honesty is the best defense against audits: Save your receipts, report all your income, and don't try to fudge things. If you're nervous about getting things right, use tax preparation software or hire a tax professional. But even if you have a pro prepare your return, review it for obvious errors. For more suggestions, check out MSN Money's page devoted to avoiding audits: *http://tinyurl.com/no-audit*.

What To Do If You Can't Pay Uncle Sam

If you have a rough year, you may discover that you can't afford to pay your taxes. It happens. In fact, it happens often enough that the IRS has very specific instructions about what to do if you're unable to pay.

First and most important, *file your tax return!* Just because you can't pay your whole tax bill doesn't mean you don't have to send in the paperwork. (If you can't complete a return, then file an *extension: http://tinyurl.com/ IRS-extension.*)

Next, pay as much as you can as soon as you can. This will reduce what you'll have to pay in penalties and interest. The IRS will then send you a bill for the balance—and will continue to do so as you make regular payments.

Finally, if you're *really* pinched, you can use Form 9465 (*http://tinyurl.com/ IRS-installment*) to set up an installment agreement—a payment plan, in other words—with the IRS. They can't turn down your request for an installment agreement if you owe less than $10,000, have paid your taxes on time for the past 5 years, you plan to pay the balance in less than 3 years, and you agree to cooperate with the IRS. (You also have to pledge to pay future taxes on time.)

 Tip You can read more about tax payment options at the IRS website: *www.irs.gov/ taxtopics/tc202.html.*

The Pros and Cons of Refunds

Every year, millions of Americans choose to have their employers withhold more than necessary from their paychecks so they'll get a tax refund at the end of the year. These people think of it as a sort of forced savings plan: If they money isn't in their paychecks, they can't spend it. Many experts hate this, and they've got some good arguments:

- **"You're giving the government an interest-free loan!"** This may not bother you—some people like letting the government use their money for a year.

- **"You're cheating yourself out of cash flow!"** If you get a refund, it's because you had too much withheld from your paychecks. For some, this money could make a real difference in their day-to-day lives. If your cash flow is tight *and* you get a big refund, you're probably better off adjusting your withholding by filing a new Form W-4. (See page 54 to learn more about the importance of cash flow.)

- **"You could invest that money at a higher rate of return!"** If the government has your money until you get your refund, you can't put that cash in a savings account, a mutual fund, or CD where it can earn interest.

With so many clear reasons *not* to get a tax refund, why do it at all? Mostly because it's a fantastic psychological trick—it's a way to force yourself to save. By having the money automatically taken out of your paycheck so you can't touch it, you can accumulate a few hundred (or even thousand) dollars every year.

I won't tell you this is a bad idea. For years, I did the same thing. I looked forward to every March because I knew that meant a big refund—which was my *only* form of savings. But now I save year-round, which is a much better tactic. As described in Chapter 7, you can "pay yourself first" by having cash from your checking account automatically put into a savings account at a different bank. This is just like using a tax refund as a forced savings plan except that you have more control over the money.

Tip Wondering when your refund will arrive? The IRS has a web page that makes it quick and easy to check the status of your refund: *http://tinyurl.com/refund-check*. You just have to provide your Social Security number, marital status, and exact refund amount.

If you get a big refund every year, consider filling out a new W-4 so that less is withheld from your paychecks. Basically, this spreads your refund out over the whole year (which is a good thing as long as you have the discipline to use this money wisely). But if a large refund makes you happy and helps you to save, then do it. Just be aware that there are better financial options when you're ready for them.

On the Money

Organizing Tax Documents

When preparing your taxes (or having someone else do them for you), it can be tough to gather up all the paperwork you need. Tax-related documents can show up any time of year, not just in the winter, and it's easy to lose important papers. Here's a simple way to keep them all together:

Every January, take a manila folder and label it with the year—"Taxes 2010," for example. Then during the year, put all your tax-related documents in the folder: investment statements, tax forms, mortgage info, receipts for charitable donations, and so on. If you'll need it to do your taxes, put it in the folder. Be sure to keep the folder someplace safe. That way, at the end of the year, it's a snap to sort these papers and submit them to your tax professional.

Where to Get More Tax Info

There's no room in this book to cover important topics like estimated taxes (*www.fairmark.com/estimate/*) and capital gains. If you need more info, go to your local library and borrow one of those gigantic tax guides like the ones from J.K. Lasser or Ernst & Young; they look like phone books and are **packed** with info. Or dig around online at tax-related sites like:

- The IRS web site (irs.gov) is surprisingly useful. It offers a library of forms and publications, an extensive list of frequently asked questions, and info on how to file for an extension. You may want to start at the Tax Topic Index: *www.irs.gov/taxtopics*.

- BankRate.com publishes an annual tax guide (*http://tinyurl.com/BR-taxguide*) that includes a handy tax calendar, forms and charts, and tips on a variety of tax topics.

- There are all kinds of useful, tax-related spreadsheets tucked on the Web. You can find two of the best at *http://tinyurl.com/tax-ss* and *www.taxvisor.com/taxes*.

- June Walker (*www.junewalkeronline.com*) has created a site filled with tax and financial advice for the self-employed.

If you really need help, your best bet is to get advice from a professional tax adviser. Yes, it'll cost money, but you'll usually find it's worth the fee—and then some.

A Brief Overview of Estate Planning

Nobody likes to think about death—especially their own. Most people don't think about creating wills until they hit middle age. But you can't always see death coming and, in addition to the emotional trauma, it can wreak financial havoc on your family.

You can make things a little easier for your family and friends by planning ahead and creating a will. A will is for anyone who wants to distribute their money and possessions according to some plan. (All that you own, including physical property and investments, is known as your **estate**. An **estate plan** is a strategy for passing your money and Stuff on to your heirs.)

Wills are extremely important. They give clear, legally-binding instructions about what you want done with your assets. Simply telling your relatives what you want to happen after you die isn't enough.

Note If you die without a valid will or living trust (lawyers call this dying *intestate*), your state's laws determine what happens to your property. Generally, your Stuff will go to your spouse and children or other closest heirs, which may not be what you intended. To have your wishes respected, you *have to* create a will.

Depending on your situation, you may need something more than just a simple will. Here's a rundown of a few of the most common estate-planning documents:

- A **will** (also called a *last will and testament*) lets you decide who inherits your property (both land and personal possessions). This is also where you designate who you want to be your children's guardian. MSN Money has a good article on mistakes to avoid when preparing a will: *http://tinyurl.com/MSN-willmistakes*.

- A **living will** (or *advance medical directive*) lets you tell your family what to do if you're incapacitated and terminally ill. This is the kind of document you need if you don't want to be kept alive on life support. The Mayo Clinic has more info on living wills at *http://tinyurl.com/LW-mayoc*.

 Note You may also want to draw up a *power of attorney*, which gives another person the legal authority to act on your behalf if you're incapacitated. For more info, visit *http://tinyurl.com/AARP-poa*.

- A **living trust** (or *revocable trust*) can help your survivors avoid *probate*, the court process used to pay your debts and distribute your property to the people who inherit it. (Some living trusts also reduce taxes or protect financial privacy.) The older and wealthier you are, the more likely you can benefit from having a trust. (But note that, even if you have a living trust, you still need a will.) You can learn more about living trusts here: *http://tinyurl.com/NOLO-livtr*.

Not everyone needs a living will or a living trust, but most folks should have a will. They're the best place to note that you want certain family heirlooms to go to specific people. If you're married and have children only by your spouse, your will can be pretty simple. (If your kids are minors, you may want to specify a legal guardian.)

The need for a will increases significantly in more complex situations: multiple marriages, multiple children by multiple partners, mixed families, and so on. You'll reduce hardships and hurt feelings in the future if you're clear in your will about what you want to happen to your property and what you want to do for specific people.

Drawing up a Will

Though modern software and various websites let you draft simple estate planning documents yourself (see the box below), you're usually better off hiring an attorney to do it for you—especially if you have complex finances. (As comedian Jerry Seinfeld says, "A lawyer is basically the person that knows the rules of the country. We're all throwing the dice, playing the game, moving our pieces around the board, but if there's a problem, the lawyer is the only person who's read the inside of the top of the box.")

Making a will isn't about walking away from a lawyer's office with a piece of paper in your hand. It's about evaluating your estate—as meager as it may be—and deciding what you want to happen to it after you die. This process is easier when somebody who knows the system is there to show you the way.

On the Money

Creating Your Own Will

Over the past decade, there's been a boom in personal estate planning as people have become increasingly comfortable downloading forms from the Internet and using legal software. If you're the do-it-yourself type, here are some good places to turn for help:

- **LegalZoom.com** is an online service that creates legal documents. You fill out a form or questionnaire, submit it to LegalZoom, and the company uses this info to create a legal will or living trust. (They can help you with other legal documents, too.) LawDepot.com offers similar services.
- **Quicken Willmaker** is a desktop program that guides you through creating your own will. Some versions can help you create living wills and living trusts, too.
- **Nolo.com** is an excellent source for books and software about legal topics. The site offers info on a variety of subjects, including estate planning. (Most public libraries have a good selection of Nolo books and other resources to help you prepare a will and other documents.)

Using resources like these, you can put together a simple will in under an hour. But be warned: These tools are aimed at those with *basic* needs. The documents they produce are certainly better than nothing, but if you have a complicated estate (if you own a business or have children by a previous marriage, for instance), your best bet is to contact an attorney.

If you use software or pre-printed forms to create your will, be sure to follow the signing instructions for your state. For more on do-it-yourself estate planning, read this article from the *New York Times*: *http://tinyurl.com/NYT-wills*.

A lot of people don't understand what will happen to their property when they die. For example, your retirement account—which is probably your single most valuable asset after your home—is generally *not* governed by a will; it's covered by a completely different set of rules. (This point is *very* important, but most people don't realize it.)

If you make your own estate plan, you may not take this sort of thing into account. And many families have been shattered by fighting that happens when a will they thought was legally binding turns out to be invalid because it wasn't properly drafted and witnessed.

A lawyer's job is to make sure everything is done properly, even if you draft the will yourself. Don't risk everything for the sake of saving a few bucks. It's better to have the documents and *not* need them than to need them and not have them.

Working with an attorney to create a will is fairly simple. Just call one up and say you're interested in planning your estate and that you need more info. He'll probably sit you down for an interview or give you a series of forms to fill out. My wife and I recently had an attorney draft our wills; you can see his blank will-planning document here: *http://tinyurl.com/GRS-will*.

The more organized you are, the easier the process is. Once the attorney has an idea of what you own and where you want it to go after you die, he'll draw up the paperwork. Though most wills share certain features, the attorney will customize it for your specific needs.

 Tip If you want to know how much an estate plan will cost, ask. The price depends on where you live and how complicated your estate is.

In a way, preparing a will is sort of anti-climactic. There's not a lot of legal mumbo-jumbo or red tape. You simply gather info, answer a few questions, and sign on the dotted line. For some people, there's more to estate planning than just creating a simple will, but for many, it really is this easy.

Once you have a will, keep it someplace safe and accessible, like a safe-deposit box, and let trusted family members know where it is. If your family can't find your will, they can't follow your wishes.

Finally, remember to update your will when things change. For example, when you first draft a will, you might designate your siblings as beneficiaries. If you get married, you'll probably want to change that. And if you get divorced, you'll want to change it again.

Estate Planning Is No Joke

Matt Haughey is the 37-year-old computer whiz behind the popular site Metafilter.com. Like many young folks, he'd never given much thought to estate planning—it was something for retired people to worry about. Matt and his wife had basic wills, but discussing anything more seemed like a sort of morbid joke.

They're not laughing anymore.

Last fall, without warning, Matt passed out at home and had a seizure. A trip to the ER revealed the bad news: Matt has a brain tumor. "I have a walnut-sized tumor sitting on my pituitary gland, at the base of my brain," he says.

"I was really mad at first. I've done my best to live well and eat right, but this is just one of those random things. Having death issues at 37 sucks. I didn't expect to have to deal with this for another 20 years."

Suddenly, estate planning is a priority. "After I got out of the hospital, we stopped talking about it and started doing something," Matt says. "We made an appointment with an estate attorney and spent 3 hours talking about this stuff." In addition to his will, Matt now has a living trust (page 240).

Matt is glad he hadn't *completely* neglected planning for the future. "Thank God that after my daughter was born, I took out a 20-year, million-dollar term life policy," he says. "The process was simple: I filled out an online questionnaire, and then a nurse practitioner came to my house to take a blood sample. After a few days, I was approved. The insurance costs like five or six hundred dollars a year. I just have to remember to pay the bill when it comes every September."

No matter how old you are, if somebody else depends on your income, you need life insurance (Matt's experience has shown him that it's important to have good health insurance, too). If you have children or any sort of estate, you need a will. And if you own a business or have sizeable assets, you may need a living trust.

"My number-one piece of advice for estate planning is to *do it while you're healthy*," Matt says. "Last summer, this was all sort of a joke: writing down the chain of command of who gets the house or retirement accounts if our entire family were to perish. Now it's not a joke, and it involves a lot of painful questions and deep thinking. When you're unexpectedly faced with the very real possibility of death, it sucks."

12 An Intro to Personal Investing

"Investment performance doesn't determine real-life returns; investor behavior does."
—*Nick Murray*

Wall Street is filled with jargon and with folks like Jim Cramer shouting at the TV camera, telling you to "Buy! Buy! Buy!" and "Sell! Sell! Sell!" But when it comes time to invest your money, it's hard to know where to start. Stocks? Bonds? Commodities? And what are those things exactly, anyway?

Investing doesn't *have* to be complicated. In fact, the investing method covered in this chapter—a method recommended by Warren Buffett and scores of other investment pros—takes just a few hours up front, and then a few hours a year thereafter. This method offers solid returns and you don't need a degree in finance to understand it.

As you'll learn in this chapter, smart investing is simple but not easy—human nature gets in the way. And before you invest a penny, you should understand some essential terms and concepts. Let's get started.

 Note This chapter gives you the basic info you need to get started with investing. For a closer look at investing and to learn more great strategies, check out Bonnie Biafore's *Personal Investing: The Missing Manual*. As with all things financial, the more you know, the better.

Why Invest?

Chapter 5 taught you how to spend less on many kinds of things, and Chapter 6 suggested various ways to increase your income. Together, these two steps can lead to positive cash flow and a monthly surplus of money that can improve your life. But although improving cash flow is the best way to build wealth in the short term, it probably **won't** be enough to let you meet your long-term goals.

For one thing, many long-term goals are expensive. You want to put your kids through college, right? According to the College Board's *Trends in College Pricing* (*http://tinyurl.com/col-costs*), it cost over $23,000 for a young adult to attend the average 4-year private school during the 2007–08 school year. That's plenty expensive already, but in recent years, college tuition costs have risen at about twice the rate of inflation. How will you be able to afford that?

And don't forget retirement. As you'll learn in the next chapter, you'll need a lot of money to retire. Just how much you'll need depends on your income, spending habits, when you start saving (the sooner the better!), and how long you live. But it's unlikely you'll have enough if you just stick your money in the bank—you need a little help from the extraordinary power of **compounding**.

 Note Compounding is the snowball effect that happens when your money earns interest over long periods of time. You earn returns not just on the amount you contributed, but on your earnings, too. To learn more about compounding, see the box on page 277.

Lurking behind all your plans for the future is **inflation**, your silent enemy. Inflation refers to the rising price of things; it's the reason a movie ticket that cost 10 cents in your grandpa's day now costs $10. Just as compounding in your bank account can help your savings grow bigger and bigger, the compounding effects of inflation constantly nibble at your wealth, making it worth less and less.

From December 1984 to November 2009, inflation averaged 2.96% per year. That probably sounds like just another boring statistic, but it's a number that has a real impact on your life. Because of compounding (which is working **against** you in this case), $100 from 1984 is worth only $48.68 today; in other words, you'd need $205.44 now to buy what $100 could get you 25 years ago.

As a rule of thumb, inflation is roughly equal to what you can earn in a high-interest savings account. So even though your money grows thanks to compounding, it's almost like you're swimming against the tide: You paddle forward as fast as you can, but inflation keeps dragging you back so you just stay in the same spot.

Savings accounts are great for short-term goals; inflation may do a little damage, but it doesn't have time to compound. If you want to achieve your big goals over the long term, you need to do more than just boost your cash flow and stick money in savings. The best way to do this is to invest in the stock market because, over the long-term, stocks offer the best possible return. (When talking about investments, your *return* is the amount you earn or lose.)

How Much Do Stocks Actually Earn?

In his book *Stocks for the Long Run* (McGraw-Hill, 2008), Jeremy Siegel analyzes the historical performance of several types of investments (economists call them *asset classes*). He tries to answer the question "How much does the stock market *actually* return?" After crunching lots of numbers, Siegel found that since 1926:

- **Stocks have returned an average of about 10% per year.** Over the past 80 years, stocks have produced a *real return* (meaning an inflation-adjusted return) of 6.8%, which also happens to be their average rate of return for the past 200 years.

- **Bonds have returned about 5%.** Adjusted for inflation, their real return has been about 2.4%.

 You'll learn about stocks and bonds starting on page 250.

- **Gold has a real return of about 1%.** "In the long run, gold offers investors protection against inflation," writes Siegel, "but little else."

 Siegel doesn't mention it but, according to my calculations, real estate has also returned about 1% per year since 1926.

Siegel goes back even further than 1926, showing that if you'd invested just one dollar in stocks in 1802, it would have been worth more than $750,000 in 2006. If you'd put that dollar in bonds instead, it would have grown to just $1,083. And if you'd put it in gold, it would be worth $1.95. (All those figures take inflation into account.)

"The dominance of stocks over fixed-income securities [like bonds] is overwhelming for investors with long horizons," Siegel writes. In plain English: Over the past 200 years, stocks have outperformed every other kind of investment. But before you rush out and sink your savings in the stock market, you need to understand a few important points.

 Note Quick reminder: A ***bull market*** is a period of generally rising stock prices, and a ***bear market*** is a period of generally falling prices.

Average is not normal

Stocks offer handsome returns because they involve a lot of *risk*, meaning their value can fluctuate a lot (that's why they're described as *volatile*). The most important thing to know about stocks is that their average performance is *not* normal.

While it's true that stocks returned an average of about 10% annually (which works out to about 7% after inflation) over the past 80 years, in only two of those years have actual returns been close to average. Recent history is more typical. The following table shows the annual return for the S&P 500 (see the Note below) over the past 15 years:

S&P 500 Annual Returns					
1995	34.11%	2000	−10.14%	2005	3.00%
1996	22.87%	2001	−12.06%	2006	13.62%
1997	23.74%	2002	−24.66%	2007	4.24%
1998	30.95%	2003	25.28%	2008	−40.97%
1999	19.81%	2004	10.59%	2009	27.76%

The average annual return for the S&P 500 for these 15 years was 6.07%.

 Note The S&P 500 is a ***stock-market index***, which is like a thermometer: It's a single number that gives you a quick reading on the value of a group of stocks. There are all sorts of indexes, including the Dow Jones Industrial Average, the NASDAQ Composite, and the S&P 500. The latter tracks the performance of 500 of the largest U.S. stocks.

As you can see from the table, stocks soared during the late 1990s' bull market, fell during the early 2000s' bear market, and had trouble deciding what to do during the past 5 years. And note that while the S&P 500 index returned an *average* of 6.07% during the 15 years between 1995 and 2009, not one of those years actually produced returns near the average (2007 came closest, but that was still nearly 2% below the mark).

These fluctuations mess with the average investor's mind: He panics and sells when prices drop, but then falls victim to what Alan Greenspan called "irrational exuberance" (basically, getting *way* too excited) and buys when prices soar. That's a sure way to lose money. Smart investors understand that average isn't normal, so they brace themselves for fluctuations and try not to buy and sell on impulse. (You'll learn more about smart investor behavior on page 255.)

The future is not the past

Overall, the value of the stock market increases with time. But over the short term, market movements are wild and unpredictable. During any given year, the stock market might return anywhere from –50% to +100%. Over long periods of time—think decades—the market is less volatile and its returns are smoother. Looking at 30-year periods, the U.S. stock market is likely to produce growth between 5–15%.

In the short term, other types of investments can and do offer better returns than stocks. During any given 1-year period, stocks will outperform bonds only 60% of the time. But over 10-year periods, that number jumps to 80%. And over 30 years, stocks almost *always* win: Siegel found that "the last 30-year period in which bonds beat stocks ended in 1861, with the onset of the U.S. Civil War." (For more on this concept, see this article at Get Rich Slowly: *http://tinyurl.com/GRS-stock-history*.)

There's just one problem: Past performance is no guarantee of future results. This is true both for individual stocks and the market as a whole. Just because the market has had average annual returns of 10% since 1926 doesn't mean it'll do so in the future. (In fact, many smart folks believe returns will be modest over the next few decades.)

Still, if history is any indication, investing in stocks is the best way for you to meet your financial goals. As long as businesses can make a profit—even when they borrow money—stocks will outperform bonds and inflation. All the same, smart investors hedge their bets and manage risk by adding a healthy dose of other types of assets, especially bonds.

But what exactly are stocks and bonds, anyhow? Let's take a brief detour to learn about the tools of investing.

 Note Risk and return are inseparable. If you want high returns, you have to accept that you'll sometimes suffer big losses, which may affect your future plans. If you're *risk averse*—not willing to risk losing money—you can find "safe" investments, but they'll offer low returns so it'll be more difficult to meet your goals.

The Tools of Investing

Assuming you're an average individual investor, you've got two primary tools at your disposal: stocks and bonds. (Other asset classes include real estate and *commodities* like gold and oil—but investing in these isn't appropriate for the average Joe.) You can buy stocks and bonds directly, or you can buy collections of them called *mutual funds*. You're probably vaguely familiar with these terms, but it never hurts to do a quick review.

Stocks and Bonds

Let's say your best friend Mary wants to open a pizza parlor, but she needs some money to do it. She comes to you with a business proposal that offers you two options. Here's the first:

- For $10,000, you can own 10% of the restaurant. In return, she'll pay you a piece of the profits every 3 months. These *dividends* don't amount to much (maybe a few hundred bucks a year), but they'll give you a reliable stream of income. Plus, you can sell your share of the ownership (your *stock*) anytime.

  If Mary's business is going gangbusters and makes good profits, you might be able to sell your stock to your friend Rhoda for $15,000 or even $20,000—much more than it cost you. But if your neighbor Phyllis opens another pizza parlor next door, it'll probably dent Mary's business. In that case, you might only be able to sell your stock for $8,000 or even $5,000.

When you buy stock, you're buying small slices of *equity* (ownership) in a business. As the company goes, so goes your investment: There's always the risk that the company will make a mistake, face stiff competition, or that the public's whims will change. When this happens, the value of the stock can drop permanently or the company can go out of business.

This sort of uncertainty might scare you. Sure, the constant stream of dividends would be nice, but you don't like the idea that the value of your investment will jump around all the time—or maybe even drop to zilch. In that case, Mary gives you another option:

- If you lend Mary $10,000 for 5 years, she'll pay you 3% interest, or $300 a year. And at the end of the 5 years, she'll repay your $10,000 loan (or *bond*). What's more, you can sell this loan just like you could sell your stock. For example, if you decide you need the $10,000, you can sell the loan to your friend Rhoda, but she may not want to pay you the full $10,000.

Again, imagine Phyllis opens a pizza parlor next door to Mary's. She, too, is asking people to lend her money, but she's offering to pay **8%** over 5 years. If Rhoda can buy an 8%, 5-year bond for $10,000, why would she pay you the same amount for a 3% bond? Instead, she might offer to buy it from you for $7,500. On the other hand, if Phyllis is only paying 1% interest on the loans she's taking, Rhoda might be willing to pay a little extra for your bond, since you're offering the best deal in town.

When you buy a bond, you're lending money to a business (or government). As with stocks, there's still a chance that the company will go out of business and you'll be left with nothing, but there are ways to reduce this risk. You could buy just the highest-rated bonds, for example, or only government bonds. (Government bonds are *generally* considered safer than corporate bonds, but there are exceptions.)

 Note Bonds are given grades—or *ratings*—based on how likely they are to be repaid. It's difficult for individual investors to buy bonds directly. For most folks, it's best to stick with bond *mutual funds* (page 252). To learn more about how bonds work, see *http://tinyurl.com/GRS-bonds* or read Chapter 7 of *Personal Investing: The Missing Manual*.

Though the prices of both stocks and bonds fluctuate based on economic and market conditions, stock prices are far more volatile: They offer the potential for greater returns—*and* greater losses. On the other hand, if you own a bond until it *matures* (that is, until the end of the time period you agreed to), you know what kind of return you'll get.

As you learned in the last section, stocks—as a group—tend to outperform bonds over long periods of time. The challenge is trying to pick which stocks will do well and which won't; even the pros get it wrong much of the time. It's not as easy as it sounds. If investors knew for sure which stock would perform best, they'd dump all their money into it. But they don't know—nobody does.

If you own just one stock, your fortunes are wholly dependent on what it does. So smart investors *diversify* (see the box on page 252) and build *portfolios* containing many stocks and bonds. You *could* build a portfolio of stocks and bonds yourself, but doing so properly requires a lot of time, effort, and money. For most people, it makes more sense to invest in mutual funds, explained next.

Don't Put All Your Eggs in One Basket

One way investors reduce risk is through *diversification*, which means not putting all your money into one investment, whether it's a stock or bond or something else altogether. By spreading your money around, you smooth out the market's wild ups and downs while getting a similar return on your investment.

You can diversify your investments in several ways, including:

- *Within* **asset classes.** The more different stocks you own, the better your diversification. Same goes for bonds.

- *Among* **asset classes.** In general, the movements of stocks, bonds, commodities (page 250), and real estate aren't strongly correlated; for example, just because the stock market is down doesn't mean the real estate market will be down, too. The same is generally true of the returns on these asset classes—they're normally independent of each other. (But sometimes, as in the recent financial crisis, there's a whole lot of correlation going on!)

- **Over time.** "Risk is also reduced for investors who build up a retirement nest egg by putting their money in the market regularly over time," writes Burton Malkiel in *The Random Walk Guide to Investing*. By using techniques like dollar-cost averaging (see page 266), you ensure that you're not investing all your money when the market is high.

There are other types of diversification, too. For example, when you buy foreign stocks, you're diversifying by geography.

How much should you diversify and how should you do it? There's no one right answer—it depends on you and your financial goals. To learn more about this concept, check out this guide from the U.S. Securities and Exchange Commission: *http://tinyurl.com/SEC-assets*.

Mutual Funds

Mutual funds are collections of investments. They let people like you and me pool our money to buy small pieces of many investments. There are a lot of benefits to doing this, including:

- **Diversification.** For less than a thousand bucks, you can buy shares in a mutual fund that owns pieces of *every* company on the stock market. Such broad exposure reduces your risk, and it's something you couldn't possibly achieve on your own.

- **Focus.** There are over 10,000 different mutual funds available in the U.S. alone. You can find funds that buy stock only in companies that support the environment, or that follow Biblical principles. You can buy bond mutual funds or funds that invest only in Canadian companies. You name it, there's probably a mutual fund for it.

- **Professional management.** When you own a mutual fund, somebody else does the research and buys and sells the stocks so you don't have to.

Because mutual funds offer these advantages to individual investors, they've soared in popularity over the past 25 years. But they're not without drawbacks. The biggest is cost: With stocks and bonds, you usually pay only when you buy and sell, but mutual funds have ongoing management costs. (You don't pay these costs directly; instead, they're subtracted from the fund's total return.) Some of these costs are obvious, but others aren't.

 Note The U.S. Securities and Exchange Commission (SEC) has a run-down of various mutual-fund fees and expenses here: *http://tinyurl.com/SEC-costs*.

One obvious cost listed in every mutual fund's *prospectus* (the booklet describing the fund) is the *expense ratio*, which is the mutual fund company's total annual cost for things like advertising and managing the fund. The company passes these costs on to investors.

Other costs are subtler; you have to look to find them. For instance, funds are required to reveal their *portfolio turnover rates*—how often they buy and sell *securities* (that's the technical term for stocks and bonds)—in the prospectus, but they don't list the costs there. Whenever the fund buys and sells securities, it has to pay commissions and taxes, just as you and I would. Studies show that a 100% annual turnover rate, which is around the average for mutual funds, adds about 1% to the cost of the fund.

Altogether, mutual-fund costs typically run about 2% annually. So for every $1,000 you invest in mutual funds, $20 gets taken out of your return each year. This may not seem like much, but as you'll see in the next section, 2% is *huge* when it comes to investments. (For more on the importance of costs, see page 258.)

Tip To find how much your mutual fund is costing you, pull out the fund's prospectus. (If you can't find your copy, go to your fund company's website and download it.) For help deciphering the prospectus, check out *http://tinyurl.com/GRS-prospectus*.

With more than 10,000 mutual funds to choose from, how do you decide which one to buy? The costs of the different funds can help you narrow the field.

The way a fund is managed plays a big role in its costs. Mutual funds can be either *actively* or *passively managed*. Actively managed funds try to beat the market and earn above-average returns. Some succeed and some don't, but as a whole, all actively managed funds earn the market average. Passively managed funds (called *index funds*), on the other hand, try to match the performance of a specific benchmark, like the Dow Jones Industrial Average or S&P 500 stock-market indexes. As you'll learn in the next section, this makes them a great long-term investment.

Index funds

Because index funds try to match an index and not beat it, they don't require much intervention from the fund manager, which makes their costs much lower than those of actively managed funds. In *The Little Book of Common Sense Investing* (Wiley, 2007), John Bogle writes that the average actively managed fund has a total of about 2% in annual costs, whereas a typical passive index fund's costs are only about 0.25%.

Although this 1.75% difference in costs between actively and passively managed mutual funds may not seem like much, there's a growing body of research that says it makes a huge difference in long-term investment results. Other advantages of index funds include diversification (see page 252) and tax efficiency. And because index funds have a low turnover rate—as described on page 253—they don't generate as much tax liability.

 Note *Exchange-traded funds* (or ETFs) are basically index funds that you can buy and sell like stocks (instead of going through a mutual fund company). To learn more about the subtle differences between index funds and ETFs, head to *http://tinyurl.com/YH-etfs*.

In *Unconventional Success: A Fundamental Approach to Personal Investment* (Free Press, 2005), David Swensen writes, "Fully 95% of active investors lose to the passive alternative, dropping 3.8% per annum to the Vanguard 500 Index Fund results." In other words, people who own index funds have typically earned almost 4% more each year than those who own actively managed funds. (This long article offers a good summary of the arguments for using index funds: *http://tinyurl.com/dowie-index*.)

By owning index funds, you can beat the returns of nearly everyone you know. But to do this, you can't let yourself get caught up in classic investing mistakes like those described in the next section. The key to successful investing—whether you own index funds or not—is overcoming bad behavior.

 Note If you're a math whiz and want to see all the calculations and proofs behind why index funds do better than actively managed funds, pick up a copy of Bogle's book or take a look at this short (but dense) paper from Stanford professor William Sharpe: *http://tinyurl.com/sharpe-rocks*.

Being on Your Best Behavior

Investing isn't rocket science; it's easy to understand the methods for reaping good returns. The biggest barrier to making those methods work is human nature. Research shows that when it comes to investing, you are your own worst enemy. In fact, according to the *Quantitative Analysis of Investor Behavior* (*www.qaib.com*) from the research firm Dalbar, Inc., the returns earned by the average investor lag far behind the returns earned by the market as a whole.

Here's a specific example: During the 20-year period ending in 2008, the S&P 500 index returned an average of 8.35%, but the average person who invested in stock-market mutual funds only earned *1.87%*, which puts him behind even the rate of inflation (2.89%). In other words, the average investor has underperformed the market by nearly 6.5% over the past 20 years. This "behavior gap"—the difference between overall market returns and individual *investors*' returns—is devastating to any hope of long-term financial success.

 Tip For more about the gap between investor returns and investment returns, visit BehaviorGap.com, where you can download "The Behavior Gap: A Snapshot" (*www.behaviorgap.com/the-lab/*), which takes a closer look at this phenomenon.

Why do investors underperform the market? Part of the problem is that so many of the mutual funds out there are actively managed. When you pay somebody else to manage your money in one of those funds, you're giving up 1–2% of your return right from the start.

Psychology and emotions play a huge role, too. Investors tend to be overconfident—they think they know more than everyone else. But according to the 2009 edition of Dalbar Inc.'s study, investors only make the best choice 42% of the time, meaning they're wrong more often than they're right.

Though it can be tough, the best thing you can do to improve your odds of long-term investment success is to admit that you're not likely to beat the market. Your best bet is to try to *match* the market, and you'll learn ways to do that on page 261. But first, let's look at how to overcome common behavioral barriers that cost the typical investor 6.5% per year.

 Note A study published in the February 2001 issue of *The Quarterly Journal of Economics* (*http://tinyurl.com/PDF-gender*) found that men trade 45% more often than women—leading to annual returns 1.4% lower. (And single men are even worse, earning annual returns 2.3% less than single women.) The reason? Overconfidence.

Know Your Goals

As you learned in Chapter 2, goals are an important part of your financial life, and investing is no exception. One way to reduce mistakes is to invest with a purpose. If you know *why* you're investing and have a long-term plan, it's easier to avoid making rash decisions that can lower your returns.

Financial advisers suggest you create an *investment policy statement*, or IPS, which is simply your target asset allocation (see the Note below) and instructions to yourself for how to set and maintain it.

 Note *Asset allocation* is the way your money is divided among your different investments; it's just a fancy way of saying "the things you've invested in." The classic example is the basic 60/40 split: 60% invested in stocks and 40% in bonds. To learn more about asset allocation, read the SEC's "Beginner's Guide to Asset Allocation" at *http://tinyurl.com/SEC-assets*. You can learn more here: *http://tinyurl.com/GRS-alloc*.

In other words, your IPS is a blueprint for your investments. It's a plan to help you build your future. An IPS helps you stay on course instead of trying to take shortcuts (by doing things like chasing hot stocks) or panicking when things fall apart (like during 2008's market crash). By keeping your goals in mind, you can avoid making financial mistakes.

It's easy enough to draft your own investment policy statement. A good place to start is Morningstar's step-by-step guide to creating an IPS (*http://tinyurl.com/mstar-ips*), which includes a free downloadable worksheet to get you started. If you want help and can afford it, pay a fee-only financial planner to help you develop an IPS. ("Fee-only" means you pay the planner directly and she doesn't get commissions for selling you stuff. For more on hiring a financial planner, see page 285.) You can also find info on setting investment goals in Chapter 2 of *Personal Investing: The Missing Manual*.

Think Long Term

Short-term returns aren't an accurate indicator of long-term performance. What a stock or fund did last year doesn't tell you much about what it'll do during the next decade.

Over the short term, index funds are, by definition, average (see page 254). But a funny thing happens the longer you hold onto them: They begin to float to the top of the stack. That's because the "hot" funds don't stay hot year after year—they cool down. So while index funds are usually in the middle of the pack in any given one-year period, they shine over the long term.

During the recent stock market tumble, some folks shouted, "Look! Buy-and-hold investing is dead!" They took the stock market's decline as evidence that passive investing with index funds doesn't work. Well, it *doesn't* work if you sell after a fall, but if you hold onto your investments, you're fine—you haven't lost anything but time. In fact, many savvy investors viewed the market crash as a chance to buy—and hold onto—even more shares of their index funds.

Investing is a game of years and decades, not months. What your investments did this year is far less important than what they'll do over the next decade (or two, or three). Don't let one year panic you, and don't chase after the latest hot investments.

The High Cost of Trading

Here's a dirty little secret: Wall Street makes money on activity; *you* make money on inactivity.

When you buy and sell securities, you have to pay somebody else to make those trades for you. And every time you pay them, you lose a little piece of your savings. This isn't a huge deal if you don't trade often, but if you buy and sell all the time, you're giving your money away.

For example, say it costs 1% each time you sell what you currently own and buy something new. If you do this once a month, you have to earn 12% more every year than the guy who sits there and does nothing. This example is an exaggeration, but studies show that speculators who trade often—usually because they're chasing the latest hot stock—tend to earn less than investors who take a long-term view.

If you want to get an idea of how much money the financial industry siphons from unwary investors, read James B. Stewart's *Den of Thieves* (Touchstone, 1992), a true-life account of the insider trading scandals of the 1980s that'll blow your mind.

Keep Costs Low

What's the easiest way to tell how well a mutual fund will do? Its past performance? The fund's manager? Nope. According to a 2002 study by Financial Research Corporation, the best way to predict a mutual fund's future performance is to compare its expense ratio (page 253) with other funds in the same class. The funds with the lowest fees tend to do better. (Remember, each mutual fund lists its expense ratio in its prospectus.)

Other experts agree. In his book *Your Money and Your Brain*, Jason Zweig notes, "Decades of rigorous research have proven that the single most critical factor in the future performance of a mutual fund is that small, relatively static number: its fees and expenses. Hot performance comes and goes, but expenses never go away." Zweig offers the following suggestions:

- Don't buy a government bond fund with annual expenses over 0.75%.
- Don't buy a blue-chip U.S. stock fund with annual expenses over 1.00%.
- Don't buy a small-stock or high-yield bond fund with annual expenses over 1.25%.
- Don't buy a foreign-stock fund with expenses over 1.50%.

You can keep things simple by sticking to index funds with expense ratios below 0.50% (or even better, below 0.25%).

And avoid buying a mutual fund with a *load*, or sales charge (basically, a commission). You already learned that actively managed funds have to overcome drag that index funds don't (page 254); why would you make things even tougher by paying a 5% load, too? It doesn't matter whether the fund is *front-loaded* (you pay the commission when you buy the fund) or *back-loaded* (you pay it when you sell the fund): studies show that load funds don't offer any advantages over no-load funds. (Some index funds carry small loads, too. The same rule holds true: You're usually better off with a no-load fund.)

Morningstar's mutual-fund selector (*http://tinyurl.com/MS-selector*) is an online tool that lets you sort funds by a variety of criteria, including expense ratio (page 253). For more on this subject, check out this article on predicting mutual fund performance: *http://tinyurl.com/RA-mfund*.

Keep It Simple

In *How a Second Grader Beats Wall Street* (Wiley, 2009), Allan Roth (no relation to your humble author) writes, "If you can't explain your investment strategy and every product in your portfolio to a second grader, you are probably doing something wrong."

People tend to think that the more complicated something is, the better it must be, especially when it comes to finances. But that just isn't the case. In fact, the *opposite* is often true—complex products caused the recent financial meltdown, after all.

So if you don't understand what your broker—the person who sells you stocks and bonds—is trying to sell you, don't buy it. Don't worry about feeling dumb or looking stupid. Remember that nobody cares more about your money than you do; it's your job to protect your savings from people with clever-sounding get-rich-quick schemes. The bottom line: Never invest in something you don't understand.

Don't Follow the Herd

People tend to pour money into stocks in the middle of bull markets—*after* the stocks have been rising for some time. Speculators pile on, afraid to miss out. Then they panic and bail out after the stock market has started to drop. By buying high and selling low, they lose a good chunk of change.

It's better to buck the trend. Follow the advice of Warren Buffett (*http://tinyurl.com/WB-greedy*), the world's greatest investor: "Be fearful when others are greedy, and be greedy when others are fearful."

In his 1997 letter to Berkshire Hathaway shareholders (*http://tinyurl.com/ BH-1997*), Buffett—the company's chairman and CEO—made a brilliant analogy: "If you plan to eat hamburgers throughout your life and are not a cattle producer, should you wish for higher or lower prices for beef?" You want lower prices, of course: If you're going to eat lots of burgers over the next 30 years, you want to buy them cheap.

Buffett completes his analogy by asking, "If you expect to be a net saver during the next 5 years, should you hope for a higher or lower stock market during that period?" You want lower prices, of course: If you'll be investing for the next decade or two, you want to buy your stocks cheap!

Even though they're decades away from retirement, most investors get excited when stock prices rise (and panic when they fall). Buffett points out that this is the equivalent of rejoicing because they're paying more for hamburgers, which doesn't make any sense: "Only those who will [sell] in the near future should be happy at seeing stocks rise." Basically, he's trying to encourage you to follow the age-old wisdom to buy low and sell high.

Following this advice can be tough. For one thing, it goes against your gut. When stocks have fallen, the last thing you want to do is buy more. Besides, how do you know the market is near its peak or its bottom? The truth is you don't. The best solution is to make regular, planned investments— no matter whether the market is high or low. (For more on systematic investing, see page 266.)

 Tip Never act on a hot stock tip—they're almost always worse than worthless. It doesn't matter if the tip comes from your broker, your brother, or your best friend; in the words of Benjamin Graham, "Much bad advice is given free."

Ignore the Financial News

Financial news can be dangerous to the health of your investment portfolio. TV and magazines are filled with hysterical hype: "Dow tumbles 400 points!" "Eight stocks to buy now!" "Pork belly prices have been dropping all morning!" But how important is up-to-date financial news to the average investor? Do daily market changes—even 400-point drops—really matter?

The May 2008 issue of the *AAII Journal* included an article called "The Stock Market and the Media: Turn It On, But Tune It Out" in which author Dick Davis argued that daily market movement is often illogical. Except in the case of obvious stuff like military coups and natural disasters, nobody knows what makes the markets move on any given day. Short-term changes are usually just random. Besides, they're not relevant if you plan to hang onto the stock over the long term anyway (and if you don't, you shouldn't own stocks in the first place!).

To the long-term investor, daily market movements are mostly just noise. "What's important is repetition or the lack of it," Davis writes. In other words, a trendline (what a stock does over a period of time) is more useful than a datapoint (what that stock is worth on any given day). "Big market moves may be inexplicable, but a long-term…approach precludes the need for explanations." In other words, when you make regular investments for the future, it doesn't matter what the market did today (or why it did it).

Davis isn't the only financial expert who believes that no news is good news—research backs him up. In *Why Smart People Make Big Money Mistakes (and How to Correct Them)* (Simon & Schuster, 2010), Gary Belsky and Thomas Gilovich cite a Harvard study of investing habits. The results? "Investors who received no news performed better than those who received a constant stream of information, good or bad. In fact, among investors who were trading [a volatile stock], those who remained in the dark earned more than twice as much money as those whose trades were influenced by the media."

Though it may seem reckless to ignore financial news, it's not: If you're saving for retirement 20 or 30 years down the road, today's financial news is mostly irrelevant. So make decisions based on your personal financial goals and your IPS (page 256), not on whether the market jumped or dropped today.

Common-Sense Investing

In this chapter, you've learned that the stock market provides excellent long-term returns, and that you can do better than 95% of individual investors by putting your money into index funds. Most importantly, you now understand that in order to have any hope of matching the market, you've got to take emotion out of investing.

But how do you put this knowledge to work? What's the best way to take advantage of the things you've learned? The answer is shockingly simple: Set up automatic investments into a portfolio of index funds. After that, ignore the news no matter how exciting or scary things get. Once a year, go through your investments to be sure your asset allocation (explained in the Note on page 256) still matches your goals. Then just continue to put as much as you can into the market—and let time take care of the rest.

That's it—that's the plan. (Told you it was simple.) Do this and you'll outperform most other individual investors over the long term.

Lazy Portfolios

The most important investment decision you can make—besides how much to invest—is *where* to invest. As with so many aspects of investing, there's no one option that works for every person.

One factor that can help you decide how to invest your money is *risk tolerance*. That's a measure of how much uncertainty—and possible loss—you're willing to deal with in your investments. If your risk tolerance is high, you can handle big fluctuations in your investment returns in exchange for the possibility of large gains. If your tolerance is low, on the other hand, you'd rather not deal with the ups and downs—even if that means giving up a chance at making higher returns.

Some of your portfolio should be in fixed-income investments like bonds and CDs, which pay interest on a regular schedule. How much depends on your goals, needs, and risk tolerance. A common rule of thumb is that the percentage of fixed-income investments in your portfolio should be equal to your age. So, if you're 30, you should have 30% in something like a bond mutual fund. (A lot of experts dislike this guideline, but it's an easy place to start.)

Most (maybe all) of the rest should be in stocks. Some of these should be stocks in American companies, and some should be in foreign companies. But there's a lot of disagreement over how much the average investor should put into foreign markets: Some say about 10%, and others say at least 30%.

These three funds—a bond fund, a U.S. stock fund, and a foreign stock fund—should form the core of your portfolio. Some folks will also want to add a smattering of other assets, like real estate or commodities, but that's beyond the scope of this book.

One good way to get started with asset allocation is to use a *lazy portfolio,* a balanced collection of index funds designed to do well in most market conditions with a minimum of fiddling by you. Think of lazy portfolios as recipes: A basic bread recipe contains flour, water, yeast, and salt, but you can build on it to get as elaborate as you'd like. The lazy portfolios that follow are great starter recipes for long-term investing—and they may be the only recipes you'll ever need.

 Note When it comes to investing, there's no shame in being "lazy." As you learned earlier in this chapter, messing around with your investments all the time—chasing hot stocks, timing the market, and so on—will get you lower returns than taking a hands-off approach. So if you're not keen on telling your friends that you're a "lazy investor," just tell 'em you're being smart with your money!

The Couch Potato Portfolio by Scott Burns

This two-fund portfolio from financial columnist Scott Burns may be the simplest way to achieve balance. It's evenly split between stocks and bonds, and should appeal to you if you're both lazy and risk-averse:

- 50% Vanguard Inflation-Protected Securities (VIPSX)
- 50% Vanguard Total Stock Market Index (VTSMX)

You can read more about this portfolio at *http://tinyurl.com/LP-potato*. Burns has also created a "couch potato cookbook" that lists several different lazy portfolios and answers some common questions; you can find it at *http://tinyurl.com/LP-cookbook*.

 Note All the portfolios in this section consist of index funds from The Vanguard Company (*www.vanguard.com*). Vanguard is a good source for index funds because they have a huge selection, but it's not the only source. Also note that those crazy letter combos—VFINX, VBMFX, and so on—are just *ticker symbols*, abbreviations that help investors name stocks and mutual funds. Ticker symbols (also called *stock symbols*) make it easier to find info on various securities. Type *MSFT,* Microsoft's ticker symbol, into Google to see for yourself.

The Second-Grader Portfolio by Allan Roth

Allan Roth is a Certified Financial Planner *and* a Certified Public Accountant, so he knows a thing or two about money. In his book *How a Second Grader Beats Wall Street*, Roth explains how he taught his son about investing. Here's his lazy portfolio, which adds foreign stocks to the mix:

- 40% Vanguard Total Bond Market Index (VBMFX)
- 40% Vanguard Total Stock Market Index (VTSMX)
- 20% Vanguard Total International Stock Index (VGTSX)

This is the medium-risk version of Roth's second-grader portfolio. For higher risk, you'd put 10% into bonds, 60% into U.S. stocks, and 30% into international stocks. A lower-risk allocation would be 70% in bonds, 20% in U.S. stocks, and 10% in foreign stocks.

The No-Brainer Portfolio by William Bernstein

William Bernstein is a retired neurologist who has turned his attention to financial matters. He wrote *The Four Pillars of Investing* (McGraw-Hill, 2002), which is one of the best books on investing published in the past decade. In his book, he suggests several different portfolios, including this "no-brainer" collection of index funds that keeps things simple:

- 25% Vanguard 500 Index (VFINX)

- 25% Vanguard Small-Cap Index (NAESX)
- 25% Vanguard Total International Stock Index (VGTSX)
- 25% Vanguard Total Bond Market Index (VBMFX)

You can read more about this portfolio at *http://tinyurl.com/LP-nobrain*.

The Coffeehouse Portfolio by Bill Schultheis

Bill Schultheis, the author of *The New Coffeehouse Investor* (Portfolio, 2009), believes that the secret to financial success is mastering the basics: saving, asset allocation, and matching the market. He says you can match the market with this lazy portfolio:

- 40% Vanguard Total Bond Index (VBMFX)
- 10% Vanguard 500 Index Fund (VFINX)
- 10% Vanguard Value Index (VIVAX)
- 10% Vanguard Total International Stock Index (VGSTX)
- 10% Vanguard REIT Index (VGSIX)
- 10% Vanguard Small-Cap Value Index (VISVX)
- 10% Vanguard Small-Cap Index (NAESX)

To read more about The Coffeehouse Portfolio, head to *http://tinyurl.com/LP-coffee*.

Other lazy portfolios

These are just a few suggestions. There are scores of index funds out there, and countless ways to build portfolios around them. In fact, there's a sub-culture of investors who love lazy portfolios. You can read more about them at the following sites:

- **Bogleheads.** *http://tinyurl.com/BH-lazy*
- **MarketWatch.** *http://tinyurl.com/MW-lazy*
- **The Kirk Report.** *http://tinyurl.com/TKR-lazy*

There's no one right approach to index-fund investing. Yes, it's simple, but you can spend a long time deciding which asset allocation is right for you. While it's important to do the research and educate yourself, you probably shouldn't spend *too* much time sweating over which choice is "best." Just pick one and get started—you can always make changes later.

If these lazy portfolios are a bit overwhelming, consider starting out with a portfolio made up of just one fund as explained next.

Single-Fund Portfolios

Building a portfolio of index funds isn't for everyone. Some folks crave greater complexity or more control—or they believe (despite evidence to the contrary) that they can outperform the market on their own. Others have no interest in building portfolios (even of just three or four funds) or can't afford the minimum investments.

If you don't want to mess with allocating assets, consider plunking down some cash for just one investment. Two good options are lifecycle funds and all-in-one funds. These might not suit your needs perfectly, but they're a fine place to start.

Lifecycle funds

Many mutual-fund companies now offer *lifecycle funds* (also called *target-date funds*), which try to create a diversified portfolio that's appropriate for a specific age group. For example, say you were born around 1970. In that case, you might consider a fund like Fidelity Freedom 2035, which includes a mix of investments that make sense for people who plan to retire in 2035 (when they'll be around 65).

Lifecycle funds have a lot of things going for them. For example, you get:

- **Automatic asset allocation,** since lifecycle funds include various asset classes.

- **International exposure.** Lifecycle funds are collections of mutual funds, including some international investments.

- **Automatic rebalancing.** Fund managers adjust lifecycle funds' asset allocation to make them more conservative as you get older.

The main drawback of lifecycle funds is that you don't have any control over them. For example, if you want the international portion of your stocks to be 50% (or more), you're out of luck. Some people are okay with that, but the lack of control drives other people crazy. And keep in mind that not all lifecycle funds are created equal. Fees and investment styles vary from company to company; some are aggressive, others more conservative.

Lifecycle funds are perfect for investors who don't want to worry about all the jargon and nonsense that usually come with investing. If you decide to buy a lifecycle fund, buy *only* that fund. If you spread your money around (especially to other lifecycle funds), you defeat the whole purpose of this kind of investment.

Note You don't have to pick a lifestyle fund that matches your likely retirement date. Instead, choose one that matches your risk tolerance. If the Fidelity Freedom 2035 is too aggressive for you, for example, go with the Fidelity Freedom 2025 instead. You can read more about lifecycle funds in this *New York Times* article: *http://tinyurl.com/NYT-tdfunds*.

All-in-one funds

If you like the idea of investing in just one fund but you don't want its asset allocation to change over time, you have a handful of other single-fund options, including:

- **Vanguard STAR Fund (VGSTX),** a collection of 11 other Vanguard mutual funds. The STAR fund is 45% U.S. stocks, 15% foreign stocks, 35% bonds, and 5% cash. (Investing in cash means putting money into things like money market accounts and CDs, which you learned about in Chapter 7.) This is a great fund to start with because you can invest as little as $1,000 into it (some funds have much higher initial investments).

- **Fidelity Four-in-One Index Fund (FFNOX),** a collection of four other Fidelity mutual funds. FFNOX is 60% U.S. stocks, 25% international stocks, and 15% bonds.

The bulk of my 401(k) (page 280) is in FFNOX because I find it fits my current needs perfectly. I may create a lazy portfolio of index funds in the future, but this fund is just right for my investment goals at the moment.

Getting Started with Systematic Investing

Now that you've picked an asset allocation—whether with a lazy portfolio or some other option—it's time to put your plan into action. While you *could* make regular investments whenever you had the spare cash, you'll have much greater success if you set up a systematic investing plan.

With systematic investing (also called *dollar-cost averaging*), you regularly contribute to your mutual funds by, say, putting $100, $250, or $500 into your investment account every month. When prices are high, your money buys fewer shares (since each one costs more); but when prices are low, your money buys more. Your constant contributions and the long-term growth of the market help you build wealth over the long run.

Discount brokers

One way to get started with systematic investing is to use a *discount broker* like ETrade.com, TradeKing.com, or Scottrade.com. Discount brokers are companies that help you buy and sell securities on the cheap. They appeal to a lot of people because it doesn't cost much to work with one. They charge lower fees than traditional brokers because all they do is buy and sell securities; they generally don't offer investment advice.

This type of broker is a good option if you want to buy stocks or ETFs (see page 254) instead of mutual funds. They're also a fine choice if you want to get started *now* and can't afford the minimum investment at one of the big mutual fund companies.

Discount brokers offer a wide range of investment options, but they have one huge drawback: They charge lots of fees. Since it's best to keep fees as low as possible, look at other options first.

 Tip If you're considering a discount broker, check out *Smart Money* magazine's annual broker survey: *http://tinyurl.com/SM-brokers*. The Digerati Life has a summary of the survey's results here: *http://tinyurl.com/DL-brokers*.

Employer-sponsored plans

If you plan to do all your investing through your employer's retirement plan, it's easy to get started:

1. **Contact HR to have retirement contributions automatically taken out of your paycheck.** As you'll learn in the next chapter, you should at least contribute as much as your employer matches, if they offer this perk.

2. **Review your fund options (which may be limited).** Many company plans don't offer index funds. In that case, use what you've learned in this chapter to find funds that have low costs and are widely diversified. You might be able to create a lazy portfolio (page 262) from your options, but often your only choice will be a lifecycle fund (page 265), and sometimes you won't even find that!

If your employer-sponsored plan doesn't offer a lot of choices, ask HR if it's possible to get more. They might say "no," but then again, they might expand the company's menu of mutual funds. Remember, it never hurts to ask!

Note Systematic investing is a good way to make regular investments, but if you have a big pile o' cash that you want to invest, it usually makes more sense financially to invest it all at once instead of spreading it out over time. This article explains why: *http://tinyurl.com/MSN-lumpsum*.

Mutual fund companies

If you plan to invest on your own—whether instead of or in addition to investing through your company's plan—contact the mutual fund companies directly instead of going through a broker. Three of the larger no-load (page 259) mutual fund companies are:

- **Fidelity Investments.** *http://tinyurl.com/FID-ind*, 800-FIDELITY
- **T. Rowe Price.** *http://tinyurl.com/TRP-ind*, 800-638-5660
- **The Vanguard Group.** *http://tinyurl.com/TVG-ind*, 800-319-4254

If you're just starting out, you should probably pick one company and stick with it; that'll make things easier because you'll be able to track all your investments in one place.

The main hurdle you'll have to clear when using a mutual-fund company is the minimum initial investment. Most mutual funds make you contribute $1,000–$5,000 (or more) to get started. For example, the Fidelity Four-in-One Index Fund mentioned earlier (page 266) has a $10,000 minimum investment, but don't let this discourage you. Minimum investments are often lower if you make them through a retirement account, like a 401(k) or Roth IRA. If that's not an option, use a targeted savings account (page 142) or a CD (page 137) to accumulate the cash. Before long, you'll have enough to buy your mutual fund.

Minimum investment requirements create another problem, too: When you first invest, you probably won't be able to afford every fund in your target portfolio. So you may have to start with just one fund instead of jumping right into your plan for three or eight, but that's okay. When you're just beginning to invest, your contributions are *far* more important than your asset allocation (page 256). So don't sweat it if you can't get your target asset allocation perfect right off the bat.

The most important step is to actually *get started investing*. If you pay yourself first (see page 145) and make investing a habit, you *will* be able to fund your future.

Make it automatic

After you've set up your investment account, it's time to remove the human element from the equation to make sure you don't sacrifice 6.5% to the behavior gap (page 255) or forget to send your investment check every month. To do that, make your investments automatic.

If you're investing through an employer-sponsored plan, you're all set— the money is automatically deducted from your paycheck. You should be fine if you're investing through a major mutual-fund company, too: Most of them offer a way to set up automatic monthly transfers from your savings account to your investment account. Some discount brokers allow this, too.

For a detailed discussion of how to automate your investing, pick up a copy of David Bach's *The Automatic Millionaire*.

Conduct an annual review

After you've opened your account and set up automatic investments, take a break—a long one (you've earned it!). Ignore the financial news. Don't check your investments every day (or even every week). Resist the temptation to buy and sell stocks frequently. Re-read the section on investor behavior (page 255), and then *leave things alone.* When you can afford to, increase your monthly contributions. And once, at the end of every year, take a couple of hours to review your investments and your IPS (see page 256).

During the year, some of your investments will have higher returns than others. For example, if you started the year with 60% in stocks and 40% in bonds, you may find that you now have 66% in stocks and 34% in bonds. What's more, your goals may have changed, or you might discover you can't stomach as much risk as you thought you could (this happened to a *lot* of folks in 2008).

At the end of the year, *rebalance* your portfolio, which simply means shifting money around so your assets are allocated the way you want them to be. Doing this is another way to take the emotion out of investing, because you're investing based on a plan instead of a whim. There are two ways to rebalance:

- You can **sell enough of your winners and buy enough of your losers** to bring things back into balance. By selling the investments that have grown and buying those that lag behind, you're following the Wall Street mantra to "buy low, sell high." Be aware, though, that you might owe taxes if you go this route, so check out the tax implications before you sell any securities.

- If you can afford it, **contribute new money to your investment account, but only to buy the assets that need to catch up.** For instance, if you only have 34% in bonds instead of your target 40%, add more bonds to bring your portfolio back into balance. By doing this, you don't have to worry about taxes, but you *will* need some cash on hand.

Though many investment professionals swear by rebalancing, some research shows that it's not as important as people once thought. In *The Little Book of Common Sense Investing*, John Bogle writes, "Rebalancing is a personal choice, not a choice that statistics can validate. There's nothing the matter with doing it…but also no reason to slavishly worry about small changes…" In other words, rebalance if your asset allocation is way out of line but don't worry about small changes—especially if you'd end up paying a lot of fees by rebalancing.

Action beats inaction

Investing doesn't have to be scary. Stick with the basics you learned in this chapter: Start with an index-fund portfolio. Do your research (you can find a list of recommended reading on this book's Missing CD page at *www.missingmanuals.com*). As you have the time and education, make adjustments that fit your style and view of the market. Move slowly. Ignore the Wall Street hype machine. Use common sense and don't take unnecessary risks. For 99% of folks reading this book, systematic investments in index funds are the way to go.

Though I've pitched index funds as a great place to start, they're also a great place to *finish*. Many smart investors make index funds the core of their portfolios and never worry about anything else. In other words, they're not a dumbed-down investment that you have to abandon for something more complicated—you can stick with index funds for the rest of your life and still get great returns.

Ultimately, the most important thing isn't how you invest, but that you *do* invest. When you're just starting out, your contributions have a bigger impact on your success than any other factor. So make a commitment to your future self: Get off the couch and set up a retirement account today. It's easy—the next chapter shows you how.

 Want to learn more about investing? Pick up a copy of Bonnie Biafore's *Personal Investing: The Missing Manual*.

13 Retirement: The Final Frontier

"Doing the garden, digging the weeds—who could ask for more? Will you still need me, will you still feed me, when I'm sixty-four?" —The Beatles

We all know we should save for retirement, but even those of us who are saving find the subject a little mystifying: How much should we save? For how long? And just where should we put our money?

You can spend a lot of time looking for the *best* options—or you can just get to work, reminding yourself that the sooner you start saving, the better. Besides, "best" is a moving target; what's best today may not be best tomorrow.

This chapter will help you sort things out. You'll learn some ways to estimate how much you need to save for retirement, and find out where to put your savings so it can grow as much as possible. You'll also get a glimpse at the pros and cons of early retirement.

What Will Retirement Look Like?

Retirement means different things to different people. To you, it may mean a house on the lake with plenty of time to garden. To your best friend, it may mean the chance to travel the world or golf every day. Just as we each have different careers, we'll have different experiences once we stop working and move on to other things. (In fact, some folks won't ever stop working!)

According to a 2002 poll from Harris Interactive (*http://tinyurl.com/HI-rpoll*), less than a quarter of senior citizens view retirement as a winding down: "Most see retirement as either a continuation of what was before retirement (40%) or as a whole new life (38%)." Based on their research, Harris Interactive classified retirees into four main groups:

- A large chunk (27%) are looking forward to a non-traditional retirement filled with exploration. These folks are generally healthy, wealthy, and well-educated, and want to use their resources to live life to the fullest by pursuing their passions.

- About 19% are looking forward to a lifestyle of comfortable contentment. These are the people who want a traditional retirement that includes travel and relaxation.

- Some (about 22%) have big plans for retirement, but they spent so much time "living for today" during their working years that they're not sure how they'll afford everything they want. These folks wish they'd saved more when they were younger.

- Finally, a large group (32%) are living the worst-case scenario: They're poor, in poor health, and generally pessimistic about the future.

 Note You may think you'll never retire, but your health may force you to reduce your work hours—and your income—as you age. According to a survey in the February 2010 issue of *Consumer Reports*, 24% of retirees stopped working "because they were made to, their health declined, or they no longer had the energy to work."

Retirement can be whatever you want it to be: You can use it to go back to school, travel the world, watch TV, or write the great American novel. But in order to afford any of those things, you have to start planning now.

Figuring Out How Much to Save

Because you can't see the future, there's no way to know *exactly* how much you'll need to save for retirement. All you can do is make your best guess, taking these variables into account:

- When will you retire?
- How long will you live? (You can get an estimate at *www.livingto100.com*.)
- How much will you spend?
- What will your health be like?
- How much will you save and how aggressively will you invest?
- What will the inflation rate be between now and when you retire?

 Tip Delaying retirement can only help your financial situation. The longer you work, contribute to your retirement savings, and go without tapping Social Security and retirement accounts, the more money you'll have later.

Most retirement calculators—both on the Web and from financial planners—estimate how much you'll need by using your income as a starting point. They'll suggest you need 70% (or 80% or 100%) of your pre-retirement income to maintain your lifestyle. But is basing this estimate on your pre-retirement income a good idea?

- Say you make $50,000 a year but spend **$60,000**. In that case, your income **understates** your lifestyle by $10,000 a year. If you based your retirement needs on your income, you wouldn't come close to supporting your lifestyle.

- On the other hand, if you make $50,000 a year but only spend $25,000, basing your retirement needs on your income would lead you to save much more than you need.

As you can see, estimating how much you'll need in retirement by looking at your current income doesn't make much sense. It's one of those rules of thumb—like "buy as much house as you can afford"—that can actually do more harm than good. There's a real danger that by following this advice, you won't have enough saved for retirement. But just as bad, there's a chance you'll have saved **too much**, meaning you missed out on using money to enjoy life when you were younger.

Instead of estimating your retirement needs based on your income, it makes more sense to base them on **spending**. Your spending reflects your lifestyle; your income doesn't. The next section explains how to do that.

Tip You can get a rough estimate of the Social Security benefits you'll receive using this Quick Calculator: *http://tinyurl.com/socsec-calc*. For a much more accurate estimate of your future benefits, check the Social Security statement you receive in the mail every year.

A Better Way

If you're going to base your savings goals on how much you'll spend in retirement, you've got to have a way to gauge your future spending. Will your expenses increase or decrease? That depends in large part on your health and your plans. If you get sick or travel a lot in retirement, for example, your expenses may go up. In general, though, your expenses will likely stay about the same. According to the Employee Benefit Research Institute's 2009 Retirement Confidence Survey (RCS):

- 49% of retirees spend *less* in retirement than before (26% spend *much* less)

- 35% spend about the same as before retirement

- 14% spend more in retirement (though 7% say their expenses are only "a little higher")

Overall, 65% of Americans spend about the same or only slightly more or less in retirement. That means their pre-retirement expenses are a good predictor of their post-retirement expenses.

 Note You can download the full EBRI report for free from *http://tinyurl.com/EBRI-rcs*. It's filled with tons of data about Americans' attitudes toward retirement—and the realities of being retired.

Expenses often drop in retirement because your kids are out of the house; your mortgage is gone—or nearly so (one of the surest steps toward retirement security is to pay off your mortgage); you have no commuting costs or other work-related expenses; and, ironically enough, you no longer have to save for retirement. Sure, you'll have other expenses—especially health care—but if you've been smart and planned ahead, you should be in good shape.

Make no mistake: You *will* need a sizable nest egg for retirement—especially if you have ambitions to travel or want to golf every day. In fact, you should save as much as you can. But don't be snookered by the constant refrain that you need 70% of your pre-retirement income. That's nonsense—base your savings goals on your projected *expenses* instead.

The moral here? Don't panic—you *can* save enough for retirement. In *Retire Well on Less Than You Think* (Times Books, 2004), Fred Brock writes:

> Most people can retire from wage slavery sooner than they think if they are willing to pay a relatively painless price for their freedom: a simpler, downsized life and, perhaps, a move to a less expensive part of the country—and it doesn't have to be remote or far away.

The key is to live within your means now, which lets you boost your cash flow so you can accumulate savings for later in life.

Retirement Calculators

Enough theory! You're probably ready for some hard numbers. In that case, you can get a quick estimate of how much you'll need to save by heading online. There are hundreds of retirement calculators scattered across the Web, and each one is a little different. Because this is all a guessing game, no one calculator is necessarily better than any other, but here are a few I've found especially insightful:

- **T. Rowe Price** has an excellent calculator that bases its results on your spending needs: *http://tinyurl.com/TRO-rcalc*.

- **The Motley Fool** has two useful calculators, one that estimates your retirement expenses (*http://tinyurl.com/fool-rexp*) and one that lets you see if you're saving enough (*http://tinyurl.com/fool-enough*).

- **Bankrate's** retirement calculator (*http://tinyurl.com/BR-rcalc*) bases its results solely on your savings. (MoneyChimp.com has a similar—but simpler—calculator at *http://tinyurl.com/MC-rcalc*.)

- **Choose to Save** has a ballpark estimate tool (*http://tinyurl.com/ballparke*) that you can use online or off. It's the best of the calculators that use income instead of expenses.

For a great combination of simplicity and complexity, check out FireCalc.com. This site may seem overwhelming at first (there's a lot of text to read), but it's actually fairly elegant. What it does is give you an idea of just how safe or risky your retirement plan is based on how it would have withstood every market condition we've ever faced since 1871. All you do is enter how much you've saved, how much you think you'll spend every year, and how many years you expect to live in retirement. Then FireCalc spits out a percentage telling you how likely your retirement plan is to succeed: 0% means that it never would have worked in the past, and 100% means it always would have succeeded.

In *How to Retire Early and Live Well* (Adams Media, 2000), Gillette Edmunds shares his formula for calculating retirement needs based on current expenses. His formula takes taxes, inflation, and investment returns into account. It's too math-y for this book, but if you'd like to calculate things by hand, track down a copy at your local library or used book store.

Looking at the results from just one retirement calculator isn't very useful. But if you compare the numbers and recommendations from several, you can get a pretty good idea of how much you'll need to save for the retirement you want. If your results are anything like mine, you may feel a little overwhelmed. In that case, make a commitment to start saving for retirement today.

 Analyzenow.com has lots of great info about sensible retirement planning. The site doesn't include a calculator, but it offers plenty of free downloadable spreadsheet templates so you can run your own numbers, as well as tons of articles about retirement planning.

Why You Should Start Saving *Today*

If you're young, you may not think you need a retirement account—you can worry about that later, right? Besides, you have better things to do with that money, like taking a trip to Vegas with your friends. But the hard truth is that, no matter what your age, you should start saving now.

According to the 2009 National Retirement Risk Index from the Center for Retirement Research, 51% of Americans are "at risk of being unable to maintain their pre-retirement standard of living in retirement" (*http://tinyurl.com/ CRR-nrri*). Part of the reason is that these folks didn't plan ahead and set aside enough when they were young.

"The amount of capital you start with is not nearly as important as getting started early," writes Burton Malkiel in *The Random Walk Guide to Investing*. "Procrastination is the natural assassin of opportunity. Every year you put off investing makes your ultimate retirement goals more difficult to achieve."

An article about retirement in the February 2010 issue of *Consumer Reports* featured a survey of more than 24,000 of the magazine's readers.

The findings won't surprise you: "Satisfied retirees planned early and lived within their means," the article noted. Those who started saving in their 30s had an average of almost *$400,000* more than those who started in their 50s and 60s. Even readers who started in their 40s typically had $200,000 more than those who waited till later in life.

The bottom line: Save early and often. People come up short of cash in retirement because they put off saving. As you'll see in a moment, the secret to getting rich slowly is the power of compounding. When you're young, time is your greatest ally. Even modest returns can generate real wealth if you start early and stick with your plan.

Frequently Asked Question

Finding Cash to Save

I know saving for retirement is important, but I can hardly find the money to pay my bills, let alone to sock away for my golden years. How can I possibly set money aside for retirement?

Saving for retirement is crucial, but if your current financial situation is precarious, it's more important to find a way to make that more stable first—to improve your cash flow (see page 54)—and *then* worry about the future. This isn't license to ignore retirement savings; it's just a reminder to take care of today before tomorrow. Be sure to:

- **Stash some cash for emergencies.** Before you save for retirement, save for the present. Without a rainy-day fund, even small disasters can sidetrack your savings for months (or years). See Chapter 7 for tips on where to put the money.

- **Pay off your credit card debt** (see Chapter 4). At the very least, make significant headway on your debt and have a plan for getting rid of it all.

After you finish paying off your debt, saving for retirement is easy: Take the amount you were putting toward debt reduction each month and—instead of spending it on Stuff—stick it in a retirement account. You've already developed the habit of using the money to improve your financial life; this is just another way to do it!

The Power of Compounding

On its surface, compounding is innocuous—even boring. How much does it matter if you start saving now? Will it truly make that much of a difference?

In the short term, compounding doesn't make a huge difference. But remember what you learned in the last chapter: Investing is all about taking the long view. Short-term results aren't as important as what will happen over 20 or 30 years.

Imagine you make a one-time, $5,000 investment when you're 20 years old. Assuming the return on that investment is 8% per year (in real life, you're never going to find an investment that guarantees this much, but bear with me), even if you never touch the investment again—never add or withdraw any money—you'll have nearly $160,000 by the time you retire at age 65. But if you wait until you're 40 to make your single investment, that $5,000 would grow to only $34,000. As you can see from this example, *time* is the main ingredient in compounding.

You can get even more out of compounding through systematic investing (see page 266). It's great that a single $5,000 investment can grow to $160,000 in 45 years, but it's even more exciting to see what happens when you make saving a habit. If you invest $5,000 each year for 45 years (for a total of $225,000 invested) and the money earns an 8% return every year, your savings will grow to over $2.24 million—nearly *10 times* what you invested!

 Note In real life, there's no way to earn a guaranteed 8% per year. As you learned on page 247, the stock market returns an average of 10% per year—but this average is *not* normal. Because stock market returns fluctuate wildly, if you invested $5,000 into a stock-market index fund every year for 45 years, you could have anywhere from less than $1 million to well over $4 million when you retired, even if your average return was exactly 8%. Confused? Just remember that, even with the power of compounding, you need to watch your progress and make course corrections along the path to retirement.

To make compounding work for you:

- **Start early.** The sooner you start, the more time compounding has to work in your favor, and the wealthier you can become. (The next best thing to starting early is starting now.)

- **Stay disciplined.** Make regular contributions to your savings and retirement accounts, and do what you can to increase your deposits as time goes on. (This is part of paying yourself first—see page 145.) Don't sabotage yourself by cashing out your retirement account when you move from one job to the next. And don't be tempted to sacrifice your future well-being for a few more bucks today.

- **Be patient.** Don't touch the money; compounding only works if you let your investments grow. You can think of it like a snowball of money: At first your returns may seem small, but eventually they become enormous.

Tip To learn more about compounding, check out the compound-interest calculator at Money Chimp (*http://tinyurl.com/MC-compound*).

A Brief Guide to Retirement Accounts

A lot of people believe that wealth is something that happens all at once, through inheritance or winning the lottery or magically picking the right stock. But in reality, you get rich slowly. The road to wealth is like a marathon: It's a long race, and the best approach is measured, even paces. To help yourself win this "race," it's important to make the most of your retirement accounts.

When you put money in a regular investment account like the ones discussed in Chapter 12, you're using after-tax money: You earned the money through your job, paid tax on it, and then used it to buy stocks and bonds. And when you sell your investment, you'll have to pay taxes on the returns the account earned. (Depending on how you invest, you may also have to pay taxes on dividends and capital gains along the way.)

One of the great things about *retirement accounts*—investment accounts specifically for retirement savings—is that they let you put off income taxes until a later date (that's why they're called *tax-deferred*), meaning you get to hold onto and profit from your money longer. And a Roth IRA (which you'll learn about shortly) lets your money grow tax-free!

There are lots of places to put your retirement savings, so it can be difficult to know where to start. Each person's situation is different, but most folks can follow these simple guidelines:

1. If you have a 401(k) or similar program at work, contribute to get the employer match (page 281). If your employer doesn't match contributions, go to the next step.

2. If you qualify, open a Roth IRA (page 282) and contribute as much as you can (up to the maximum allowed).

3. If you have money left, put as much as you can into your 401(k) (see page 280).

4. Once you've done all of the above, *then* put your money in regular investment accounts (see Chapter 12). You might also consider paying down your mortgage.

Following these steps is one the best ways to take control of your financial future. The following pages cover each step in more detail.

Funding Your Future with a 401(k)

According to the Congressional Research Service, nearly half of American workers participate in retirement plans offered by their employers (*http:// tinyurl.com/CRS2007pdf*). About one-third of these folks have defined-benefit plans, while two-thirds have defined-contribution plans.

With a *defined-benefit plan*—which most people simply call a *pension*—when you retire, you receive a fixed monthly payment for the rest of your life. (The amount you get paid is based on how long you worked for the company and how much you earned.) With a *defined-contribution plan*, on the other hand, your benefits aren't fixed; they're based on how much you (and your employer) put into the plan and what kind of returns your investments earned.

The *401(k)* is a specific type of defined-contribution plan that, over the past couple of decades, has become much more common than traditional pension plans. (The name 401(k) comes from the section of the tax code that defines these plans.) Let's look at the pros and cons of 401(k)s.

 Note There are a variety of defined-contribution retirement plans out there. For-profit companies offer 401(k) plans, while nonprofit organizations and governments offer 403(b) plans. And if you work for the federal government, you may have access to the Thrift Savings Plan. Though these plans aren't identical, they're similar, so you can generally apply the advice in this chapter about 401(k)s to other defined-contribution plans, too.

Advantages of 401(k)s

401(k)s have a lot going for them. For one, they make contributing to your retirement automatic: Once you sign up for your company's 401(k) plan, your retirement saving comes directly out of your paycheck. You can "set it and forget it," only making changes when you want to increase (or decrease) your contributions. This takes the human element out of the equation, preventing you from gumming things up (and that's a good thing—see page 255).

Even better, your contributions and earnings are tax-deferred. In plain English, that means you don't have to pay taxes on the money you put into a 401(k) until you withdraw it. You're not taxed on the profits (the returns the account earns) until then, either. This is a big advantage over a regular investment account. For example, if you earn $50,000 per year and you put $5,000 into your 401(k), your taxable income drops to $45,000; if you're in the 25% tax bracket (see page 233), say, that would save you $1,250 in taxes. And you won't be taxed on that $5,000 contribution (or any returns it earns) until you take the money out at retirement, so your investment has a chance to grow even faster than in a regular investment account.

But the biggest advantage of 401(k)s is the **employer match:** Many companies match at least a part of what their workers set aside for retirement. IBM, for example, currently matches employee contributions dollar for dollar up to 6% of their income! Most company matches aren't so generous, but they're still worth taking full advantage of. In effect, you can give yourself a raise by taking advantage of the employer match—though you won't see the effects of the "raise" until you retire.

Disadvantages of 401(k)s

Alas, 401(k)s aren't perfect. For one thing, once you put money into a 401(k), you can't easily access the cash if you end up needing it for something else. Except in cases of hardship (see *http://tinyurl.com/401k-hsw*), if you pull the cash out before age 59 and a half, you'll be socked not only with taxes, but also a 10% early withdrawal penalty. (On the other hand, you **have** to begin pulling money out by the time you're 70 and a half, unless you're still working for the company that sponsored the plan.)

Also, find out the details of your company's vesting policy. **Vesting** is the process by which you gain "ownership" of any contributions your company makes to your 401(k) (as with an employer match). You **always** own the money you've put into the plan yourself, but you only gradually gain ownership of your company's contributions. You might own none of them during the first year you participate, for example, 20% the second year, and so on. If you leave the company before you're fully vested, you won't get 100% of the money they contributed. Check with your company's HR department to learn more.

But the biggest problem with 401(k)s is that they often offer only limited investment options. The firm that manages your company's retirement accounts probably gives you a small menu of mutual funds from which to choose. Your challenge is to find the one best suited to your needs (which, as you learned in the last chapter, is likely to be the lowest-cost fund; favor index funds, if possible).

If your company's 401(k) plan is lousy (it has high fees and poor selection, say), move the money into an IRA (page 282) when you leave the company. But no matter how bad the plan, it's probably not bad enough to pass on the employer match. For more info on how to deal with a bad 401(k) plan, read this article from **Money** magazine: *http://tinyurl.com/bad401k*.

Every company's 401(k) plan is different. Your best bet is to read up on how yours works and do what you can to make the most of it. And whether or not your company offers a 401(k), you should definitely take a look at the investor's best friend: Roth IRAs.

 Tip At some point, you may want to shift money from one retirement account to another, like moving the money in a 401(k) from your old job to a Roth IRA. (The technical way to say this is that you want to *roll over* your 401(k).) Be warned: These moves can be tricky. The IRS has a handy chart that shows which accounts can roll over into other accounts: *http://tinyurl.com/IRS-ropdf*. For more info, read the Get Rich Slowly article at *http://tinyurl.com/GRS-401kmove* and contact a financial planner (see page 285).

Learning to Love Roth IRAs

Even if your company doesn't offer a retirement plan, you can still save for the future. One of the best ways to do so is with a Roth IRA.

An IRA is an *individual retirement arrangement*, a retirement plan that gives you tax advantages when saving for retirement. There are two types of IRAs:

- With a **traditional IRA** (first introduced in 1975), the money you put in is typically tax deductible, but the money you pull out at retirement will be taxed at the then-current rate.

- With a **Roth IRA** (first introduced in 1997), you contribute after-tax dollars, but when you retire, you don't have to pay taxes on the returns the money earned. (These IRAs get their name from Delaware senator William Roth, who helped pass the law that created them.)

In other words, money in a traditional IRA is taxed when you withdraw it, but the money in a Roth IRA is taxed before you contribute it. (For more on the difference between Roth IRAs and traditional IRAs, see the box on page 287.)

You make investments in an IRA through an individual retirement *account*. Many folks use the term "IRA" interchangeably to refer to both individual retirement arrangements and individual retirement accounts, but there are some important differences. You have just one Roth IRA, for example, but you can have many Roth IRA accounts. That is, you can have a Roth IRA account at your credit union and one with your mutual fund company, but they're both part of the same IRA. (It's kind of like how this page and the last one are both part of the same book.)

One important thing to realize is that an IRA isn't itself an investment—it's a place to *put* investments. When you open an IRA account, it's like an empty bucket just waiting to be filled. The things you put into your IRA bucket are investments. You might, for example, buy stocks to put into your bucket, or maybe bonds. Some people use their IRA accounts to buy investment real estate, and some simply let their cash sit there, earning interest in CDs, just as it would if it were deposited in the bank down the street (which may actually be where they keep their IRA account!).

As you might expect after reading the last chapter, smart people mix up the contents of their IRA accounts over time. Their buckets might contain a combination of stocks, mutual funds, bonds, and real estate. (When you start out, your bucket will probably hold just a single investment, and that's fine.)

For many people, Roth IRAs are the perfect place to put retirement savings. They're an easy way to contribute to your financial future, and they're such a good deal that it's worth taking an extended look at them.

 Note Some companies offer *Roth 401(k)s,* which are like a cross between a Roth IRA and a regular 401(k): You put in after-tax dollars so that you can withdraw them tax-free. You can learn more about Roth 401(k)s at *http://tinyurl.com/yh-401k.*

Roth IRA rules and requirements

There are some restrictions on who can contribute to Roth IRAs. These arrangements are designed to help ordinary working folks to save for retirement by giving them a significant tax break. They're not meant for people with really high incomes.

If your tax filing status is single and you earn more than $105,000 but less than $120,000 in 2010, the amount you can contribute is limited. And if you earn more than $120,000, you can't contribute to a Roth IRA at all. If you're married and filing jointly, your contributions are limited if your household income is more than $167,000 but less than $177,000 in 2010. And if you and your spouse earn more than $177,000, you can't contribute to a Roth IRA at all.

These income limits are based on your *modified adjusted gross income*. (If you don't know what that is, don't worry about it unless you think you're close to the limit.) Also note that the Roth IRA income limits usually increase every year. A few other important facts:

- If you're younger than 50, you can only contribute $5,000 to your Roth IRA in 2010 (if you're 50 or older, you can contribute up to $6,000).

 Tip These contribution limits increase from time to time to keep up with inflation, so you should check every year to see whether they've gone up.

- To invest in a Roth IRA in any given year, you (or your spouse) need to have earned income; in other words, you can't fund a Roth IRA if all of the money you received that year came from an inheritance.

- You can use a Roth IRA even if you have a 401(k) or other retirement plan.

- You have to make your contributions by the tax deadline each year. For example, you have until April 15, 2011 to make your Roth IRA contributions for 2010. (But it's a good idea to fund your account as early as possible.)

- You can convert traditional IRAs to Roth IRAs. There used to be income limits on these conversions, but those limits are gone as of 2010. If you think you might like to convert a traditional IRA to a Roth, contact a financial planner. (The topic is beyond the scope of this book.)

- You can withdraw your *contributions* at any time without penalty. But if you try to withdraw your *earnings* (the returns on your contributions) before you're 59 and a half, you'll have to pay taxes *and* a 10% early-withdrawal penalty (except in special circumstances).

- Lastly—and this is important for many people—you can withdraw up to $10,000 in earnings without penalty to buy your first home, as long as your IRA spans at least 5 tax years. Check out *http://tinyurl.com/mf-irahome* for more info.

There are other arcane guidelines and provisions, but these are the basics. If you want more info, check out Publication 590 at the IRS website (*http://tinyurl.com/IRS-iras*) or contact your friendly neighborhood financial planner (see the box on the next page).

How to Hire a Financial Planner

If you don't have the time or knowledge to create a roadmap for your financial future, consider calling in a pro. A *financial planner* can help you put the pieces of your investment puzzle together in a way that makes sense for your personal goals and values. Even if you do most of the work yourself, you may want to have a planner check things over to make sure your investment plan will work as you intend. Planners can also make recommendations and give advice on how to implement your plan.

Before hiring a planner, decide how much help you want or need. Different planners charge different rates, typically based on one of these methods: by the hour (best if you need minimal help), by the project (best if you need help in a specific area), on retainer (best if you want ongoing help), or based on a percentage of the assets they're managing for you. (Watch out: This last method has a built-in conflict of interest.)

The more research you do on your own (like reading this book!) and the more you're willing to do yourself, the less you'll end up paying. Most planners will give a free initial consultation, which will let the two of you get a feel for each other. (Be sure to ask these 10 questions: *http://tinyurl.com/CFP-questions*.)

As you look for a planner, watch out for potential conflicts of interest. Ask yourself if the recommendations she gives you could somehow benefit her. Those paid by commission tend to be salespeople rather than actual planners. So ask questions, read the fine print, and assume nothing.

It's important to know that the term "financial planner" isn't regulated—anyone can call themselves that. But Certified Financial Planners (often simply called CFPs) *are* regulated and have to agree to uphold a set of standards and follow a code of ethics.

You can find a CFP using the Financial Planning Association's PlannerSearch website (*http://tinyurl.com/FPA-search*). The Garrett Planning Network (*www.garrett-planningnetwork.com*) has a searchable directory of financial planners who charge by the hour. The National Association of Personal Financial Advisors (*www.napfa.org*) also has a searchable directory.

For a financial planner to give investment advice, she has to be a registered investment adviser (RIA). RIAs are required to place your interests above their own; stockbrokers—even if they're CFPs—don't have to do that.

How to open a Roth IRA account

Opening a Roth IRA account is easy. If you've ever filled out a job application, applied for a credit card, or opened a bank account, you've got what it takes to open a Roth IRA account.

Deciding *where* to open your Roth IRA account is the toughest part of the process. If you already have an investment advisor, ask her for recommendations, but look for other options, too. Many banks and credit unions offer IRA accounts (though you'll usually be able to invest only in deposit accounts, like CDs). If you're willing to make some decisions on your own, you can open an IRA account through a discount broker or mutual fund company. There are a lot of good options out there, but you might start your search with these firms:

- **Fidelity Investments.** *http://tinyurl.com/FID-ind*, 800-FIDELITY
- **T. Rowe Price.** *http://tinyurl.com/TRP-ind*, 800-638-5660
- **The Vanguard Group.** *http://tinyurl.com/TVG-ind*, 800-319-4254

Set aside an hour or two some Saturday morning to explore the options over a cup of coffee. With a little research, you should be able to find a company and program that suits your needs. When you're shopping around for a place to open an IRA account, ask the following questions:

- Is there a minimum initial investment?
- What sorts of fees will they charge on your account?
- Can I make automatic contributions?

 Tip Making regular automatic investments to a Roth IRA account is a fantastic way to build wealth. Most brokers and mutual-fund companies provide some sort of program that'll pull money from your bank account every month. If you make this a habit, you won't even notice the money is missing; it'll be a regular expense in your monthly budget. Do this and you'll put yourself far ahead of your peers.

- What investment options will I have? Can I invest in index funds?
- Will I be able to download statements?

Search for a company that suits your needs. But don't fret about finding the *perfect* match—find a good match, and then get your IRA account in motion. You can move your money to a new IRA account if the first company you choose isn't a good fit.

Once you pick a place to open your IRA account, it's time to fill out the application. Some firms want you to download forms, and then mail or fax them back, but most companies provide online applications. To complete the application, you'll need your Social Security number, bank account info (so you can transfer funds), info about your current employer, money in a bank account (depending on where you open your IRA account, you might need anywhere from $25 to $3,000), and about half an hour of free time.

When you've gathered all that info, you're ready to fill out the paperwork. You'll probably have to answer some simple questions about your investment plans and goals. Once you complete the application, they'll ask you to transfer money to your new Roth IRA account. (This money will probably earn interest until you choose an investment.) That's all there is to it!

Extreme Retirement Saving

If you've already put enough into your 401(k) to get the full employer match *and* you've maxed out your Roth IRA, congratulations—you're in great shape! What you do after this depends on your priorities.

If you think you need to save more for retirement, then pump up your 401(k) as far as you can. In 2010, you can contribute up to $16,500, including your employer match. If you're 50 or older, you can contribute up to $22,000.

You might also consider accelerating your mortgage payments (see page 215); many retirees find that owning their home free and clear gives them tremendous peace of mind. A final option is to use targeted savings accounts (page 142) to pursue other goals. These are all great options, and Super Savers can't go wrong by pursuing any—or all—of them. They'll each put you that much closer to retirement.

Early Retirement and Other Dreams

For most of us, a job is a necessary evil. Many folks dream of retiring early—finding a way to leave the workplace in their 40s or 50s instead of sticking it out until age 65 (or older). In fact, the 2009 EBRI Retirement Confidence Survey (page 274) found that 18% of retirees left the workforce before age 55 (and another 17% retired before they turned 60).

Early retirement is a fantastic goal, but it's tough to do because of four main obstacles. When you retire early:

- **You have less time to earn money.** If you start working at 20 and retire at 65, you have 45 income-producing years. But if you retire at 45 instead, you only have 25 income-producing years to achieve the same results.

- **Your investments have less time to compound.** As you learned on page 278, the longer you go without touching your savings, the more you benefit from the power of compounding.

- **You'll be drawing on your savings for longer.** The average American will live to be nearly 80. So if you retire at 65, your savings will probably need to last only 10–20 years; but if you retire at 45, your savings may have to support you for 30–40 years.

- **You won't have some of the traditional perks of retirement (at least not right away).** If you retire young, you won't be able to draw on Social Security or Medicare for many years. You'll also face penalties if you want to tap your retirement accounts before you reach the minimum age requirements.

In short, if you retire early, you'll have less money saved and it'll have to last longer than if you waited. Even if you stay healthy and the economy cooperates, that's asking a lot.

That's not to say you shouldn't plan to retire early. It's a laudable goal (and one I've set for myself). If you're serious about doing it, you need to be extra diligent about living frugally now so you can save as much as possible for the future.

After Philip Greenspun retired in 2001 at the age of 37, he wrote an article about some of the joys, challenges, and practical aspects of his decision: *http://tinyurl.com/PG-retired*. And at MSN Money, Liz Pulliam Weston profiled people who retired early. In one article (*http://tinyurl.com/rb50-one*), Weston looks at what it takes to retire by age 50. In another (*http://tinyurl.com/rb50-two*), she shares how three couples made this dream a reality.

To learn more about early retirement, check out the Early Retirement Forum (*www.early-retirement.org*) or track down a copy of **How to Retire Early and Live Well** by Gillette Edmunds. Edmunds' book pays special attention to the financial challenges faced by early retirees—including the psychological impact of a market crash.

Because early retirement presents so many financial hurdles, some people choose *semi-retirement* instead. Semi-retirement is like early retirement except that you continue to draw income from some sort of work. In **Work Less, Live More**, Bob Clyatt explains the advantages of this option:

> With a modest income from part-time work, early semi-retirees may not have to face the dramatic downshifting in spending and lifestyle that so often confronts those who live only on savings or pensions. And semi-retirees learn that a reasonable amount of work, even unpaid work, keeps them energized, contributing, and sharp.

Though semi-retirement is more realistic than early retirement, it's still not for the faint of heart. You have to be dedicated and work hard to make it happen. Semi-retirement typically involves:

- **Ample savings.** Semi-retirees plan far in advance, accumulating a large nest egg before they make the leap.

- **Modest living.** Semi-retirees tend to be frugal and use techniques like those in Chapter 5.

- **Ongoing work.** Though semi-retirees aren't employed full time, they do keep working for a number of reasons: The added income means they don't have to draw down their retirement savings as quickly as they would otherwise, and the work lets them spend time with people while doing something worthwhile.

 According to the EBRI Retirement Confidence Survey, one-third of retirees worked for pay in 2009.

- **Exploration.** People in semi-retirement give themselves permission to explore new interests by doing things like going back to school or taking a part-time job in a completely new field.

- **Purpose.** Most importantly, semi-retirees can pursue projects and passions that align with their core values. Instead of slogging away selling pharmaceuticals, for example, you may finally have time to volunteer at the local health clinic.

If you're interested in semi-retirement, Clyatt's *Work Less, Live More* is an excellent place to start. It's full of brilliant advice and practical examples.

The Final Frontier

Ultimately, deciding when and how to leave the workforce isn't about some number in a retirement account. Think about your goals and what makes you happy. It may be that you're satisfied with your current job and you hope to keep at it for years to come. Do what's right for you.

And remember: A happy retirement is about more than money. Intangibles like health, hobbies, and habits will help you fend off boredom and increase your overall satisfaction after you leave the workforce. More than anything, close ties with friends and family will ensure your long-term happiness. So as you build financial wealth for retirement, build social wealth as well. The next chapter has tips for doing exactly that.

14 Friends and Family

"When you get to my age, you'll measure success in life by how many of the people you want to have love you actually do love you. That's the ultimate test of how you've lived your life." —Warren Buffett

This book has given you the knowledge and tools you need to build a better financial future. Using what you've learned, you can boost your cash flow to pay off debts from the past, provide for the needs of today, and fund your dreams for the future. If you put in the work and do the right things, you *can* get rich—slowly.

But to what end? Money is valuable because it can help you meet your goals. The point of building wealth isn't the Stuff you buy or the money itself—these things are secondary. What matters is that money can give you *freedom:* freedom from worry, freedom to pursue your goals, and freedom to spend time with the people you love.

Living a rich life isn't about making money; it's about your relationships with other people. Because friends and family play a vital role in your happiness, this chapter explores some ways to balance love and money.

Financial Blueprints

In *Secrets of the Millionaire Mind*, T. Harv Eker writes that each of us has a "money blueprint," a built-in set of attitudes and beliefs that affect how we deal with money. This blueprint is created by exposure to messages about money from friends, current events, TV and movies, and especially family. Unfortunately, most of our financial blueprints have flaws that prevent us from having healthy relationships with the stuff.

For example, when I was a kid, my family was poor. Dad sometimes had trouble putting food on the table, yet he always found ways to spend on expensive toys—sailboats, stereos, and so on. From his example, I learned to put wants before needs, and so ended up deep in debt as a young man. It took years to change this part of my money blueprint.

Our financial blueprints don't just shape how we interact with money; they also define how we relate to other people when money is involved. Do you lend money to friends? Do you give to charity? How much do you tip in restaurants? How do you feel if your spouse is a spendthrift?

When your money blueprint comes into contact with folks who have different money blueprints, you might have conflicts. The following sections explore ways to handle common situations where your financial values (especially the new ones you have after reading this book) are different from those of the people around you.

Friends with Money

As adults, most of our friendships tend to be with folks in financial situations similar to our own. The people we work and play with come from similar groups, and generally have similar incomes. Still, you probably have a few friends who are in different financial circumstances: Some seem to be loaded, while others struggle to get by.

These differences in income can lead to awkward moments. You need to go clothes shopping this weekend, say, but your best friend wants to hit the mall instead of browsing thrift stores. Or maybe your coworkers want to celebrate every birthday by going out for drinks, but the cost is killing you. Even minor differences in income (and in financial blueprints) can lead to misunderstandings and hurt feelings.

Though most financial interactions with friends are minor, there are two topics that deserve special attention: peer pressure and borrowing (or lending) money.

Handling Peer Pressure

Peer pressure is a real and powerful force: If your friends value fashionable clothes, you may start to value fashionable clothes; if your friends like expensive wine, you'll likely become fond of expensive wine, too. It can be tough to make smart financial choices when everyone around you is spending—you feel pressured to spend too in order to belong.

But it *is* possible to spend time with friends without going broke. The key is to recognize that peer pressure is mostly internal; it comes from a desire to fit in. When you realize that you don't have to spend to impress your friends, most of the pressure goes away. Here are some ways to cope with social spending situations:

- **Explain your goals.** Let your family and friends know you're trying to get out of debt or saving to buy your first house. Be straightforward about past regrets and future plans, and ask them to help you make smart financial decisions. Once they understand your goals, they'll likely be supportive.

 Note A lot of people think that talking about money is taboo. But it's something we all deal with, so why not give and get help from the people around you? You shouldn't pressure your friends to talk about their finances if it makes them uncomfortable, but there's no shame in sharing your situation with others. Who knows? Your friends might have some great advice!

- **Suggest low- or no-cost alternatives.** Bike or run together. Go hiking. Kick a soccer ball around. Organize a picnic or a mother-daughter tea party. A one-time investment in a board game or a deck of cards is a great, cheap source of entertainment. If your friends want to go to a movie, suggest a matinee. If they want to dine out, pick a restaurant you know you can afford (or better yet, suggest a potluck).

- **Budget for social spending.** If your circle of friends makes a habit of a specific activity, build it into your budget so it doesn't catch you by surprise. If your coworkers go out for happy hour on the first Thursday of every month, for example, set aside $20 to join them.

- **Leave your money at home.** If you're worried that you'll cave to peer pressure, create a self-imposed limit. Take $5 or $10 or $20 with you, but leave the plastic behind. If you don't have the money with you, you can't spend it.

- **Limit yourself.** Do things with friends, just spend less. Join your friends for happy hour, for example, but munch on the free food and buy just one drink. If your friends want to buy more, let them—but you don't have to.

- **Opt out.** If your friends regularly do expensive things, politely bow out from time to time. By playing poker only once a month instead of once a week, for example, you reduce your costs by 75%. If your friends like to go shopping, join them for the companionship, but make it clear that you're there for the company, not the buying. (If the temptation to spend will be too great, don't go at all.)

- **Don't keep score.** Don't obsess about what others do or don't have—focus on the relationships, not the Stuff. This can be tough, but it doesn't do any good to ask yourself why you don't live in a fancy 4,000-square-foot house on five acres. Remember: Life isn't a competition. Your goal isn't to keep up with the Joneses, it's to do what's best for you.

The most important thing is to be honest—with your friends *and* with yourself. Don't cave to peer pressure just to impress people. This can be tough if you're a people-pleaser, but it's vital to your long-term happiness.

And remember that peer pressure works both ways: Your friends influence you—and you influence them. So try to be aware of ways that your actions subtly affect those around you. Don't put people in situations where they're forced to compare themselves to you. Respect your friends when they say "no," and don't try to push them to do things they're not comfortable with. Don't suggest expensive activities to friends who have other financial priorities, and don't brag about money or flaunt it.

Each of us comes from different circumstances. Don't judge other people (or yourself) based on what they do and don't buy. Make smart financial choices for yourself and gently encourage your friends to do the same.

Lending and Borrowing

"Neither a borrower nor a lender be," Shakespeare wrote in *Hamlet*, "For oft loan loses both itself and friend." When a friend or family member asks to borrow money, your first inclination is probably to help out. But many people have learned the hard way that friendship and finances don't always mix. You can save yourself a lot of grief by knowing in advance how you'll handle these situations.

Some people decide that they'll never make personal loans: They know that if they're asked, they'll simply say, "Sorry, but it's my policy never to lend money to people I know." If you think this is harsh, you can follow it with something like, "But I'd be happy to help in some other way, if I can. What do you need?"

 Note Think very carefully before co-signing on a loan. As a co-signer, you're legally obligated for the debt, so if something goes wrong, you'll be stuck with the payments, a black mark on your credit report, *and* a broken friendship. If you want to help, it's usually better to lend money than to co-sign.

Not all loans between family and friends end in disaster. In fact, although there aren't any stats on the subject, it's likely that most loans go smoothly. But the potential for trouble is so great that you should think twice before lending (or borrowing) money. Ask yourself what would happen if the borrower never repaid the loan. How would it affect your finances—and your friendship?

You're likely better off saying "no" rather than putting yourself in a position where you have to hound a friend for money. Which would make you feel worse: the momentary pain of telling a friend "no," or the ongoing anguish of having the loan destroy the friendship?

Despite these warnings, there will undoubtedly be times you're tempted to lend money. When you do, be smart about it:

- **Discuss other options.** Is there any other way you could help your friend? Sometimes people think money is the only way to deal with problems when there are actually other solutions.

- **Only lend money you can afford to lose.** You may never see the money again, so don't put your own financial well-being on the line just because you feel sorry for your cousin Joe. Make sure you're taken care of before you lend money.

- **Be clear about your expectations.** Draw up a payment schedule and discuss what happens if something goes wrong.

 Tip Use this loan calculator at Bankrate to create a payment schedule: *http://tinyurl. com/BR-loancalc*.

- **Get it in writing.** Don't just hand over the money without some sort of record. At LawDepot.com, you can fill out a web form, and for 12 bucks you get a completed promissory note: *http://tinyurl.com/LD-pnote*. There's also a free sample template at Expert Law: *http://tinyurl.com/ EL-pnote*.

- **Deal with problems right away.** You may feel like a nice guy by not reminding the borrower that they're 30 days past due, but you're just setting yourself up for trouble. Keep the lines of communication open.

If you can afford it (and it doesn't seem weird), consider *giving* the money instead. That way there's no ickiness on either side. If your friend pays you back, great; if not, you can feel good about helping her out. And remember: It's always okay to politely refuse.

At some point, *you* may be the one borrowing money from a friend or family member. (You should do this only if you can't boost your income or tap an emergency fund.) When you borrow, explain exactly why you need the money, put the deal in writing, and then stick to your word.

Keeping your word is the most important part. That means repaying the loan as promised—or sooner, if possible. Take this as seriously as you would any other financial obligation; in fact, take it *more* seriously. If you don't pay the bank back, you'll damage your credit score. But if you don't pay back a friend, you'll damage that friendship and your reputation.

Don't make promises you can't keep: If you say you're going to pay back an extra $200 when you get your Christmas bonus, do it. And use the borrowed money for the stated purpose. If you need cash to buy a car because yours was just totaled, then buy a car; don't go out and use the money to buy a new plasma TV. If your friend comes over and sees you have a new car *and* a new TV but you haven't been making your payments, it's going to make his blood boil.

Love and Money

Money management can be difficult even when you're on your own. But throw a life partner into the mix and things get much more complicated. Financial conflicts can cause major problems in relationships—including divorce.

Spreading the Word

Making positive changes to your financial life gives you an awesome sense of power and control. Like any new believer, you want to share what you've learned. That's a good thing—but you need to be careful.

If you try to share your newfound wisdom with others, you may find they're not as excited as you thought they'd be; in fact, some will be insulted. Though you may have friends and family who could profit from what you've learned, if they're not ready to listen, you risk doing more harm than good by offering advice. (Parents, especially, aren't always thrilled about being corrected by their own children.)

Fortunately, there are some subtle ways you can help those who are struggling:

- **Lead by example.** Suggest cutting back on family gift exchanges this year. When you go out to dinner, lobby for cheaper alternatives. Start walking to the grocery store instead of driving. Bring home books, CDs, and DVDs from the library. Don't make a big deal out of these things—just do them. Rather than goading your friends and family into saving, simply be an example of what can happen through smart choices.

- **Be willing to answer questions.** When your friends who struggle with money see that you've got things under control, they're going to have questions. They'll want to know how you paid off your debts, how you got started investing, and why you bought a used car. Be available as a resource to those who want help.

- **Use the soft sell.** When your friends complain about money, don't make a big deal out of it. Share your story, and mention the tools that helped you turn things around (like this book!). Don't lecture them, and don't try to convert anyone. Just spend a few minutes explaining how you solved your problems, and then let it go.

It *is* possible to encourage your family and friends to make smart choices without making them defensive or angry. But be careful about offering your opinion unless someone asks for it. When you see somebody is ready to make a change, be there to help.

The best way to balance love and money is to communicate—a lot. Writing in the **New York Times** (*http://tinyurl.com/NYT-moneytalks*), Ron Lieber listed four financial issues that couples should discuss before marriage (if you're already married, they're still well worth exploring with your partner):

- **Ancestry.** What's your money blueprint (page 292) like? What did your parents teach you about money? How your family modeled money plays a huge role in your own relationship with the stuff. If your attitude toward money is different from your partner's, it can cause friction.

- **Credit.** Although it's not romantic, partners in a committed relationship ought to pull their credit reports and credit scores together and discuss the results (Chapter 8 tells you how). Don't think of this as a competition to see who has the better score; instead, consider it a way to be completely honest with each other so you feel like you're on the same team.

- **Control.** Before you get married, decide on the family financial structure and who's responsible for which household accounts. (In many families, one person plays the role of CFO.) Know what your budget will be like and how much each partner may spend freely without asking permission.

- **Affluence.** Finally, discuss your goals. How wealthy do you, as a couple, want to be? What are you willing to sacrifice to get there? (See the box on page 29 for an example of a couple that worked hard toward a shared financial goal.)

As you consider these factors, strive for trust, honesty, and open communication. Without them, it's difficult to work together toward common goals. And that's really what success in a long-term relationship is all about: Working as a team.

 Note If you're not married but want help working out your finances with your partner, pick up a copy of the truly excellent book *Money Without Matrimony* (Dearborn, 2005) by Sheryl Garrett and Debra Neiman.

The Importance of Teamwork

You'll always have some personal goals that don't align with those of your partner. (My wife rolls her eyes at my comic book collection, for example.) That's fine, but put shared goals first. No matter whether your finances are joint or separate (see page 299), make sure your common objectives are met before pursuing personal passions.

Here are some ways to ensure that both partners are on the same page and that nobody feels singled out as the bad guy:

- **Regularly review accounts.** Schedule regular times to go over the household finances. Some couples do this weekly, others once or twice a month. At each session, look at upcoming income and expenses, and deal with any unexpected budget items. These reviews let you make course corrections.

- **Don't be controlling.** Take "you" and "I" out of your budget conversations and replace them with "we" and "us." Each partner needs to feel like they're involved in the household finances. If you unilaterally tell your husband he can't spend money on his motorcycle hobby, for example, he's just going to be resentful. So work together to find common ground.

- **Be supportive.** Find ways to encourage each other toward your shared and separate goals. If your wife asks you to call her out on bad behavior, do it. If she wants advice, give it. Don't lecture and don't act superior; help each other improve.

- **Play to your strengths.** Some people hate looking at the big picture: They don't care about retirement savings, interest rates, or the Dow Jones Industrial Average. Others don't like nitty-gritty stuff such as clipping coupons and looking for sales. Let each partner be in charge of the stuff they're good at. (I'm not very good at grocery shopping, for example; that's my wife's bailiwick. But I love being in charge of refinancing the mortgage and choosing mutual funds.)

It's rare that partners agree completely on how to handle their money. The key is to find as much common ground as possible, and then compromise on the rest.

Joint or Separate Finances?

Perhaps the biggest question facing married couples is whether to merge their money or keep it separate. Most people getting married for the first time merge their finances; many folks entering their second marriage keep things separate.

Really, though, the degree of merging is up to you. Some couples have only a single joint account where they put all their money. Others keep a seldom-used joint account for certain needs but otherwise maintain complete financial autonomy. Most couples fall somewhere in between. Don't let anyone tell you that there's only one right way to merge finances. Each relationship is different, so the correct choice is the one that works best for you and your partner.

Many couples find that the ideal solution is some sort of blended system; they share a joint account for household finances, but each partner has a personal account to do with as they please. When you take this hybrid approach, the real decision is about how to divide the household income:

- **If you and your partner make roughly the same amount,** you could contribute equally to the joint account, and then keep what's left over in your personal accounts.

- **If one partner makes significantly more than the other,** she could fund the joint account entirely on her own and keep the remainder in her personal account. Her husband could simply keep his own income in his personal account to do with as he wishes.

- Some couples **use a proportional system:** If one partner earns two-thirds of the household income, say, he contributes two-thirds of the joint account. After funding the joint account, the partners can do whatever they want with the leftovers.

- A final option is to **use the "adult allowance" system.** In this case, both spouses put their entire paycheck into the joint account, and then withdraw a fixed amount into their personal accounts every month.

If you use a hybrid system, it's absolutely vital to let each person use the money in their personal accounts however they want. (And it's also good to have rules about what expenses are paid from the joint account.)

Kids and Money

According to the U.S. Department of Agriculture's *Expenditures on Children by Families* (*http://tinyurl.com/USDA-kids*), the typical middle-income family will spend about $11,610 per year to raise a child born in 2008. (For low-income families, the average will be $8,500 per year, and for high-income families, $19,250 per year.)

These costs only increase as the kid gets older. The typical middle-class household will spend over $200,000 to raise a child from birth to age 18. That's nearly *$300,000* when adjusted for inflation, and these figures don't even include college!

 Tip How much will it cost to raise *your* kids? The USDA has a handy cost-of-raising-a-child calculator that gives you a rough estimate of expected annual expenses based on where you live, your income, and your kid's age: *http://tinyurl.com/USDA-kidcalc.*

These numbers aren't meant to scare you out of having kids, just to give you some idea of the costs involved. There are ways to reduce expenses (cloth diapers, hand-me-down clothes, and so on), but there's no getting around the fact that raising kids requires a serious commitment of emotion, time, and money.

When a new baby arrives, if both parents work, couples face a big decision: Should one parent stay home with the child? (If so, which one: The mother? The parent with the smallest salary?) Or should both parents stay on the job? This decision is often about more than money—personal values may determine the best course of action—but sometimes both parents continue to work because they believe they need the income.

In her book *Miserly Moms* (Bethany House, 2001), Jonni McCoy notes that because childcare is so expensive, there's frequently no financial advantage for both parents to continue working. Between the cost of childcare and the cost of working (food, transportation, clothing, and so on), the second salary may be effectively negated. But how can you know if you're one of those couples that can afford for one parent to stay home?

The Parents.com stay-at-home calculator (*http://tinyurl.com/SaH-calc*) may help. Enter your income, expenses, and what you spend for childcare and work, and the calculator estimates whether living on one income is feasible.

If it's a priority for one parent to stay home with the children, how can you make that happen? It's important to discuss these questions early: Will you need to make cutbacks? How big will your emergency fund need to be before one partner leaves the workplace? Will you have enough insurance? You may need to scale back your lifestyle so one parent can stay home with the kids; many folks are willing to make these sacrifices because they feel that being a parent is the most rewarding career they could ever have.

Raising money-smart kids

Teaching your children about money is one of the best things you can do to ensure their success. Financially aware kids become financially aware adults.

In order to raise money-smart kids, you need to be open about your family's financial situation. Some parents try to shield their kids from the family finances, but this does more harm than good. Teach children about money from a young age by letting them see how and why you make various financial decisions. If they see the challenges you face, they can prepare for them in their own lives. Here are some other tips:

- **Set an example.** Model the behavior you want your kids to learn: If you want them to save, save. If you don't want them to become compulsive shoppers, try to curb your own impulse spending.

- **Be prepared.** Have answers before you need them. Know how you're going to handle specific situations like allowances or begging for candy in the grocery store. (I know one couple who turns their kids down by simply saying, "Sorry, but that's not in the budget.")

- **Be consistent.** Kids do best with clear, consistent expectations, so think carefully about your family's money rules before setting them. Don't be so rigid that there's no wiggle room—be willing to mold your system to fit your needs—but once you've set a policy, apply it consistently and fairly.

- **Be honest.** Share your successes *and* failures. Tell your kids what you did right and what you wish you'd done differently. Explain your thought process each step of the way.

Most of all, make this learning process interactive. Involve your kids in frugal activities that teach them self-sufficiency, like gardening, baking, home repair, and so on. Teach them to comparison shop by having them help at the grocery store. As they get older, make them financial apprentices: Show them how to pay bills, check a credit score, and buy a car. Teach them that managing a household is a team effort.

Allowances

A regular allowance teaches children how to handle money. When kids have their own money to manage, they're better able to learn the value of saving and the difference between wants and needs.

You can dole out allowances in a zillion different ways. How much do you pay? What age do you start? Do you stop once your child is old enough to work after school? How often do you pay? Some parents pay big allowances and expect their kids to buy their own clothes. Others pay small allowances but pay for their children's clothes and school activities.

Most of these decisions are beyond the scope of this book, but there are two topics that deserve special attention. The first is whether to base allowances on behavior. There are two schools of thought:

- **Tie the money to grades, chores, and behavior.** This gives kids an incentive to do the right thing, but critics argue that tying an allowance to these actions sends the wrong message. Kids should strive for good grades regardless of what (or whether) they're paid for doing so, they argue, and doing chores is simply part of being a family member.

- **Give the allowance without expecting anything in return.** Using this method, kids learn about money even if they don't make good grades or do their chores. But critics worry that it creates an "entitlement mentality," meaning the kids expect something for nothing.

Most families are probably best off with some sort of hybrid approach: Provide a minimal base allowance that's paid without expecting anything in return, and then add "commissions" for certain chores and behaviors.

 Tip Instead of paying for good grades, consider giving something else your child values: a later curfew, a trip to a pro sporting event, golf lessons, more time with friends. This encourages the behavior you want without tying it to money.

However you distribute it, use the allowance as a chance to teach kids the value of money. Instead of just letting them spend it on whatever they want, consider a system that divides the money for specific goals. You might, for example, use three jars (or envelopes) labeled like this:

- **Save (30%).** The cash in this jar is for long-term goals, like buying a bike or baseball mitt. Let the child decide on the goal—with your help.

- **Share (10%).** This money is for giving to someone else. Your kid can decide where it goes—whether it's a charity or just somebody else in need (even a sibling!)—but the point is to share it with others.

- **Spend (60%).** There are no restrictions on this money. Your child can spend it on books or bubblegum—whatever strikes her fancy.

For example, if you pay your kids a weekly allowance equal to 50 cents per year of age, you might have your 6-year-old (who gets $3.00 per week) put 90 cents into Save, 30 cents into Share, and $1.80 into Spend. As long as your kids follow the rules for each jar, let them make their own choices and mistakes. It's better for them to learn a lesson now with $10 than later with $10,000.

 Note You can read more about segmenting allowances at Get Rich Slowly: *http://tinyurl.com/GRS-allowance*. A company called Money Savvy Generation makes a special piggy bank (*http://tinyurl.com/money-pig*) that has slots for Save, Donate, and Spend, and even one for Invest.

Making the Most of a Windfall

Once in a while, you get lucky: You win the Super Bowl betting pool, get a bonus at work, or unexpectedly inherit a fortune from a long-lost aunt. It can be tempting to spend these windfalls on fun stuff—it's "extra" money, after all—but doing so can be a huge mistake. If you receive a windfall of a few thousand dollars or less, follow these guidelines:

- **Let yourself spend 5% of it on fun.** Treat yourself to a fancy dinner maybe, or buy that collector's-edition DVD set you've been wanting.

- **Use the rest to pursue your financial goals.** If you're working on a debt snowball (see page 160), use the windfall to knock off another big chunk. If you've set up a targeted savings account (page 142) for a down payment, put it there. If you have a Roth IRA (page 282), put it there.

The important thing with small windfalls like these is not to fritter them away. It's easy to spend them on things that don't matter in the long run. So give yourself a small treat and then be smart with the rest.

With a big windfall, such as an inheritance, first set aside enough to cover any taxes that haven't been withheld. (You'll be able to afford a tax professional to calculate this for you—it's worth hiring someone to do this.) Then, let yourself spend up to 5% on fun. If you have debt, use the windfall to pay it off; as unglamorous as it sounds, it's the best course of action. This will free up your cash flow so you'll essentially enjoy a prolonged, time-release windfall.

Next, put the rest of the money into an account where it can earn interest while you decide what to do (a 3- or 6-month CD is a good choice—see page 137). Then, do nothing: Don't touch the money. Take time to let your emotions pass so you can get over the initial urge to spend it all on a big house or a fancy car. Live your life just as you did before.

Meanwhile, get professional help. *Don't* seek advice from anyone who might profit from your money, like a commissioned broker. Instead, find a good CPA or fee-only financial planner (page 285) who doesn't sell investment products.

Ultimately, you'll want to use the money to pursue your goals. Everything you've dreamed about doing will now be within reach, so take the time to make a plan and then follow through.

Church, Charity, and Community

Just as children should allocate their money for spending, saving, and sharing (page 303), so should adults. You've learned a lot about smart spending and saving; let's finish the book with a brief look at sharing.

In *It's Not About the Money* (HarperOne, 2009), Brent Kessel writes that the act of giving is "the yoga of money": "The yoga of money is the act of using money to affirm and enhance our sense of unity, with money itself, and ultimately with something greater than all physical forms."

That sounds like a lot of New Age nonsense, but Kessel has a point. This book has focused on how you can develop a healthy relationship with money to improve *your* financial situation. But there's more to it than that: By improving your finances, you're in a better position to help others.

If you feel called to give, there are three great ways to do so.

- **Donate to charity.** There's a lot of need out there. If you're concerned about child abuse, hunger, homelessness, heart disease, or earthquake victims in Haiti, one way to help is by contributing to charities that assist the victims and prevent the problems. When you give money to an organization like the Red Cross or Salvation Army, your money does real good in the world.

 Charity Navigator (*www.charitynavigator.org*) lets you search for financial info and mission statements from over 5,000 U.S. charities. And VolunteerMatch.org connects volunteers with more than 74,000 nonprofits that need help.

- **Contribute to your community.** If you worry about giving money to charity because you don't know how it'll be used, then help people you know. If a friend does a walk-a-thon for breast-cancer research, make a pledge. If you hear a coworker is struggling with medical bills, make a contribution (doing so anonymously is fine—sometimes even better). If a local homeless shelter needs help, make a donation. Helping people you're connected with can feel awesome.

 Even if you can't afford (or don't want) to give money, there are other ways to help. Many folks contribute used clothing and other household goods to charities that sell the items in thrift stores or give them directly to those in need. And don't forget, you can always donate your time: Charities are desperate for people to lend brains and brawn to help their cause.

- **Tithe.** Many religions—including Judaism, Christianity, and Islam—encourage believers to donate a portion of their income to their church. This money is generally used to support the local ministry and congregation. Tithing can be a great way to use your money to back your beliefs.

If your money blueprint (page 292) doesn't include giving, it can be tough to get started. And even if you want to give, you may not know where to start. Try taking some baby steps. Starting small with giving works the same as starting small with saving: You give a few bucks a month, as you're able. The amount won't really affect your budget, but it'll teach you the habit and mechanics of contributing. Once you see that you *can* give to charity, begin to increase the amounts.

Some folks can be sanctimonious about charitable giving; ignore them. Don't let anyone make you feel guilty for not giving or tell you where to send your money. Create your own personalized giving policy based on your goals and values. Think about the kind of world you want to live in and act accordingly. Your actions may not give you any direct financial benefit, but they'll generate social capital (explained next) and make life better for everyone.

Social Capital

You create *social capital*—mutual goodwill—when you volunteer at a soup kitchen, help your neighbor move a piano, have your Sunday School class over for a barbeque, or join a softball league. Any time you participate in your community, you're generating social capital, both for yourself and the other people involved. People with lots of social capital can find help when they need it; those with little social capital can spend a lot of time frustrated and alone.

The classic Christmas film *It's a Wonderful Life* is a great illustration of social capital. Jimmy Stewart plays George Bailey, a man who repeatedly foregoes his own interests to help his friends and neighbors. It costs him—financially and mentally. When disaster strikes, Bailey decides he's worth more dead than alive, and plans to commit suicide so that the proceeds from his life-insurance policy can set things right.

In the end, Bailey is saved when all the folks he's made sacrifices for over the years come to his aid. Sure, it's a schmaltzy, feel-good moment, but it's a fine example of social capital in action. When Bailey's brother declares that George is "the richest man in town," he's not joking: Bailey may not have much financial capital, but he's flush with social capital.

You don't have to sacrifice your own interests to create social capital. You can often create win-win situations where everyone profits. But the best way to build social capital is to help others without expecting anything in return.

There's more to wealth than just money. Social capital is just as real as financial capital—and often more valuable.

Note For an in-depth look at social capital, pick up a copy of *Bowling Alone* (Simon & Schuster, 2001) by Robert Putnam.

True Wealth

It's easy to believe that having more money is the key to a better life—but it's not. The key to a better life is increased *happiness*.

Wealth and happiness aren't mutually exclusive, of course. In his final column for the *Wall Street Journal* (*http://tinyurl.com/wsj-final*), Jonathan Clements wrote that financial stability improves well-being in three ways:

- **If you have money, you don't have to worry about it.** By living below your means, you get a degree of financial control—even if you aren't rich. Avoiding debt gives you options.

- **Money can give you the freedom to pursue your passions.** What do you want out of life? What gives you a sense of purpose? These are the sorts of things you'll want to pursue in retirement. Better yet, structure your career so you can do the things you love now.

- **Money can buy you time with family and friends.** In fact, Clements says, true wealth comes from relationships, not from dollars and cents. In other words, social capital is worth more than financial capital.

Money is a tool. As with any tool, a skilled craftsman can use it to build something amazing: a meaningful life filled with family and friends. But if you're not careful and don't have a plan, the life you construct with your money can be fragile—even dangerous.

Really, there's only one way to ever be satisfied with the money you have: knowing how much is Enough (see page 12). True happiness comes when you learn to be content with what you have. If you never take the time to figure out what Enough means to you, you'll *always* be unhappy with your financial situation.

Enough is different for each of us. It's not just different amounts of money, but different types of wealth. For me, Enough is having my home paid off and cash set aside to let me buy comic books and go out to dinner with my wife once in a while. For you, Enough may mean renting a small apartment but owning a boat and having the freedom to go sailing for months at a time.

To find Enough, you've got to set goals and look inside to find your core values. It can take months or years to get clear on what makes life meaningful for you, but once you've done this, you can make choices that reflect your priorities.

After all, that's why you're doing this. You're not building wealth so you can bathe in buckets of gold; you're doing it so you don't have to worry about money, so you can pursue your passions and spend time with your family and friends.

Remember: True wealth isn't about money—it's about relationships, good health, and ongoing self-improvement. True wealth is about happiness. Ultimately, it's more important to be happy than to be rich.

Index

Get even more for your money.

Join the O'Reilly Community, and register the O'Reilly books you own. It's free, and you'll get:

- 40% upgrade offer on O'Reilly books
- Membership discounts on books and events
- Free lifetime updates to electronic formats of books
- Multiple ebook formats, DRM FREE
- Participation in the O'Reilly community
- Newsletters
- Account management
- 100% Satisfaction Guarantee

Signing up is easy:

1. Go to: oreilly.com/go/register
2. Create an O'Reilly login.
3. Provide your address.
4. Register your books.

Note: English-language books only

To order books online:

oreilly.com/order_new

For questions about products or an order:

orders@oreilly.com

To sign up to get topic-specific email announcements and/or news about upcoming books, conferences, special offers, and new technologies:

elists@oreilly.com

For technical questions about book content:

booktech@oreilly.com

To submit new book proposals to our editors:

proposals@oreilly.com

Many O'Reilly books are available in PDF and several ebook formats. For more information:

oreilly.com/ebooks

O'REILLY®

Spreading the knowledge of innovators   www.oreilly.com